Organized Interests
and American Government

Critical Topics in American Government Series

Understanding the U.S. Supreme Court: Cases and Controversies
By Kevin McGuire

Organized Interests and American Government
By David Lowery and Holly Brasher

Voice of the People: Elections and Voting in the United States
By Alan Abramowitz

Organized Interests and American Government

David Lowery
University of North Carolina
at Chapel Hill

and

Holly Brasher
University of Alabama
Birmingham

Boston   Burr Ridge, IL   Dubuque, IA   Madison, WI   New York
San Francisco   St. Louis   Bangkok   Bogotá   Caracas   Kuala Lumpur
Lisbon   London   Madrid   Mexico City   Milan   Montreal   New Delhi
Santiago   Seoul   Singapore   Sydney   Taipei   Toronto

Higher Education

ORGANIZED INTERESTS AND AMERICAN GOVERNMENT
Published by McGraw-Hill, a business unit of The McGraw-Hill Companies, Inc.,
1221 Avenue of the Americas, New York, NY, 10020. Copyright © 2004 by McGraw-Hill
Companies, Inc. All rights reserved. No part of this publication may be reproduced or
distributed in any form or by any means, or stored in a database or retrieval system,
without the prior written consent of the McGraw-Hill Companies, Inc., including, but
not limited to, in any network or other electronic storage or transmission, or broad-
cast for distance learning.

Some ancillaries, including electronic and print components, may not be available
to customers outside the United States

This book is printed on acid-free paper.

1 2 3 4 5 6 7 8 9 0 DOC/DOC 0 9 8 7 6 5 4 3

ISBN: 0-07-246786-X

Publisher: *Lyn Uhl*
Senior sponsoring editor: *Monica Eckman*
Editorial coordinator: *Angela W. Kao*
Marketing manager: *Katherine Bates*
Senior media producer: *Sean Crowley*
Project manager: *Destiny Rynne*
Production supervisor: *Carol A. Bielski*
Associate designer and cover design: *George Kokkonas*
Supplement associate: *Kathleen Boylan*
Art director: *Jeanne M. Schreiber*
Permissions: *Marty Granahan*
Typeface: *10/12 Palatino*
Compositor: *ColorType*
Printer: *R.R. Donnelley and Sons Inc.*

Library of Congress Cataloging-in-Publication Data

Lowery, David.
   Organized interests and American government / David Lowery, Holly Brasher.
      p. cm.
   Includes index.
   ISBN 0-07-246786-X (softcover : alk. paper)
      1. Pressure groups—United States. 2. Lobbying—United States. I. Brasher, Holly. II.
   Title.

JK1118.L64 2004
322'.0973—dc21
                                                                    2003052735

www.mhhe.com

Brief Contents

Contents

List of Tables and Figures

TABLES

FIGURES

Preface

CONFLICTING IMAGES OF ORGANIZED INTERESTS

When teaching our courses on the politics of interest representation, we pose a specific challenge to our undergraduate students: we ask them to find a political cartoon offering a positive view of organized interests. Students have no difficulty finding political cartoons featuring interest groups, yet these drawings seem to always cast organized interests in a very harsh light. This consensus stretches right across the ideological divide that separates Americans on political issues. To conservative cartoonists, liberal interest groups are depicted as the loony fringe of politics, while liberal cartoonists, in turn, emphasize the themes of coercion and corruption when spotlighting conservative interest organizations, especially those representing big business. To date, none of our students has ever answered our challenge by identifying a single political cartoon in which organized interests are presented as anything more than instruments of greed and selfishness. Many of these same students, however, are affiliated with one or several organized interests and freely identify with the policy aspirations of many others. Indeed, students typically and rather fiercely defend the role these specific organizations play in democratic politics. And they are not alone. Many political scientists argue that organized interests constitute one of the major conduits — along with voting and political parties — through which citizens first come to understand and then express their policy preferences to public officials. Which of these two images is closer to the truth? This is the question we explore in this book.

ORGANIZATION OF THE BOOK

Our exploration of the politics of interest representation is organized along two tracks. First, underlying the image of organized interests as the Jeckyll and Hyde of American politics is a long running and sometimes intensely contentious social science debate about their role in democratic government. This three-sided debate between pluralists, transactions, and neopluralist scholars is introduced in the first chapter and then carried through all of the topics we examine, albeit more strongly with some than others. More than most political science texts, we also try to identify who the players are in this debate, what they argue, and how they buttress their claims with research. Both the broad frame provided by the three perspectives on organized interests and the details about their arguments are important. It is very difficult to comprehend the large body of research on organized interests if these studies are not organized in some framework that lends meaning to the questions they pose and the answers they offer. But a framework without specific content is a shallow substitute for really understanding and appreciating the debate over the politics of interest representation. In this sense, our needs are no different than those of someone wishing to understand a football game. We cannot fully appreciate the game unless we understand the specific strengths and weaknesses that individual players bring to their teams' efforts. But even with such detailed knowledge, we will be missing something rather important if we do not understand first that these players are organized on teams with competing objectives.

The second organizing theme of the book follows the stages of what we label in the first chapter "the influence production process." In some respects, this is a very fancy name for the series of topics typically addressed in introductory courses on American politics, running from an individual's political participation, through the legislative, executive, and judicial branches of government, to a consideration of public policies. Our chapters follow this conventional outline. Indeed, we hope that this book will find use in such courses as a specific lens through which to understand American politics more generally. In another respect, however, our label suggests something quite new for texts on organized interests. That is, most texts treat the subject's many topics—such as interest group mobilization, lobbying, and campaign spending—as separate and distinct, often ignoring how the lobbying and campaign contributions of organized interests are related to each other or how both are conditioned by the way in which interest organizations were initially formed or mobilized. One of the central premises of our book is that these topics are best understood as interconnected parts of a whole. How interest groups are mobilized directly influences the lobbying tactics they employ. In turn, how political institutions structure lobbying opportunities may well influence incentives to mobilize. And in the end, both the nature of mobilization and the use of influence tactics determine how successful organized interests are in shaping public policy. Sometimes, anklebones really are connected to shinbones, and the quality of that connection plays a big part in determining how well we can dance. The sequential order of the chapters and the connections among them are purposefully designed to provide students with an integrated view of the politics of interest representation.

PEDAGOGY

Taken together these two organizing themes highlight the central idea of our pedagogical approach to understanding the politics of interest representation. This book provides students with an *integrated* understanding of the long *debate* over the role of organized interests in American politics. Many of the specific topics we consider within this structure will be familiar to students of interest organizations. Still, we introduce two new topics that are not commonly addressed in texts on interest groups. First, Chapter 3 focuses on the dynamics of interest community growth and diversity. Based on cutting edge research, this is the first time that this topic has been examined systematically in a text on organized interests. We argue in Chapter 3 that the density and diversity of interest communities play an important role in linking the mobilization of organized interests to their use of influence tactics. Second, unlike almost all other texts, we discuss the role of organized interests in both state and national politics throughout the book. Indeed, we argue strongly that research on state interest organizations offers important leverage for understanding some issues that are difficult to address when focusing solely on national politics.

Our text also employs two pedagogical tools to help students to better understand the debate over the role of organized interests in American politics. First, we have already noted that we do not shy away from discussing competing theories guiding research on organized interests. At times, as in Chapter 3's discussion of interest communities, the very abstractness of these theories will challenge students. We try, therefore, to ground our discussion in many specific examples of current policy controversies and a number of examples of specific interest organizations. Some of these discussions of specific interest organizations are presented in text boxes. But many contemporary examples of controversies involving interest organizations drawn from the front pages of America's newspapers and the nightly news — including 2002's financial and accounting scandals, the abuse crisis in the Boston Archdiocese of the Catholic Church, and the debate over the passage and implementation of the Bipartisan Campaign Finance Reform Act — are discussed throughout the body of the text. Second, each chapter ends with a number of questions for students to consider about a specific organized interest that they might be interested in. As noted earlier, a bit of probing almost always identifies groups or organizations that students are members or even leaders of or with which they closely identify or have a strong antipathy toward. Our questions — along with the sources identified in the appendix — are designed to enable students to link these specific interest organizations to the larger debate over the politics of interest representation.

Ultimately, we do not expect students to adopt our views about any specific interest organization, nor do we expect them to adopt one or another side in the larger debate about the role of organized interest in American politics. We do hope, however, that this textbook will help them to be better prepared to participate in that debate as informed citizens.

ACKNOWLEDGMENTS

We are grateful to those who reviewed various versions of our manuscript:

Kenneth Kollman, University of Michigan — Ann Arbor

Robert Lowery, Michigan State University

Dale A. Newman, University of Missouri — Kansas City

Russell Renka, Southeast Missouri State University

Robert Spitzer, SUNY Cortland

Gary Wekkin, University of Central Arkansas

Clyde Wilcox, Georgetown University

Thomas P. Wolf, Indiana University Southeast

The readers provided copious and unusually thoughtful comments that made the text both stronger and more engaging. They also helped us to avoid a number of egregious errors. We hope that we got all of them. If not, it will not be due to a lack of diligence on the part of the readers. Their assistance and hard work are greatly appreciated. Many others contributed to this work, our own undergraduate students foremost. Many of our colleagues at the University of North Carolina at Chapel Hill read all or parts of the manuscript. We especially appreciate the assistance of Virginia Gray, Kevin McGuire, Isaac Unah, Adam Newmark, Susan Webb Yackee, Andrea McAtee, Jennifer Anderson, Chris Witko, Jenny Wolak, and the American Politics Research Group. We also thank the McGraw-Hill team of Monica Eckman and Angela Kao for their patience, enthusiastic coaching, and the ease with which the manuscript moved from idea to print. Finally, we thank Audrey and Gianna for their unswerving support (meow!) throughout the writing process.

DL/HB
January, 2003
Chapel Hill, North Carolina
Washington, D.C.

CHAPTER 1

Representing Interests — An Argument

The economy had already been in a downward slide for seven months when terrorists struck the Twin Towers and the Pentagon on the morning of September 11, 2001. Economic prospects sharply dimmed as the stock market collapsed and unemployment rose in the following weeks. The U.S. Congress and the president immediately focused on an economic stimulus package as the remedy. However, the bipartisan unanimity that characterized the immediate aftermath of the terrorist strikes evaporated over the months Congress worked on the stimulus plan. Months of struggle ensued, but a bill was eventually sent to the president.

The politics that shaped the final bill, however, appalled many. Lost in the patriotic fervor following September 11, the stimulus bill was for too long stuck in a maze of special interest pleading. As the *Washington Post* noted, "The major impact of the Republican economic stimulus bill so far has been to stimulate lobbyists to scurry around the halls of Congress like Energizer bunnies, hat in one hand, begging tax breaks for their industries, and campaign contributions in the other."[1] The bill proposed would repeal the corporate alternative minimum tax, which would provide tax refunds of $1.4 billion for IBM, $833 million for General Motors, and $671 million for General Electric. Another proposal would have deferred taxes on overseas corporate profits until they were repatriated, costing the U.S. Treasury $21.3 billion over the next decade. The *Post* concluded that, "We see, once again, why lobbyists are so munificently paid. Critics in and out of Congress are making the point that the Republican economic stimulus is mutating into a general tax bill — a Christmas tree full of goodies hung there by and for special interests."[2]

Was the *Post's* assessment correct? Was this episode just another example of special interests exploiting a national calamity for narrow advantage? Or was Congress responding to the public's demand for an economic stimulus package with real punch, even if it necessitated providing tax breaks for a few? These conflicting interpretations hinge on a number of factors, including different views of how the economy works. But they also raise important questions about democratic governance. When is an interest a special interest? Can special interests really influence public officials to the point that the common or general interest is ignored or abused? And what — if anything at all — should be done about the influence of special interests?

These issues and the debates about them are not new. Indeed, they address one of the very problems that James Madison, Alexander Hamilton, and John Jay examined in *The Federalist Papers* as they promoted adoption of a new constitution.[3] The essential problem of self-rule, Madison argued in "Federalist No.10," lies in reconciling our natural, inevitable pursuit of self-interest with the dangers of any one **faction** or interest using government for its own narrow purposes. The solution the founders designed did not abolish self-interest. Rather, as Hamilton, Madison, and Jay argued, the new government would simply make it more difficult for factions, for special interests, to capture the instruments of public authority. Sovereignty was to be shared by state and national governments, each exercising a check on the other. Authority within these governments was further divided between the executive, legislative, and judicial branches. And distinct electoral constituencies and lengths of terms were specified in order to vary the motivations of those securing appointment to public office. To the founders, the resulting system of checks and balances was first and foremost a defense against special interests.[4]

The problem of faction did not disappear, however. As Madison recognized, the pursuit of self-interest is natural and inevitable, and democratic governments, by their very nature, must allow its pursuit through government. Citizens of the United States are guaranteed opportunities to seek redress of grievances and the right of free speech. So, while the institutions of the new constitution may have made it more difficult for one faction to control all of the instruments of government, they could neither prohibit nor much restrain clamoring for redress of grievances.

Such clamoring is especially vigorous in the United States. During his travels in the United States in the early 1830s, Alexis de Tocqueville famously observed that it was a nation of joiners. "In no other country in the world," he noted in *Democracy in America*, "has the principle of association been more successfully used, or applied in a greater multitude of objects, than in America."[5] This tendency only grew after the Civil War as the railroad and telegraph allowed previously local organizations to attain continental scale.[6] And it continues today. A 1981 Gallup poll of citizens in 12 advanced industrial democracies found that 76 percent of Americans were members of voluntary associations. This far surpasses participation in other industrial nations, such as Great Britain at 52 percent and Japan at 29 percent.[7] This proclivity to join is often praised, as by Tocqueville, as a special strength of the American political system. Most recently, a number of observers have followed Robert Putnam in arguing that a strong civil society based on these associative tendencies is a prerequisite of democracy.[8]

Americans applaud their strong associative tendencies as evidence of robust levels of participation in civic life. But praise often shifts to blame when the organizations arising from the tendency to associate try to influence public policy. To many critics, organized interests are the modern embodiment of the factions so feared by Madison. When Union veterans of the Civil War mobilized as the Grand Army of the Republic to seek more generous pensions, they were accused of exploiting the "bloody shirt" for narrow self-interest.[9] They were not the last organization to be so accused. Indeed, nearly every organized interest has been accused of representing special interests. This criticism intensifies, however, when those pursuing influence represent elite interests. Mistrust of elite interests is a recurring theme in American politics. Theodore Roosevelt's trust-busting crusade promised to rein in the large corporations that exploited American workers. Franklin Roosevelt's decrying of Wall Street plutocrats was popular with those who held them as responsible for the Great Depression. And Dwight Eisenhower's warnings about the military-industrial complex identified the potential of the arms industry and military interests to acquire an unwholesome power. Madison's fear of faction is now most commonly expressed as alarm about the role of organized interests.

For much of our history, however, debate about the role of organized interests was framed in what now seem somewhat narrow terms. That is, with the exception of purely local civic groups, the role played by organized interests in the political process was viewed largely in the same light as Madison's understanding of faction. Organized interests represented special interests antithetical to the public interest. The central issue of the debate was how best to provide opportunities both to seek redress of grievances and to associate freely while insuring that the instruments of public authority were not captured by special interests. In the early 20th century, for example, the Progressive Movement advocated grafting several new institutions — the initiative, referendum, and recall, the civil service system, and independent regulatory authorities — onto the founders' constitutional framework. These new institutions, they argued, were needed either to circumvent elected officials, should they be overly influenced by special interests, or to remove public decisions from their hands into those of professionals attentive to the public interest. The new instruments of government would, it was argued, better control the power of special interests too weakly constrained by the checks and balances of the founders.[10]

Few analysts of American politics were willing to argue that organized interests were anything better than a necessary evil. This changed with new interpretations of democratic government developed by political scientists in the last century. Arthur Bentley was the most significant voice in inaugurating this new interpretation with his 1908 book, *The Process of Government*.[11] To Bentley and like-minded observers who were later identified as pluralists, the key task of democratic government was balancing the competing interests of society. In this view, interests were not an impediment to self-rule, but its raw material. To pluralists, competition among organized interests were seen as the primary instrument through which competing interests in society are discovered and expressed.[12] Thus, far from being a curse on the democratic body politic, organized interests were vital to its health.

Older fears about faction did not disappear. But the great argument was now bifurcated. While at one time we argued only about whether our political institutions sufficiently controlled special interests, we now debate the antecedent proposition that they are antithetical to collective interests or the public good. Both arguments are now more intense than ever. This book is about these arguments. We introduce these disputes in this chapter. We first consider the object of the argument—organized interests. We then introduce the several players in the debate—politicians, journalists, and academics—and the varied evidence they employ. And last, we summarize the arguments themselves by outlining three distinct schools of thought about organized interests in American politics.

WHAT WE ARGUE ABOUT

We have yet to define what interest organizations are. Before doing so, it is worth spending some time considering why such definitions matter. Doing so is important because many different terms have been used to describe the modern embodiment of factions, such as interest groups, voluntary associations, pressure groups, special interests, and social movements. The terms *lobbyist* and *political action committee* (PAC) are also commonly employed in discussions about interest representation. Which term we employ matters in two ways.

First, each term specifies the boundaries of the topic differently. Two types of organizations, collectively identified as **voluntary organizations,** have members. **Membership groups**—such as the National Rifle Association, the American Association of Retired Persons, and the American Medical Association—enroll individual citizens as members. **Associations,** in contrast, enroll **institutions** as members. Members of the National Manufacturers Association are firms, and cities and towns are members of their state's League of Cities. While some scholars study only voluntary organizations (e.g., membership groups and associations),[13] they are now a minority of organizations. In the 50 states, for example, membership groups and associations now comprise only 40 percent of lobby registrations by organizations. The remaining 60 percent are institutions—corporations, local governments, universities, churches, and so on—lobbying on their own behalf.[14] Institutions may have employees, customers, and clients, but they do not have voluntary members in the same sense as membership groups and associations. Exclusive attention to those organizations with members (including interest groups, pressure groups, or voluntary associations) would, therefore, lead us to ignore many of the most important players in the politics of interest representation.

Another term, **social movements,** while also ignoring institutions, has the opposite effect of leading us to consider more than intended. Social movements are broad, loosely organized collections of individuals purporting to represent the interests of those traditionally outside of the political establishment.[15] When we speak of movements such as the environmental movement, women's liberation, Christian right, civil rights, or the gay and lesbian movement, we refer to more than just the organizations purporting to represent these interests. We also refer to the many unorganized citizens holding positive views about the goals and objectives of a movement. Thus, social movements are more encompassing than interest organizations. Sociologists study social movements to understand the demographic and cultural roots that eventually lead to political demands. But our purpose lies in examining how interests are expressed to government collectively beyond the political activities of individual citizens. However, the organizations speaking for social movements, and sometimes coordinating voting, contacting, and protest behaviors, are interest organizations. Thus, the National Association for the Advancement of Colored Persons and the National Organization for Women are part of the subject matter we must consider.

The second reason definitions matter is that they can frame controversial issues in such a manner that a term prejudices our conclusions about them. The concepts of **pressure groups** and **special interests** may invoke such prejudice. We will see that many interest organizations are entirely passive most of the time, largely monitoring the course of public policy and only occasionally seeking to influence public officials. Even more importantly, there is considerable controversy about just what these organizations do when seeking influence. Some students of interest representation suggest that their activities are limited to providing information in order to strengthen the ties between the preferences of citizens and their elected officials, an activity that only rarely entails pressure in the colloquial sense of the term. To focus on pressure groups, then, would prejudge our assessment of the evidence on this dispute. The term *special interest*, one we have already used in the first sentence of this chapter, is equally troubling. While some organizations represent narrower interests than others, all interest organizations are special interests in the sense of representing some subset of the general public. But special interest further implies that organizations invariably and inevitably work against the general interest. We will see, however, that some scholars view conflict among interest organizations as an essential part of the discovery of the general interest. Still others dispute the notion that a general interest is definable in any meaningful sense. Thus, defining our topic as the study of special interests could well lead us to prejudge debates about the politics of interest representation.

Two other terms are often used in discussions about interest organizations — **lobbyists** and **PACs**. We will spend some time defining and examining the behavior of lobbyists and PACs in later chapters, but they are not our subject matter per se. Rather, with the exception of the tiny minority of PACs not sponsored by interest organizations, lobbyists and PACs are better viewed as instruments interest organizations use to acquire influence.[16] This book focuses on interest organizations and how they use these instruments. Moreover, counting lobbyists or PACs is a poor way of defining the universe of organizations engaged in politics. Some organizations employ many different kinds of lobbyists. For example, the lobbyists representing Microsoft in Washington in 2002 included employees working directly for the firm, but many others worked for the 15 contract lobbying firms hired by the company or were employed by trade associations the firm has joined. In contrast, some contract lobbyists represent many different interest organizations. Similarly, not all interest organizations operate PACs, organizations that contribute money to political candidates or campaigns.

What, then, are **interest organizations?** Three conditions signal our understanding of the term. First, interest organizations must in the first instance be organized. This distinguishes our subject matter from studies of individual political behaviors not linked to organizations. In the 1996 presidential election, for example, many political commentators highlighted the pivotal role of "soccer moms." But while clearly important to the successful electoral coalition constructed by Bill Clinton, the interests of soccer moms are not represented exclusively by an interest organization, nor did such an organization mobilize them on behalf of the Clinton campaign. In contrast, the United Steel Workers of America and the National Rifle Association actively represent the interests of their members on an ongoing basis and mobilize their members in support of political candidates and issues. Our understanding of organizations, however, is not exclusive. Organizations come in many forms — schools, business firms, golf clubs, professional sports leagues, academic associations, advocacy organizations, nonprofit agencies, and so on. Potentially, all of these examples are interest organizations.[17]

Although we define organizations quite broadly, not all organizations are interest organizations. Thus, the second condition of our definition refers to the meaning of **interest** as an active intersection of an organization's preferences with public policy. Political scientist Robert Salisbury provided one of the most influential statements of this condition when he wrote: "I hold the view that an interest arises from the conjunction between some private value . . . and some authoritative action or proposed action by government. Neither private value nor government action (actual or potential) can by itself generate the interest. Likelihoods and potentials may abound, but unless the conjunction occurs there is no interest."[18] That is, organizations take on the status of interest organizations only when private interests actively intersect with public policies. Passive observation of government by organizations is not enough. Undertaking some minimal action to influence the course of public policy, such as lobbying or sponsoring a PAC, is necessary to achieve the status of interest organization. An important implication of this condition is that the population of interest organizations is likely to be fluid. While many organizations seek to influence public policies on a continuous basis, many others lobby government officials only once on a single narrow issue and then abandon the ranks of interest organizations. Or they may be active on an ongoing but infrequent basis.

The final condition of our definition serves to distinguish interest organizations from the other major institution of democratic politics mediating the preferences of citizens and the actions of governments—political parties. Political parties and interest organizations share many traits, and the two topics are often considered together in political science courses. But interest organizations differ from political parties in one key respect: They do not themselves seek elective office. Indeed, the primary "interest" of political parties is winning elections. The representation of private values by political parties, therefore, is more fluid than via interest organizations. While the platforms of political parties do not change in a capricious manner over the short term, electoral calculations may lead parties to adopt very different policy stances over the long term. For example, Teddy Roosevelt's Republican Party better represented civil rights and environmental interests than did the Democratic Party of his day, the opposite of contemporary issue-party alignments. And it was not at all obvious following the 1973 *Roe* v. *Wade* decision of the Supreme Court which party would become associated with the prolife movement and which would adopt a prochoice stance. The key interest of political parties that is constant is winning elections. In contrast, it is unlikely that the National Rifle Association will ever advocate stricter gun control or that the Sierra Club will lobby to weaken environmental regulations. Even so, the boundaries between parties and interest organizations may still be fuzzy at times. It is not clear, for example, whether Ralph Nader's effort to win the presidency in 2000 under the banner of the Green Party was a realistic bid to win elective office or an effort to pressure the Clinton-Gore administration to be more active on environmental issues. If the latter, the Green Party is better viewed as an interest organization than a political party.

Even with this definition, it is still very difficult to identify the population of interest organizations operating in American politics. They seek influence in many different venues — legislatures, bureaucratic agencies, and the courts. And they operate at all levels of government — federal, state, and local. Still, as Salisbury noted, "Although most interest groups will tend to prefer one institutional branch to another, most of them will try to attain and utilize access across the whole system."[19] Accordingly, venues maintaining the most comprehensive lists of interest organizations should provide us the most valid census of interest organizations. The most comprehensive, if still incomplete, lists of interest organizations now available are provided through the lobby registration requirements of Congress and the state legislatures.

Congress enacted the Lobby Disclosure Act in 1995. It requires that all organizations directly contacting legislators and spending at least $20,500 over a six-month period register with Congress. Frank R. Baumgartner and Beth L. Leech analyzed the 1996 registrations and report that 5,907 interest organizations lobbied Congress in 1996.[20] Of course, not all registered organizations are equally active. The top of Table 1-1 lists 12 interest organizations that lobbied on at least 12 issues in 1997 and a sample of those lobbying on just one. The most important thing to note about Table 1-1 is the range of organization on lobbying rolls. Many big players familiar to us from news reports about politics — the AFL-CIO, General Motors, the Sierra Club, and the American Civil Liberties Union — are on the list of most active organizations. But less well-known organizations, such as West Publishing Company, the Long Island Savings Bank,

TABLE 1-1 Sample of Most and Least Active Interest Organizations at Federal and State Levels

FEDERAL INTEREST ORGANIZATIONS, 1996	
Most Active Organizations *Lobbied on at Least 12 Issues*	Least Active Organizations *Lobbied on Only a Single Issue*
Sierra Club IBM Corporation American Farm Bureau Federation General Motors Corporation National Association of Broadcasters National Taxpayer Union American Petroleum Institute American Civil Liberties Union National Manufacturing Association AFL-CIO American Cancer Society Associated General Contractors of America	American Association of Nurserymen Association of Community College Trustees Government of India City of San Antonio Americans for Tax Reform Airline Pilots Association Long Island Savings Bank Coalition to Stop Gun Violence Northwestern Memorial Hospital Rocky Mountain HMO West Publishing Company Business Executives for National Security

STATE INTEREST ORGANIZATIONS, 1997	
Most Active Organizations *Lobbied in Most States*	Least Active Organizations *Lobbied in Only a Single State*
Anheuser-Busch Companies, Inc. (49) AT&T (49) Bankers Association (48) AFL-CIO (47) Association of Realtors (47) MCI Telecommunications (47) National Association of Independent Business (47) The Tobacco Institute (46) Optometric Association (44) American Psychological Association (44) Pharmaceutical Research and Manufacturers Association (44) Smokeless Tobacco Council, Inc. (43)	San Jacinto River Authority (TX) Golden Age Fisheries (AK) Thunder Basin Coal Company (WY) Binions Horseshoe Hotel and Casino (NV) Ramapo College of New Jersey (NJ) Randolph Jewelry and Loan (NE) Public Parking Association (CA) Watkins-Shepard Trucking (MT) Alliance for Responsible Driving (AZ) Yankee Gas Services Company (CT) Village of Johnson Power and Light Department (VT) Boston Bank of Commerce (MA)

and the American Association of Nurserymen also seek political influence. Thus, the Washington interest community is far more inclusive than commonly acknowledged. It encompasses all of the organizations listed at the top of Table 1-1. If they are organized in some minimal fashion, seek to influence public policy, and are not a political party, they are interest organizations.

All 50 states require interest organizations to register with their legislatures. While registrations requirements vary somewhat across states, all are more restrictive than the federal Lobby Disclosure Act, capturing a broader range of interest organizations. Thus, they provide a very good census of interest organizations active in the states. Jenny Wolak and her colleagues report that 21,103 distinct interest organizations registered in the states in 1997.[21] Again, their level of activity can be measured in many different ways. But one indicator is the number of states in which an interest organization seeks influence. The 12 organizations registered in the most states are listed in the bottom left of Table 1-1. Clearly, these include many of the usual suspects in stories about lobbying—Anheuser-Busch, AT&T, and the AFL-CIO. But the bottom right of the table includes a sample of the much larger number of organizations registered in only a single state. These include Ramapo College of New Jersey, Golden Age Fisheries of Alaska, and Randolph Jewelry and Loan of Nebraska. While hardly household names, these interest organizations, too, are full-fledged members of the community of organized interests.

THE PLAYERS AND THEIR EVIDENCE

To many political observers, little has changed since Madison warned of the destructive power of factions or the Populists warred with railroad and banking interests at the turn of the last century. That is, the debate is still framed in very narrow terms. Interest organizations are viewed as a pernicious influence on democratic government. The debate is restricted to two narrow questions. Will a particular reform—such as campaign finance reform—successfully reduce the influence of organized interests? And, if so, are the costs acceptable in terms of new limits imposed on free speech? But few politicians or journalists consider whether a vigorous system of organized interests inevitably poses a threat to democratic self-rule.

This narrowly framed argument certainly seems characteristic of the rhetoric of politicians. Senator Mitch McConnell of Kentucky, for example, spent little time praising the virtues of organized interests while opposing campaign finance reform legislation over recent sessions of Congress. Rather, he propounded the somewhat contradictory arguments that the proposed reforms would not work and violated rights of free speech. McConnell even labeled the *New York Times* and the *Washington Post* as the "biggest special interests in America" for editorializing for the passage of the bill.[22] Politicians use such labels for competitive political advantage, if in a highly selective manner. Republicans revel in chaining Democrats to the agendas of the American Civil Liberties Union, trial lawyers, and radical environmentalists. And Democrats ardently assert that Republicans are captives of the Christian right, big business, and the National Rifle Association. While defining which interests are "special interests" is very much in the eye of the beholder, special interests, all agree, are inimical to democracy.

Yet the other part of the great argument over interest representation—that vigorous contention over policy by interest organizations is a necessary part of healthy democratic politics—remains implicit in the many ways politicians solicit and attend to organized interests. This divergence between politicians' rhetoric and behavior is often credited to crass cynicism. But it may reflect instead a real tension between their deep appreciation of the necessary and legitimate role of organized interest in American politics and their constituents' antipathy toward them. That is, few politicians have ever lost votes by attacking the power of special interests. In any case, we are unlikely to uncover the full dimensions of the debate over the role of organized interests in American politics by attending to political rhetoric.

Nor are we likely to find a defense of organized interests in journalists' accounts of American politics. Like the radical pamphleteers of the revolutionary era, today's journalists are nearly uniform in denouncing organized interests. This is evident in the titles of recent works by journalists: Ken Silverstein's *Washington on $10 Million a Day: How Lobbyists Plunder a Nation,* Elizabeth Drew's *The Corruption of American Politics: What Went Wrong and Why,* and David S. Broder's *Democracy Derailed: Initiative Campaigns and the Power of Money.*[23] It seems that journalists rarely question whether we are going to hell in a handbasket, but only ask how soon, how fast. Still, a few journalists have recounted some notable failures by organized interests to achieve their goals. But as with Jeffrey H. Birnbaum and Alan S. Murray's *Showdown at Gucci Gulch,* an analysis of lobbyists' unsuccessful effort to derail the Tax Reform Act of 1986, these failures are touted as especially striking because they are so rare.[24]

This antipathy toward organized interests is especially evident in political cartoons. Cartoonists, dating back to the Civil War, have made targets of interest organizations. Some of their contemporary themes are evident in the four cartoons presented in Figure 1-1. The McKinnon cartoon in the upper left of the figure suggests that some politicians are owned by special interests. The means by which their souls are purchased are highlighted in the cartoons in the upper right and lower left of Figure 1-1. Oliphant suggests that politicians are coerced, while Wasserman's cartoon suggests that money is the root of this particular evil. The final cartoon suggests that these activities have real consequences. In this case, lobbying by automakers is a substitute for substantively addressing the need for energy conservation. These themes are nearly universal in political cartooning.

Politicians and journalists' negative views of organized interests are likely both a cause and a consequence of the suspicions many Americans harbor about organized interests. We have seen that antipathy to faction is well rooted in American political culture. This antipathy is as strong as ever, as seen in Figure 1-2. The figure reports responses to an American National Election Study question asked since 1964: "Would you say the government is pretty much run by a few big interests looking out for themselves or that it is run for the benefit of all the people?" Since 1970 a majority of Americans, at times exceeding three-quarters of respondents, agreed that the government is run by a few big interests looking out for themselves. Common wisdom, then, is decidedly skeptical of the power of organized interests in American politics.

Politicians and journalists reflect this common wisdom and, by doing so, surely reinforce it. But their negative view of organized interests also likely arises from the kinds of evidence they employ—stories, anecdotes, cases, and telling examples of scandalous behavior. These are the raw materials journalists and politicians use to illustrate their brief against special interests. Unfortunately, nonsystematic collections of horror stories, while serving well as illustrations of more general principles, are inadequate for testing them. Such cases are typically selected precisely because their outcome supports a proposition rather than potentially challenging it. We require more systemic evidence if we are to dispassionately understand the nature and consequences of the political activities of organized interests. The other side of the great argument over organized interests—that they are a necessary and vital part of a well-functioning

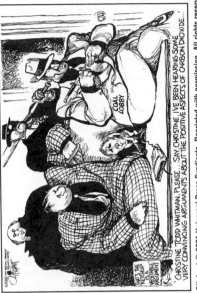

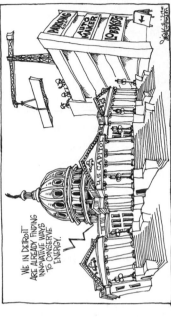

FIGURE 1-1 A Sample of Political Cartoons on Organized Interests.

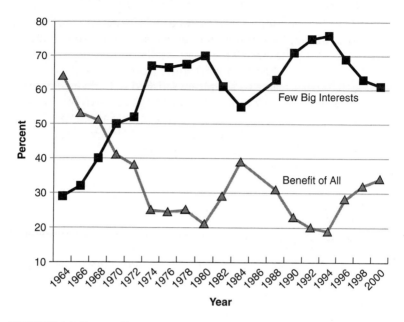

FIGURE 1-2 Survey Responses on Government Run by Few Big Interests or for Benefit of All

Source: The National Election Studies, Center for Political Studies, University of Michigan, *The NES Guide to Public Opinion and Electoral Behavior* (Ann Arbor: University of Michigan, Center for Political Studies, 1995–2000). The values in the two series do not add to 100 because of "don't know" responses.

democracy — is unlikely to find expression in an echo chamber filled with anecdotes.

The full debate over the politics of organized interests is best reflected in the work of social scientists. Scholars are less constrained by popular opinion than are journalists and politicians. But, more importantly, the evidence social scientists employ is better designed to test general propositions. We will see that political scientists and economists, like politicians and journalists, sometimes examine specific cases. But the subjects of academic case studies are ideally selected not because they illustrate a proposition, but because their outcome is uncertain in advance and can therefore provide a test of it. More often, however, social scientists rely on systematic samples of the behaviors of politicians and organized interests. These samples allow us to determine whether a particular behavior is common or exceptional. Further, they allow us to assess the conditions that give rise to one type of behavior rather than another.

Lest we seem too harsh toward journalists and politicians, we must note that social scientists are rarely satisfied with their own work on organized interests. A number of important reviews of scholarly work on interest organizations are quite pessimistic about the state of our knowledge on the topic.[25] We do not share this view. First, a great deal of new research has been conducted on interest representation in just the last few years. This new research has highlighted a number of consistent themes about how interest organizations form and pursue influence. Much of it addresses directly the concern of the critics that knowledge about interest organizations is fragmented and incomplete. Second, many of the complaints about academic research on the politics of interest representation are better understood as recognition of the broad range of potential questions about interest organization politics. Neither political science nor economics has a single theory or set of theories describing and explaining the role of organized interests in American politics. Instead, we have a host of sharply competing perspectives that mirror the full range of issues raised throughout the great debate on organized interests in democratic politics.

THE ARGUMENT IN PERSPECTIVE

We have now defined the object of our long-standing argument— interest organizations—and have a list of the players—scholars, politicians, and the media—doing all of the arguing. But what is it about interest organizations that either makes them essential to democratic politics or a profound threat to it? What is the argument about? The argument's many nuances will be fully known, of course, only when we reach the end of the book. But since this is not a mystery novel, a preliminary summary should help us appreciate those nuances as they unfold. Our summary is organized around two elements: the four stages of the influence production process and three perspectives on interest representation.

The Influence Production Process

Debates about the politics of interest representation range widely across a variety of topics. Why are some interests in society well represented by many interest organizations but others by only a few? Are communities of interest organizations biased against some kinds of interests or broadly representative of interests in society? Do interest organizations alter the content and ultimate resolution of the policy agendas governments consider or merely respond to those agendas by reinforcing the link between elected representatives and citizens? These questions can be usefully organized into a series of specific topics addressing the stages of the **influence production process,** as seen in Table 1-2. Organizing the questions in this way should remind us that the several elements of the influence process are not unrelated to each other. Therefore, our answers to the questions raised above should be consistent with each other. The cells of the table identify how each of the three perspectives understands a given stage of the process, and they cite a single work that best expresses that view.

To exercise influence, whether that influence undermines democratic representation or is essential to securing it, interests in society must first organize and then survive. The first stage of the influence production process concerns, then, the mobilization and maintenance of individual interest organizations. How do latent interests in society come to be represented by specific interest organizations? What are the essential tasks they must perform if they are to survive as organizations? With the exception of the third stage of the influence production process, scholars have devoted more time to answering these and related questions than to any other set of topics about the politics of interest representation. But many controversies remain.

Once interest organizations are mobilized for political action, they enter a population of other interest organizations. This is the interest community stage of the influence production process. Many, perhaps most, of the older members of the interest system are unlikely to interact with its newest member; they will be concerned about very different issues. Yet some of these older organizations may be quite similar to the new member of the community, competing with it for resources needed for survival and/or acting as allies on issues both support. Other members of the community will be opponents in the policy process. Thus, the community of organizations a new entrant joins will be filled with many organizations— some allies, some opponents, and many indifferent to it. We will see that their interactions with each other have important implications

TABLE 1-2 Three Perspectives on the Influence Production Process

Perspective	The Mobilization and Maintenance Stage	The Interest Community Stage	The Exercise of Influence Stage	The Political and Policy Outcome Stage
Pluralist perspective	Mobilization is a natural product of shared concerns. David B. Truman, *The Governmental Process* (1951)	All salient interests are represented in community. David B. Truman, *The Governmental Process* (1951)	Organizations provide only information. Raymond Bauer, Ithiel de Zola Pool, and Lewis Dexter, *American Business and Public Policy* (1963)	Pluralist Heaven Robert A. Dahl, *Who Governs?* (1961)
Transactions perspective	Mobilization is biased by collective action problems. Mancur Olson, *The Logic of Collective Action* (1965)	The interest community is biased in favor of elites. E. E. Schattschneider, *The Semisovereign People* (1960)	Public policy is bought and sold like any commodity. Fred S. McChesney, *Money for Nothing* (1997)	Pluralist Hell Mancur Olson, *The Rise and Decline of Nations* (1982)
Neopluralist perspective	Collective action problems can be solved. Jack L. Walker, Jr., *Mobilizing Interest Groups in America* (1991)	Community is a complex organization ecology. Virginia Gray and David Lowery, *The Population Ecology of Interest Representation* (1996)	Influence is contingent and most often limited. John P. Heinz, Edward O. Laumann, Robert L. Nelson, and Robert H. Salisbury, *The Hollow Core* (1993)	Pluralist Purgatory Frank B. Baumgartner and Bryan D. Jones, *Agendas and Instability in American Politics* (1993)

for both their survival prospects and their ability to influence public policy.

The third stage of the influence production process entails the exercise or attempted exercise of influence. Lobbying and campaign finance activity represent the most well-known and controversial tools used by interest organizations to influence public policy. But they are hardly the only means by which interest organizations seek to shape political outcomes. Two broad questions guide research on influence tools. How do interest organizations select among and then employ the various influence tools available to them? And do they influence the political behaviors or policy decisions of legislators, political executives, and judges or the preferences of the public? We will see that there is no shortage of answers to these questions.

The final stage of the influence production process is the policy and political outcome stage. Here we are concerned about the aggregate consequences of the use of influence tools by organized interests. How does the interest system as a whole influence political participation by citizens, the operation of government, and the course of public policy? The last stage of the influence production process addresses at the broadest level the core of the long argument about interest representation. Do organized interests facilitate or undercut democratic representation?

In addition to the issues raised at each stage of the influence production process, we will also consider several issues about the process itself. The most important of these concerns is the independence of the four stages. Because those studying the politics of interest representation tend to specialize in one stage or another, their linkages are rarely considered. Yet it seems clear that each stage of the process might condition outcomes at later stages. Does the mobilization of individual organizations fully determine the density and diversity of interest communities, or do interest communities have their own emergent properties meriting distinct explanation? Does the density or diversity of interest communities condition the kinds of influence tools interest organizations use? And do the linkages between the stages of the influence production process go in only one direction from mobilization through aggregate policy and political impacts? Or do they feed back through the influence production process? Does the character of the interest community, for example, condition the later mobilization efforts of new interest organizations? Examining the linkages and feedbacks will be an essential part of our analysis.

Three Perspectives on Organized Interests

Three broad perspectives dominate research on interest representation. A summary of these approaches is presented in Table 1-2. The **pluralist school**, the oldest of the three, largely shaped how political scientists understood interest representation through the 1950s and 1960s. The pluralist perspective developed as scholars sought new explanations of how democracies function in the face of emerging social science evidence that questioned the civics book model of government. That is, evidence from public opinion surveys suggested that citizens were more often than not very poorly informed about politics.[26] They were, therefore, unlikely to fulfill the democratic ideal of a fully informed citizen who makes choices in his or her own interest. Further, voting is a poor signaling device. It is an imprecise way to communicate preferences. To use a contemporary example, during the 2000 presidential election the two major parties staked out positions on a complex market basket of issues—taxes, abortion, national defense, and the environment. But voters were presented with only two real choices: Al Gore or George Bush. Given the positions of the parties, it seems unlikely that a prochoice, anti-tax, prodefense, and proenvironment voter could precisely signal his or her policy preferences by voting for either candidate. How, then, can citizens exercise control of government if not through informed choices made at the polls? The new explanation developed by political scientists focused on the critical role played by two intermediary institutions—political parties and interest organizations. These institutions, they argued, both articulate and organize the inchoate preferences of citizens and communicate those preferences to government. They provide a complementary solution. Parties aggregate preferences; interest organizations provide specificity. David Truman forcefully developed the interest organization side of the argument in his very influential 1951 book, *The Governmental Process.*

Pluralists like Truman viewed interest organizations as an essential part of the machinery of democracy. At the mobilization stage of the influence production process, pluralists assumed that if citizens felt sufficiently threatened by problems amenable to governmental solution, they would band with others to seek redress. Accordingly, all salient interests in society would be represented within the community of interest organizations, the second stage of the influence production process. While this community would not be a mirror image of all interests in society, it would well reflect those of real concern to citizens arising from social and economic disturbances. At the third stage of the influence production process, interest organizations were thought to exercise only a limited but crucial form of influence on government officials. That is, interest organizations could not readily alter the preferences of either citizens or elected officials. Instead, pluralists thought they could provide information to strengthen the link between them. And this school's interpretation of the last stage of the influence production process can be characterized as pluralist heaven. This vision of heaven is not a peaceful one. As Truman noted, "The activities of political interest groups imply controversy and conflict, the essence of politics."[27] But as intermediary institutions, organized interests, along with political parties, structure this conflict so as to insure that the preferences of citizens are fully expressed by government even in the face of the noise and ambiguities of democratic politics.

The second perspective is the **transactions school.** This perspective is derived from two sources. First, a few political scientists were dissatisfied with what they perceived as the palliatives of pluralist theory, dissatisfaction perhaps best expressed by E. E. Schattschneider in his 1960 book, *The Semisovereign People.*[28] The second and more influential source was economists, who naturally applied their discipline's concept of transactions to the analysis of politics. Indeed, we label this school as we do because the economic concept of transactions runs throughout much of this work. Transactions scholars focus on the specific exchanges that go on between interest organizations and both their members and government officials.

The transactions school differs from pluralism in ways that can hardly be more stark. Rejecting the notion that mobilization is natural, transactions scholars—most notably, economist Mancur Olson in his 1965 book, *The Logic of Collective Action*—suggested that latent groups with small numbers but large stakes are far more likely to overcome barriers to organization than those with large numbers and diffuse stakes.[29] In the latter case, individual incentives to "free ride" by letting someone else pay the costs of organizing while enjoying the benefits of their efforts are so powerful that mobilization is unlikely. The resulting community of interest organizations will overrepresent the former and underrepresent the latter. This would not matter much if interest organizations only provided information to public officials. Transactions scholars argue, however, that organized interests manipulate the preferences of the public and the actions of public officials. As Fred S. McChesney has stated it, "The essential insight of the economic model is that legislation and regulation are sold to the highest bidder in political markets, just as other goods and services are sold in more familiar commercial markets."[30] The cumulative impact of such sales is something akin to a pluralist vision of hell. Collectively, interest organizations undermine the confidence citizens have in government and the control they exercise over it. Ill-considered policies, adopted at the behest of a biased set of organized interests, weaken the economy supporting what are only nominally democratic political systems.

The **neopluralist school** is a more recent and heterogeneous collection of hypotheses. While some of the key research in the neopluralist perspective is decades old, much of it appeared only recently. But if a single work signaled the start of recent neopluralist scholarship, it was the 1993 book, *The Hollow Core*,[31] written by John P. Heinz, Edward Laumann, Robert L. Nelson, and Robert Salisbury. Borrowing from and building on both the pluralist and transactions approaches, the neopluralist perspective takes a middle ground between the pluralist and transactions schools. That is, the neopluralist approach suggests that under specific conditions the world of interest organization politics might appear consistent with either of the other two perspectives.

Three aspects of neopluralists' understanding of organized interests are especially important to keep in mind. First, while chronologically the most recent of the three perspectives and now the dominant approach within political science, neopluralism has not fully replaced the earlier approaches. Examples of all three approaches are evident in both current research and public debates about the politics of organized interests. Second, we will see that important elements of both the pluralist and transactions approaches are incorporated into the neopluralist perspective. To fully understand the neopluralist approach, then, we must first understand how pluralist and transactions scholars view the politics of organized interests. For both reasons, we cannot simply jump to the end of the story by focusing solely on the neopluralist approach.

Third and most importantly, the neopluralist approach offers more than a Goldilocks compromise between the transactions and neopluralist perspectives. Two concepts running throughout neopluralist research—variation and contingency—distinguish it from the two earlier perspectives, both of which see the world of interest organizations in rather stark terms. Variation is simply the notion that the world is neither black nor white, but a complex pallet including all shades of gray. Sometimes interest organizations are influential and sometimes they are not. Contingency is the notion that influence is conditional on circumstances. In a world dominated by variation and contingency, research must focus on explaining why otherwise similar latent interests experience quite different mobilization outcomes, why some interest communities are more crowded or diverse than others, why certain influence tools are used by some organizations and not others, and why the use of a given influence tool is only occasionally effective. In sum, the neopluralist research program tries to identify the specific conditions that influence how organized interests behave as they do and when they are successful.

Turning to the influence production process, neopluralists acknowledge the collective action problem highlighted by Olson. But they view it as neither so severe as Olson thought nor beyond solution. Neopluralist analysis of the mobilization and maintenance stage of the process is largely about mapping the clever ways in which organization leaders overcome barriers to collective action. Neopluralist's also argue that interest communities are more than the sum of mobilization events. Rather, interest communities are better understood as complex organization ecologies with their own dynamic properties that merit distinct explanation. The concept of contingency is nowhere more powerfully expressed than in neopluralist analysis of the use of influence tools. How organizations select among the influence tools available to them and how effective they are depend greatly on the specific circumstances in which organizations find themselves. Mapping these circumstances, therefore, is a key element of neopluralist research. Finally, the neopluralist assessment of the cumulative impact of organized interests might be labeled pluralist purgatory. That is, the strength of the linkage between citizen preferences and government actions is variable. Under specific conditions, interest organizations can weaken or distort that link, but, overall, neopluralists tend to view such distortions as rare when the public cares about an issue.

We have presented the three perspectives as if they are unified sets of propositions across the four stages of the influence production process. This is, in fact, a fairly realistic portrait of the three-sided academic debate about organized interests. In some cases, this consistency arises from obvious linkages between the stages. If, for example, influence tools are highly effective in manipulating public preferences and the actions of elected officials, then the cumulative impact of interest organizations on democratic politics is unlikely to be benign. Picking and choosing from among the perspectives does not, however, always produce inconsistencies. One might well conclude, for instance, that the transactions school makes a strong case that impediments to mobilization associated with free riding bias the composition of interest communities but reject its claims about buying legislation. If so, then biases in mobilization will have little ultimate consequence for public policy. Thus, at least some mixing and matching of the positions of the perspectives across the stages of influence production process is viable. Students, therefore, should evaluate the evidence for each school's position on each stage of the process.

CONCLUSION

This book explores in a more detailed manner how these three perspectives understand the several stages of the influence production process. The mobilization and maintenance of individual interest organizations is the subject of Chapter 2. We turn to the interest community stage in Chapter 3. Considerably more attention is given to the exercise of the influence stage, given the many venues in which interest organizations operate. Chapter 4 explores how organized interests seek to influence public opinion and citizens' voting choices. Chapter 5 turns to the legislative venue. Chapter 6 examines lobbying the executive branch of government, while Chapter 7 addresses the judiciary. Chapter 8 considers the last stage of the influence production process, assessing how the interest system as a whole influences the play of democratic politics and the policies governments produce. The last chapter also considers reforms that have been proposed regarding what should be done about the politics of interest representation. We describe several reform proposals and consider what our three perspectives can tell us about their merits and prospects.

Finally, understanding complex ideas is often easier when they are grounded in specific cases. In each chapter, therefore, we highlight two interest organizations, considering how the topic in the chapter is expressed in the specific circumstances in which they find themselves. We encourage students to track these topics similarly by discovering how a specific interest organization is governed, exploring the interest communities in which it operates, examining the influence tools it employs, and charting its policy successes and failures. All but the last chapter will end, then, with a list of questions about interest organizations that students can pursue. To assist this effort, the appendix provides a list of accessible information sources.

KEY TERMS AND CONCEPTS

Faction

Voluntary Organizations

Membership Groups

Associations

Institutions

Social Movement

Pressure Groups

Special Interest

Lobbyists

PACs

Interest Organizations

Interest

Influence Production Process

Pluralist School

Transactions School

Neopluralist School

QUESTIONS ABOUT YOUR INTEREST ORGANIZATION

Selecting an interest organization to track through the influence production process is easy. Identify an organization that you are a member of, think favorably—or not so favorably—of, or about which you are just curious. But remember, not all organizations are interest organizations. So having identified a candidate organization, check a few of the websites listed in the appendix to see if your organization engages in at least some influence activities. Sites that may be especially useful are those recording lobbying or PAC registrations. The website of the organization itself can be used to answer the following questions.

1. Describe your organization. What is its official name? Is it a profit or nonprofit corporation, a government organization, a club, or some other kind of organization?

2. Describe the origins of your interest organization. When was it founded? Who founded it?

3. How is your organization governed? Who is in charge and whom do they report to?
4. How important is influencing public policy to your organization? Is this its major function or only a minor part of its activities?

NOTES

1. Judy Mann, "The Needy Fare Poorly in GOP Stimulus Bill," *Washington Post*, October 24, 2001, C12.
2. Mann, "The Needy Fare Poorly in GOP Stimulus Bill."
3. Alexander Hamilton, James Madison, and John Jay, *The Federalist Papers* (New York: Mentor, 1961).
4. Gordon S. Wood, *The Creation of the American Public: 1776–1787* (New York: W. W. Norton, 1969).
5. Alexis de Tocqueville, *Democracy in America* (New York: Mentor, 1956), pp. 95–96.
6. Theda Skocpol, Marshall Ganz, and Ziad Munson, "A Nation of Organizers: The Institutional Origins of Civic Volunteerism in the United States," *American Political Science Review* 94: 527–546 (2000).
7. Sidney Verba, Kay Lehman Schlozman, and Henry E. Brady, *Voice and Equality* (Cambridge: Harvard University Press, 1995), pp. 79–81.
8. Robert Putnam, *Bowling Alone* (New York: Simon and Schuster, 2000).
9. Scott Ainsworth, "Lobbyists as Interest Group Entrepreneurs: The Mobilization of Union Veterans," *The American Review of Politics* 16: 107–129 (1995).
10. Jack H. Knott and Gary J. Miller, *Reforming Bureaucracy* (Englewood Cliffs, New Jersey: Prentice Hall, 1987).
11. Arthur Bentley, *The Process of Government* (Chicago: University of Chicago Press, 1908).
12. David R. Truman, *The Governmental Process* (New York: Alfred A. Knopf, 1951).
13. See, for example, Jack L. Walker, Jr., *Mobilizing Interest Groups in America* (Ann Arbor, Michigan: University of Michigan, 1991).
14. Virginia Gray and David Lowery, "The Institutionalization of State Communities of Organized Interests," *Political Research Quarterly* 54: 265–284 (2001).

15. Anne N. Costain and Andrew S. McFarland, *Social Movements and American Political Institutions* (Lanham, Maryland: Rowman and Littlefield Publishers, 1998).

16. Thomas Gais, *Improper Influence* (Ann Arbor: University of Michigan Press, 1996).

17. The only exclusions we make are governmental organizations seeking influence within their own governments. A few state governments, for example, require that their own departments and agencies register as lobbyists when discussing policy with legislators. While this is certainly an example of lobbying, it is not conducted by an independent interest organization. We view such interactions as a form of bureaucratic politics, not the politics of interest organizations.

18. Robert Salisbury, "Interest Structures and Policy Domains: A Focus on Research." In *Representing Interests and Interest Group Registration*, eds. William J. Crotty, Mildred A. Schwartz, and John C. Green (Lanham: University Press of America, 1994), pp. 12–13.

19. Robert H. Salisbury, *Interests and Institutions* (Pittsburgh: University of Pittsburgh Press, 1992), p. 97.

20. Frank R. Baumgartner and Beth L. Leech, "Interest Niches and Policy Bandwagons: Patterns of Interest Group Involvement in National Politics," *Journal of Politics* 63: 1191–1213 (2001).

21. Jennifer Wolak, Adam Newmark, Todd McNoldy, David Lowery, and Virginia Gray, "Much of Politics Is Still Local: Multi-State Lobbying before State Legislators," *Legislative Studies Quarterly* (2002, in press).

22. Mitch McConnell, Interview with Jim Lehrer on *Newshour*, April 2, 2001.

23. Ken Silverstein, *Washington on $10 Million a Day: How Lobbyists Plunder the Nation* (Monroe, Maine: Common Courage Press, 1998); Elizabeth Drew, *The Corruption of American Politics: What Went Wrong and Why* (Woodstock, New York: Overlook Press, 1999): David S. Broder, *Democracy Derailed: Initiative Campaigns and the Power of Money* (New York: Harcourt, 2000).

24. Jeffrey H. Birnbaum and Alan S. Murray, *Showdown at Gucci Gulch* (New York: Vintage Books, 1987).

25. See, for example, Douglas R. Arnold, "Overtilled and Under-tilled Fields in American Politics," *Political Science Quarterly* 97: 91–103 (1982); Mark P. Petracca, *The Politics of Interests* (Boulder,

Colorado: Westview Press, 1992); David Knoke, "Associations and Interest Groups," *Annual Review of Sociology* 12 (1986); William C. Mitchell and Michael C. Munger, "Economic Models of Interest Groups: An Introductory Survey," *American Journal of Political Science* 35 (1991), p. 513; Frank R. Baumgartner and Beth L. Leech, *Basic Interests* (Princeton: Princeton University Press, 1998).

26. Philip E. Converse, "The Nature of Belief Systems in Mass Publics." In *Ideology and Discontent,* ed. David Apter (New York: Free Press, 1964).

27. Truman, *The Governmental Process,* pp. 502–503.

28. E. E. Schattschneider, *The Semisovereign People* (New York: Holt, Rinehart, and Winston, 1960).

29. Mancur Olson, *The Logic of Collective Action* (Cambridge: Harvard University Press, 1965).

30. Fred S. McChesney, *Money for Nothing* (Cambridge: Harvard University Press, 1997), p. 1.

31. John P. Heinz, O. Laumann, Robert L. Nelson, and Robert Salisbury, *The Hollow Core* (Cambridge: Harvard University Press, 1993).

CHAPTER 2

Organization Mobilization and Maintenance

The Moral Majority, founded by Reverend Jerry Falwell to represent the interests of conservative Christians, claimed over 400,000
members and a multimillion-dollar budget in 1979. The Moral Majority, however, folded a decade later, even as the Christian Coalition, founded by Reverend Pat Robertson, prospered. Why did one
organization succeed and the other fail? And why do some organizations not form at all? The percentage of Americans who are homosexuals, for example, has almost certainly remained constant over
time. And public policy has more often than not imposed heavy burdens on the lives of gays and lesbians. Yet prior to 1950 gay and lesbian interests were essentially unrepresented in the political process.
After 1970, however, many organizations representing the interests
of homosexuals were founded yearly, only leveling off in the 1990s.
Why were they successful at one time but not another? These cases
highlight a fundamental fact about interest representation. Before
an organization can lobby a legislator for a favorable vote, employ
an issue ad to influence public opinion, prepare an amicus brief on a
judicial decision, sponsor a political action committee, or engage in
any other kind of influence activity, it must first be constituted and
survive.

A great deal of research, not surprisingly, has been conducted on
understanding the formation or mobilization of interest organizations and how they then survive and maintain themselves. However, this research has not produced a single explanation of either

mobilization or maintenance behaviors. Rather, the differences among the pluralist, transactions, and neopluralist perspectives discussed in Chapter 1 are nowhere more evident than in accounts of mobilization and maintenance behaviors. We consider first how individuals and organizations are mobilized and then turn our attention to the maintenance problems that organizations face once mobilized.

THE MOBILIZATION OF INTEREST ORGANIZATIONS

Except for the study of lobbying, no other question about organized interests has attracted more attention than the issue of **mobilization** — explaining why some become active to try to influence the course of public policy while others do not. But not all questions of mobilization have attracted the same level of scrutiny. We will first consider the frequently examined question of why individuals join interest organizations. We then turn to the less common effort to explain variations in the mobilization of institutions — those organizations without members.

Mobilizing Individuals

The question of why individuals join organizations, many of which become interest organizations, was not a great puzzle for pluralists. Joining with others to secure common goals seemed entirely natural to David Truman. As he wrote in *The Governmental Process*, "Men, wherever they are observed, are creatures participating in those established patterns of interaction we call groups."[1] If there were any variation in this innate proclivity, it occurred across cultures. As Tocqueville noted in *Democracy in America*, Americans have from the start seemed to have a special proclivity to engage in collective efforts to solve problems, a pattern that continues to be observed in contemporary research on political participation.[2] But whether or not Americans are really different from citizens of other countries, Truman recognized that a willingness to join with others is not itself sufficient to explain mobilization. That is, innate associative tendencies are a resource that can be called upon to secure membership in group efforts to secure a goal. But a goal still has to specified and articulated.

Disturbance Theory   To pluralists, such goal-directed mobilization arises from disturbances in society. Indeed, Truman's understanding of mobilization is often labeled **disturbance theory.** Disturbances are conflicts that develop in society, and they arise from any number of sources associated with technological, social, economic, demographic, and even cultural change. Resolving conflicts entails, in the first step, recognizing and defining a disturbance and then joining with others to seek solutions. As Truman noted, "Any mutual interest, . . . any shared attitude, is a potential group. A disturbance in established relationships anywhere in society may produce new patterns of interaction aimed at restricting or eliminating the disturbance."[3] When solutions are sought via government policy, the group assumes the status of an interest organization. Further, proposed or actual solution of an initial disturbance may itself constitute a further disturbance by threatening those benefited by the initial problem or threatened by the consequences of a shift in government policy. Thus, a disturbance may set off a chain or wave of group mobilizations until a new social or economic equilibrium is established.

Environmental organizations provide a good example of disturbance theory. Greater recognition of environmental problems developed slowly during the 1950s, but accelerated following publication of Rachel Carson's *Silent Spring,* a devastating analysis of widespread use of pesticides.[4] Consistent with Truman's analysis, this disturbance generated a three-fold increase in the number of environmental interest organizations and a ten-fold increase in the staff size of all environmental organizations since 1960.[5] The policy successes of the environmental interest organizations — passage of the Environmental Protection Act of 1969, establishment of the Environmental Protection Agency in the next year, and the adoption of federal air quality standards with amendments to the Clean Air Act in 1970 — engendered a countermobilization by business interests concerned about the costs of environmental regulation. Most notably, a number of new conservative legal foundations were established by the late 1970s to challenge the growing pace of environmental legislation and regulation.[6]

Truman's disturbance theory of mobilization was widely accepted by political scientists. But they also nibbled at its edges in several ways. Perhaps the most bothersome flaw in pluralist theory was that considerable variation could be observed in associative tendencies across individuals. As with almost all forms of political participation, men, whites, the employed, and those who are older and have more income, education, and sense of political efficacy are more likely to join voluntary organizations. As Steven J. Rosenstone and John Mark Hansen said in summarizing four decades of research, "people with more abundant resources participate more in governmental politics than those with less abundant resources."[7] Given this class bias in participation, not all disturbances are likely to generate the same level of joining. Others questioned the extent of Americans' associative tendencies. Americans join groups in relatively higher numbers compared to citizens in other countries. But in absolute terms, their level of participation is still quite low. Although the use of the term *political* in questions surely biases responses downward, surveys since 1950 indicate that only two to four percent of Americans admit to being members of a political club or organization.[8] And some scholars, most notably Robert Putnam, assert that joining is now less common than in the past.[9]

The rate at which individuals join groups has been partially addressed by more recent, comprehensive studies of joining. While still finding a class bias in participation in voluntary organizations, Sidney Verba, Kay Lehman Schlozman, and Henry F. Brady in their 1995 book, *Voice and Equality*, indicate that joining remains characteristic of Americans, as expected by pluralists. Their survey reports of affiliations with many different kinds of voluntary organizations are reported in Figure 2-1. When voluntary organizations are defined this broadly, participation rates are far more extensive than critics allow. Fully 79 percent of their respondents reported being members of voluntary associations, and 41 percent belonged to four or more organizations. Moreover, involvement is quite active; 42 percent of respondents reported that they were active members, 65 percent attended a meeting in the prior 12 months, and 55 percent contributed funds to organizations. And fully 61 percent of these members indicated that the associations they belonged to take stands on political issues, a figure that is probably an underestimate given the broad range of organizations actually engaged in lobbying. We will see in Chapter 3, for example, that nearly all of the kinds of organizations studied by Verba, Schlozman, and Brady and reported in Figure 2-1 are found on lobby registration rolls. Organization participation is wide, if not evenly, spread across the American public. The empirical support for pluralism is, therefore, mixed.

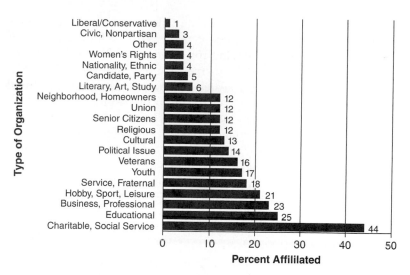

FIGURE 2-1 Voluntary Organization Affiliations
Source: Sidney Verba, Kay Lehman Schlozman, and Henry E. Brady, *Voice and Equality* (Cambridge: Harvard University Press, 1995), pp. 62–63.

The Logic of Collective Action   Mancur Olson provided a more serious challenge to the pluralist view of mobilization in 1965 in *The Logic of Collective Action*. Olson launched a simple but devastating attack on the pluralist assumption that participation is natural and provided the underpinning for the transactions perspective on mobilization. He accepted Truman's claim that interest organizations try to resolve via public policy the disturbances leading to their mobilization. He pointed out, however, that such policies are **collective goods.** Any new policy solution will benefit everyone who was disturbed under the old status quo, whether or not they were members of the organization agitating for change.

    Collective goods have two important characteristics that allow **free riding,** benefiting from the collective good without contributing to its provision. First, potential beneficiaries cannot be excluded from benefiting from collective goods. Second, collective goods are jointly consumed. That is, the good cannot be divided and it cannot be consumed to exhaustion. An often-cited example of a collective good is clean air. If environmental organizations pressure government to pass policies that ensure clean air, citizens who are not members of the environmental organizations and have not contributed to their effort still fully enjoy the benefit of clean air. It is a good that is available to all the citizens; there is no way to exclude certain citizens to keep them from enjoying the cleaner air. Air also cannot be divided, with some citizens consuming more than their share and others less, nor, outside of a sealed room, can it be used up. In all practical terms one person's consumption of clean air does not diminish someone else's enjoyment of it. The tax code provision allowing deductions for mortgages is also a collective good. This is not a benefit that all Americans can enjoy, since it is limited to homeowners. However, if an organization such as Citizens for Tax Justice works to protect this tax deduction, then its benefits are available to all homeowners, not just those who support the provision in the tax code. No American homeowner can be excluded from enjoying this benefit simply because he or she has not worked to ensure that it was provided. And again, the good is jointly consumed. It cannot be divided; if one homeowner has a large deduction because she has a large expensive home, it does not leave less of the benefit for other taxpayers. And it cannot, in practical terms, be consumed to exhaustion. Regardless of how many homeowners take the tax deduction on their income tax, it is still available to more taxpayers.

Olson then delivered a blow to pluralism by asking what rational individuals would do when asked to join an effort to secure a collective good. His answer was that they would do nothing. Since they would benefit from the adoption of a new policy whether or not they worked to secure it, they would decide to free ride on others' efforts. But since all of the potential members of a voluntary organization are presumed to be rational, all would make similar calculations. According to Olson's logic, then, no one should undertake the costs of forming and maintaining organizations to pursue even widely shared objectives as long as they concern collective goods.[10]

This is a very simple argument. Indeed, it has been presented in only a few paragraphs, but its key implication is immense — the formation of membership organizations is far from natural. The opposite, in fact, is more nearly true. Absent other forces promoting mobilization, we should not expect interest organizations to form based solely on shared concerns of their potential members. But many membership organizations do in fact form. So Olson then turned to considering the forces that actually promote mobilization. He identified three ways in which organizations may overcome the problem of collective action.

The first is prohibition of free riding. If all of the potential members of an organization that might benefit from its success are compelled or coerced to join, then no free riding will occur. Those who will benefit from the collective good must contribute to the effort to obtain it. Labor unions, according to Olson, are classic examples of **forced riding.**[11] Since all employees of a firm would benefit from the higher wages and better working conditions resulting from union activity, each employee would have an incentive to free ride by not joining and by retaining their union dues. Accordingly, forming unions is very difficult even when potential members acknowledge their benefits. Unions solve this problem by advocating laws ensuring a closed shop in which every employee is required to join the union. Unfortunately, this solution is not readily available to all organizations. And this solution is further complicated by a chicken and egg dilemma. The adoption of closed shop laws for unions, for example, presupposes that unions are strong enough to force their passage through state legislatures. But how do unions become sufficiently strong to force their passage in the absence of a closed shop?

A second solution suggests only a partial avoidance of the problem of free riding. While free riding is always a potential problem, it is more severe in some cases than others. For several reasons, it is least troubling for small groups, groups pursuing large stakes, and, especially, small groups with large stakes. For very small potential memberships, collective goods begin to take on some of the attributes of selective goods, those that are consumed by only a single person. That is, each member's share of the collective good increases as group size decreases; a million dollar pie is more attractive if it is to be sliced into five pieces rather than five million. Since it makes little sense to free ride on yourself, incentives to participate will, therefore, increase as each person's share of the collective good increases. Further, social norms against free riding become more powerful as the potential members of an organization decline in number. It is easy to free ride by not joining a consumers' organization when there are 280 million consumers in America. Nonparticipation will be hard to observe. But it is much harder to hide if there are only five potential beneficiaries of a collective good. And, last, incentives to join will be more powerful as stakes become larger. No matter how many potential members there are of a group, any single member's payoff will increase if the collective return to the group is 100 million dollars instead of a thousand dollars. The key implication of this "solution" is that it is more difficult for some organizations to overcome the collective action problem than others. Organizations with smaller numbers of potential members and/or pursuing larger stakes are more likely to mobilize than those with large potential memberships and/or smaller stakes.[12]

This partial solution can be illustrated by the American oil and gas industry, which is dominated by several large firms. If the individual corporations worked together to pressure the federal government to allow tax deductions for depleted oil wells, then each company would benefit financially a great deal. If there were many firms, each firm's return from the tax break would be less substantial. Consider again the oil and gas industry, but this time from the perspective of the consumer. Should they become organized, they could well force a reduction in gasoline taxes, making gas cheaper for every driver. However, the benefit that accrues to any individual consumer would be a very small amount of money — pennies on the gallon — and would not create a strong incentive for the vast numbers of gasoline consumers to organize; hence, the firms are better organized than consumers.

The third and most general solution to the problem of collective action identified by Olson lies in the provision of **selective benefits** by organizations. Selective benefits, unlike collective benefits, are those we consume individually. Olson argued that organizations engage in a transaction with members, exchanging selective benefits for membership. He used the example of the American Medical Association (AMA), suggesting that its provision of low cost malpractice insurance, publication of medical journals, and development of training programs at medical conventions better explains why doctors join than their concern about the collective benefits derived from the health care policies for which the AMA lobbies. Doctors who do not join the AMA cannot secure the selective benefits of insurance, journals, and training, even if they still benefit from collective goods provided via lobbying. Indeed, Olson argued that selective incentives are so important to securing membership that collective goods are produced by organizations only as a **by-product** of their provision of selective benefits. Members join to obtain selective benefits, and the surplus resources accrued by the organization are then used for lobbying. Accordingly, there may be little or no connection between the reasons motivating individuals to join voluntary organizations and the collective goods for which they lobby.[13]

Publication of Mancur Olson's *The Logic of Collective Action* in 1965 is ironic in some ways. Even as the book took academe by storm, events in the real world seemed to conspire against Olson's argument. Critics of the Vietnam War were just beginning the initial stages of organizing for sustained protest. But the civil rights movement—and many civil rights organizations—had been underway for more than a decade. And the women's liberation, consumer, and environmental movements and resurgent Christian right and good government causes would give birth to many new organizations over the next 15 years—the National Organization for Women (1966), Friends of the Earth (1969), Moral Majority (1979), Common Cause (1970), and Greenpeace (1971). Given Olson's argument, the shared interests associated with these movements should not have been sufficient to promote the emergence of interest organizations. Doubts emerged as well within academe. Tests of Olson's model in controlled laboratory settings found only mixed evidence of free riding. Experimental subjects often contributed to producing collective goods, even if participation was incomplete across all members and contributions were lower than pluralists might have expected.[14] As persuasive as Olson's ideas were, they could not fully explain why individuals joined interest organizations.

Sidestepping the Logic   Much of the research done on mobilization over the last three decades has involved trying to understand why Olson's model was incomplete. A variety of explanations have been developed. But it is important to note that few of these answers reject Olson's analysis entirely. The collective action problem is quite real and it conditions many of the behaviors of voluntary organizations. Still, enough modifications, amendments, and addenda to Olson's analysis have accumulated over time to constitute something new. We label this the neopluralist view of individual mobilization. In essence, the neopluralist approach suggests that the collective action problem is neither as severe as originally thought nor immune to solution.

There are four parts to the neopluralist claim that the problem of collective action is not as severe as Olson thought. The first lies in his narrow definition of selective incentives. In the case of the AMA, for example, Olson mentions only collective goods the medical organization lobbies for and a narrow list of selective **material benefits**— low-cost insurance, journals, and professional training. But Robert

Salisbury, building on the work of Peter B. Clark and James Q. Wilson, argued that selective incentives are not restricted to material benefits.[15] Those who join may also receive an **expressive benefit**— a benefit from feeling that they are acting on an issue they care about. This is a psychological gratification from participation, not a material benefit. Many of those who joined the Million Mom March did so for the benefit of working to support gun control, not for some sort of discount or publication. Those who join may also receive **solidary benefits** from participation—camaraderie from affiliating with like-minded people, social status, or a sense of accomplishment. The Sierra Club, for example, regularly plans outings, giving members frequent opportunities to socialize with fellow Sierrans.

Critically, expressive and solidary rewards are, like material incentives, selective benefits. Therefore, unlike collective goods, they cannot be accrued by free riding; one must join the organization. Solidary and expressive benefits, therefore, sidestep the collective action problem in the same manner as material selective incentives. But unlike strictly material incentives, solidary and expressive benefits are plausibly related to the collective benefits pursued by organizations. Solidary benefits are likely to be higher from interacting with those who share our interests. The satisfaction we derive from expressing ourselves on things we care about is even more clearly related to the collective goods provided by voluntary organizations.

We can gain some idea of the importance of these several kinds of incentives by examining the range of benefits organized interests actually provide their members. Figure 2-2 identifies the typical benefits provided by federal and state voluntary groups.[16] Nearly all organizations provide collective goods in the form of lobbying and coordination with similar voluntary groups. And some of the material benefits identified by Olson are clearly important. Many organizations provide conferences, training, and publications. Relatively few, however, offer the narrower types of incentives identified by Olson: insurance, discounts on consumer goods, or tours. But reliance on the solidary and expressive benefits associated with issue advocacy, participation, friendship, and opportunities for professional contacts is widespread. The importance of this last set of benefits was made clear when interest group leaders were asked to identify how important each benefit was to attracting members. The expressive and solidary benefits were rated equally as important as conferences, training, and publications and far more important than

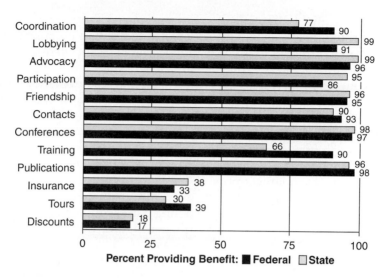

FIGURE 2-2 Benefits Provided by Federal and State Interest Organizations with Members

Sources: David C. King and Jack L. Walker, Jr., "The Provision of Benefits by Interest Groups in the United States," *Journal of Politics* (54: 394–426, 1992); David Lowery and Virginia Gray, "How Similar are State and National Interest Organizations?" *Comparative State Politics* (18: 1–16, 1996).

tours, discounts, and insurance.[17] In short, membership depends on more than either the provision of very narrow selective benefits or broad collective goods. There is an intermediate category of benefits that can only be secured by participation, but that are still related to the collective goods interest organizations provide.

A second way in which free riding problems might be mitigated lies in the context in which most groups form. Both Truman and Olson implied that those who might work together on the basis of shared concerns act as atomistic individuals with no prior interaction. This allows for cool calculation of the costs and benefits of participation, especially in large groups. Lacking both the powerful social norms of small groups and their relative ease in detecting defectors, free riding is easier in larger groups. Many voluntary organizations, however, arise from within existing organizations — churches, schools, and places of work — where members of the group already have a variety of ties. Verba, Schlozman, and Brady's analysis of civic volunteerism, for example, highlights the importance of such contexts in promoting mobilization.[18] It is through organizations, they argue, that individuals first become engaged with issues, linking them to their personal lives. Personal ties within organizations then provide modes by which individuals are contacted and recruited into voluntary groups. And last, working within organizations provides individuals the critical skills and resources they need to participate effectively in political activity, such as the ability to organize ideas and speak in public. Within such settings, issue engagement, personal recruitment, and resource development sharply reduce both opportunities and motivations to free ride even when groups are not small. In effect, such contexts facilitate mobilization by allowing even large groups to act as if they were small groups.

Some contexts, of course, are especially conducive for developing the kinds of social norms promoting participation and reducing free riding identified by Verba, Schlozman, and Brady. In Dennis Chong's analysis of the civil rights movement, he identified that the movement's roots in black churches, contexts in which strong social norms operate, enabled it to effectively sidestep problems of collective action and mobilize large numbers of black citizens.[19] The same is almost certainly true for the modern Religious Right represented first by the Moral Majority and then the Christian Coalition. Other evidence also suggests that norms promoting participation can develop even in narrower economic contexts. Terry Moe's surveys of members of voluntary groups in Minnesota representing the professional interests of farmers, retailers, and printers indicate that feelings of responsibility and obligation were very strong motivations for joining.[20] Similarly, Verba, Schlozman, and Brady's survey of organization activists across a variety of groups reports that they rate such civic rewards as doing one's duty to the community as a more important source of gratification than the material or social benefits of membership.[21] The importance of social norms that arise naturally within a wide range of organizational settings suggests that they must be an essential part of any explanation of mobilization.

The third part of the neopluralist argument that barriers to collective action may not be as strict as Olson thought concerns his image of individuals as rigorous calculators of costs and benefits. The decision to free ride involves a calculation that one's contribution to a group will not be missed. The group will still produce collective benefits the free rider can enjoy while pocketing his or her unpaid membership dues. But Moe's survey of members of Minnesota voluntary groups indicates that joiners often overestimate the importance of their contributions in securing collective benefits.[22] While each member's contribution was objectively only a drop in the bucket, a majority of the members of all five organizations claimed that its absence would increase the chance of the organization's failure. John Mark Hansen's analysis of the histories of three national interest organizations further suggests that this kind of misperception is especially likely when the collective good involves defending members from a threat.[23] This is important in light of Olson's distinction between the operation of collective incentives in large and small groups. In small groups, we have seen, each individual will gain a larger share of a collective benefit, making it something more like a selective good in promoting membership. If individuals overestimate the importance of their contributions, especially when the collective good involves a threat, then members of even large groups may act as if they were part of a small group. In such small numbers they see a direct link between their contribution and receiving a benefit.

Fourth, resources also lessen barriers to collective action, at least for some. Money, education, and social status are important predictors of whether an individual participates in political activities such as voting or joining an interest group.[24] Ultimately, the decision of whether or not to free ride is based on a cost-benefit analysis. What is the return I will receive on my investment of time or membership dues? When the reward is a collective benefit, the return may be inadequate to warrant the investment. However, costs of participation are a smaller fraction of the available resources of those with higher levels of education, income, or high status occupations. Although this hardly solves the free rider problem, it does make it less problematic for some individuals. One implication of this, however, is that this biases organized political participation in favor of those who already have more of society's resources.

The collective action problem is not a trivial concern. As Terry Moe concluded, "the evidence clearly supports the basic outlines of Olson's critique of pluralism: group membership is not simply a manifestation of political support . . . Politically based membership, however, is much more common than Olson's model would predict."[25] Recognition of the mixed attributes of solidary and expressive benefits, the fact that many membership groups form in contexts conducive to issue engagement and personal recruitment, and our tendency to miscalculate the importance of individual contributions to group success accounts, in part, for why this is so.

Even if not as severe as suggested by the transactions school, the collective action problem remains a serious barrier to mobilization. The second part of the neopluralist model of mobilization, therefore, highlights ways in which organizations—or potential organizations—try to overcome free riding. Olson, of course, noted one such mechanism in his discussion of forced riding, coercing those benefiting from the provision of collective goods to join the organizations promoting them. Neopluralists add to this analysis by identifying a second major strategy to overcome barriers to collective action—**subsidization.** If some outside agency reduces the costs to potential members of forming or joining organizations, then successful mobilization will be more likely. Several forms of subsidization have been noted by neopluralists, most notably by Jack Walker based on surveys of profit and not-for-profit associations, whose members are institutions, and citizens groups, whose members are individuals.[26]

Among the most important sources of support is that provided by individual **patrons,** wealthy individuals who care intensely about an issue. Examinations of the early histories of membership groups indicate that many were either founded or initially sustained by the contributions of one or a handful of wealthy individuals. This was confirmed by Walker's findings as seen in Figure 2-3. While only 3.8 percent of the profit associations received aid from individual patrons, fully 29.9 percent of not-for-profit associations and 47.7 percent of citizens' organizations received such support. Walker noted especially the importance of patron support for liberal citizens organizations, results more recently emphasized in Thomas Gais's analysis of support for left-leaning PACs.[27] But patron support for conservative interest organizations became more common during and after the Reagan administration.[28]

While considerable attention has been focused on wealthy patrons, Walker's data miss another type of individual subsidization of membership groups provided by interest organization **entrepreneurs.** Many organizations are founded by dedicated individuals who, far from wealthy, sacrifice mightily to subsidize the founding of organizations they care deeply about. Robert Salisbury, for example, found that entrepreneurs were vital to overcoming

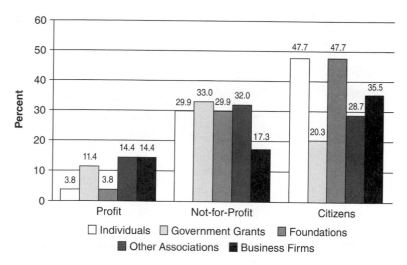

FIGURE 2-3 Percent of Member Organizations Receiving Five Sources of Aid at Time of Founding
Source: Jack L. Walker, Jr., *Mobilizing Interest Groups in America* (Ann Arbor: University of Michigan Press, 1991), p. 79.

problems of collective action in many farm organizations. He notes, for example, that "Newton Gresham, having failed as a newspaper publisher, fed his family on credit and neighbors' largess for more than a year until his Farmers Union began to attract enough dues-paying members to sustain him."[29] Histories of many organizations highlight this special role of founding entrepreneurs.

A second source of subsidization is government. As seen in Figure 2-3, 11.4 percent of profit and 33.0 percent of not-for-profit associations initially relied on government grants, while 20.3 percent of citizens' organizations also relied on public funds. But grants do not tell the full extent of public support for membership organizations. Organization histories again highlight the crucial role of initial government sponsorship even for many organizations that would seem to be unlikely dependents of the public sector. Walker, for example, noted that "the American Farm Bureau Federation began as a network of official advisory committees to county agents organized by the Department of Agriculture, the National Rifle Association was launched in close consultation with the Department of the Army during the 19th century to encourage familiarity with firearms, . . . and the American Legion was begun during World War I with government support to encourage patriotism."[30] More recently, the National Organization for Women "was founded in 1966, shortly after one of the annual national conventions of State Commissioners on the Status of Women, by a group of commissioners frustrated by the limits on political action placed upon them by their official status."[31] This pattern of public support continues today as local governments privatize the production of many social services. In many cases, the new providers of social services are nonprofit organizations created with the encouragement of local governments so that they might bid for service contracts.[32]

Other organizations offer another source of subsidies. As seen in Figure 2-3, foundations, other membership associations, and business firms **sponsor** all three types of membership organizations studied by Walker. But this support is especially crucial for citizens' groups. Of the citizens groups founded between 1960 and 1983 surveyed by Walker, 47.7 percent received financial aid from foundations, 28.7 percent from other associations, and 35.5 percent from business firms. Support from other organizations is often vital. Indeed, the federal structure of American government has long promoted such subsidies, with national membership groups often supporting the establishment of state affiliates.[33]

Similarly, both direct and nondirect (e.g., foundation) corporate contributions support many groups that act as interest organizations. The motives underlying this support are varied. Sometimes they reflect the chief economic concerns of a firm. An insurance company, for example, started the American Association of Retired Persons as a marketing device.[34] But contributions are sometimes motivated by explicit political goals, as in the case of many conservative legal foundations and think tanks. Corporate giving also less overtly includes political contributions to environmental groups and those representing minorities, support some critics suggest are payoffs to avoid attacks by these organizations. Anthony Nownes and Allan Cigler estimate that these politically overt and covert types of financial aide account for two-thirds of foundation grants.[35] But charitable altruism, while promoting a positive corporate image, surely accounts for many grants to social, health, art, and education groups.

A final source of subsidies, one not tapped by Walker's survey, lies in the efforts of political candidates. Recent studies of electoral mobilization have emphasized the crucial role played by political elites in raising voters' concerns about issues and getting them to the polls.[36] Simply put, candidates need votes. Rather then sitting at home and hoping for the best on election day, they seek out and mobilize voters. We will see in Chapter 4 that membership organizations provide an important source of votes. It is not surprising, then, that political elites seek the support of interest organizations. In some cases, however, they sponsor them. Walker points out, for example, that the National Council of Senior Citizens was founded in 1960 through the joint efforts of the AFL-CIO and the presidential campaign of John F. Kennedy.[37]

We have seen, then, that many interest organizations are founded with substantial help. Subsidies are important because they strike at the core of both Truman and Olson's implicit understanding of mobilization as the coming — or often not coming — together of like-minded, autonomous individuals. If Olson's theory is accurate, **collective action** issues surely inhibit organization foundings. But subsidies effectively sidestep problems of free riding. That is, the types of benefits sought by patrons, entrepreneurs, corporations, politicians, and the government in subsidizing mobilization are often selective rather than collective goods. Patrons care about expressive benefits. And the votes provided to politicians, the income and positions provided to entrepreneurs, and the corporate profits accruing to firms are powerful selective incentives. But they are selective incentives that lead to the provision of collective benefits. With initial subsidization, many voluntary organizations overcome the collective action barrier.

Mobilizing Institutions

Most studies of mobilization focus on explaining why individuals join membership groups. Although Olson discussed firms, his theories of collective behavior have most often been applied to individuals. While Walker surveyed voluntary organizations, including associations with institutions as members, his analysis emphasized the decisions of individuals. But mobilization issues bear on the decisions of institutions as well, whether that mobilization takes the form of an institution joining an association or deciding to act on its own. The decision by institutions to act on their own is all the more important now given that they now comprise the majority of lobby registrants.[38] Yet direct institutional mobilization is rarely studied. The primary goals of most institutions—churches, schools, business firms, and state and local governments—do not lie in the pursuit of public policy. So why do some institutions lobby while others stick to producing automobiles, providing religious services, or educating students? There are many more institutions in society than there are institutions actively pursuing political goals. Which subset chooses to become politically active? As we will see, many of the same issues we have discussed in regard to individual mobilization are also relevant for understanding the mobilization of institutions.

Institutions are not individuals, however. This makes applying these explanations to organizations more complicated in some ways and easier in others. The task of understanding organizational-level mobilization is made easier by the likelihood that institutions are less subject to some of the cognitive biases and social norms that influence individual-level mobilization. As Robert Salisbury notes, "Institutional leaders estimate that investment in political representation would be beneficial to the interest of the organization. One might treat this as a rational calculus problem."[39] This is, of course, the same kind of calculus problem that leads to free riding by individuals. But institutions are likely to make even colder calculations of costs and benefits. This simplifies our understanding of institutional motivation.

The main complication is that institutions participate in politics in many ways, including lobbying or sponsoring a PAC on their own or in an association with similar organizations. Indeed, many institutions pursue public policy goals both through associations and on their own. Mapping the full range of institutions' political activity is not easy. Unfortunately, we know less about the mobilization of institutions than we should. Most studies of direct institutional mobilization have examined the sponsorship of PACs by large business firms. Thus, they consider a relatively narrow form of political participation[40] by only one type of institution.

While somewhat limited in focus, the majority of studies of PAC sponsorship by business firms find that two factors important to both Olson and Truman seem to influence this form of political activity.[41] First, stakes seem to matter a great deal. Firms that are heavily regulated, have significant contracts with government, and/or have been charged with criminal activity sponsor PACs more frequently than those with fewer stakes in public policy. In short, firms employ PACs as an investment strategy, engaging in politics to secure economic returns. Second, resources matter too. Firms with more assets, greater sales, and/or more employees are more likely to sponsor PACs. As with individuals, political participation by institutions increases as policy stakes rise and resources for political activity are more readily available.

The collective action problem and free riding also present a complication for the study of the mobilization of institutions. Some have argued that firms are fully exposed to incentives to free ride since government policies, especially government regulations, bearing on one firm in an industry are likely to influence all of them.[42] Policies, in this view, are collective goods, and the collective action should apply here as well as to individuals. Others, however, suggest that many of the items business firms lobby for, especially contracts from government, are selective benefits available only to the firms that lobby for them. Further, all firms within an industry may not share a common interest. Larger firms, for example, because they can more easily bear the costs of regulation, may seek more stringent regulation as a useful competitive strategy against smaller firms within an industry.[43] If true, then large firms may view more stringent regulation as a selective good worth lobbying for. Unfortunately, PAC studies provide us with few firm answers. Some studies find that firms in more concentrated industries—those with fewer firms—are more likely to sponsor PACs than those with many firms and greater opportunities to free ride on the political activities of others. But several other studies find no evidence of free riding.

This ambiguity may arise from the limited usefulness of PAC sponsorship as a measure of the political activities of institutions. If PACs are, as suggested by a number of studies, a minor and infrequent means by which institutions lobby, then perhaps a more valid picture of the extent of free riding can be obtained using lobby registration data. Many more institutions lobby than sponsor PACs. Figure 2-4 examines 1997 lobby registrations by manufacturing firms in the 50 states. The x-axis measures the number of manufacturing firms in a state. The y-axis indicates the lobby participation rate—the number of lobby registrations by manufacturing firms divided by the number in such firms in a state. The figure supports

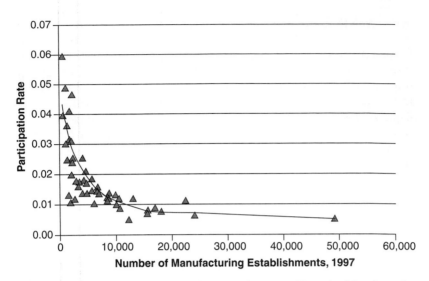

FIGURE 2-4 Lobby Participation by Manufacturing Firms by Number of Firms in Sates, 1997
Source: Compiled by the authors.

the collective action hypothesis. That is, four to six percent of all firms tend to register in states with few numbers of firms. But in states with many firms, participation rates fall to one percent or less. As opportunities to free ride increase, participation rates decline.[44]

It may surprise some that tendencies to free ride may have greater bearing on explaining variations in the mobilization of institutions than individuals. Olson assumed the opposite. Yet the institutions comprising many economic sectors exhibit the same pattern of declining participation rates as number of institutions increase that we observed in Figure 2-4. Still, these findings remain more suggestive than definitive.[45] The larger conclusion that should be drawn from these results is that we know very little yet about institutional mobilization, especially the mobilization of nonbusiness institutions across the full range of their political activities. This represents perhaps the single largest gap in the study of the politics of interest representation.[46]

MAINTAINING INTEREST ORGANIZATIONS

Once formed, organizations must survive if they are to influence public policy. But organization survival has not always seemed an important issue. To Olson, the most serious crisis any organization faces lies in overcoming the problem of collective action. Once mobilized, he assumed that they would face smooth sailing. James Q. Wilson similarly assumed that "organizations tend to persist."[47] Based on more systematic tallies of lobby registrations, we now know that this assumed persistence is illusionary. Most organizations do not survive for long. As we will see in Chapter 3, Table 3-1 shows that 59.78 percent of the interest organizations registered to lobby with state governments in 1990 were no longer on registration rolls in 1997. And a study of Minnesota organizations that ceased lobbying between 1980 and 1990 found that 45.78 percent of the institutions, 79.07 percent of the membership groups, and 84.40 percent of the associations withdrawing from registration rolls ceased to exist as organizations.[48] The **maintenance** of interest organizations, obviously, is not something to be taken for granted.

Recognition of the importance of survival does not, however, make it easy to say much about it. The key difficulty lies in the sheer range of organizations seeking political influence, as reported in Table 1-1 of Chapter 1. The scale of the maintenance problem for organizations like AT&T or the Sierra Club is astoundingly different from that of the Village of Johnson Power and Light Department or Randolph Jewelry and Loan. And the maintenance problems of institutions, associations, and membership groups differ markedly, as do the maintenance tasks of interest organizations in the private and public sectors. And last, seeking political influence is a core task of some organizations. For others, it is a minor adjunct of their primary tasks of producing tires, flying airplanes, or providing religious services. In short, interest organizations are very heterogeneous. Saying much beyond generalities about their maintenance is very perilous.

Instead of listing specific research findings applicable to only a narrow range of cases, therefore, we present two tools that are useful in diagnosing the maintenance problems of a wide range of interest organizations: niche theory and exchange theory. Niche theory provides a useful way to describe the maintenance problem. Exchange theory describes how organization leaders, managers, and entrepreneurs deal with it. Both theories are quite general in the sense that they can accommodate pluralist, transactions, and neopluralist perspectives on organization maintenance. Each of the perspectives, however, offers its own distinctive flavor to both theories.

Niche Theory

To understand **niche theory,** we must temporarily leave the world of lobbyists and politicians and enter the world of population biology. Niche theory was developed by population biologists to understand how species survive in complex environments. Biologist G. Evelyn Hutchinson described the niche as a multidimensional set of attributes of a population in relation to its environment.[49] That is, the survival of a population of a given species depends on access to a number of distinct resources in its environment — food, nesting space, mates, and so on. The access a species has to each resource is potentially extensive. A species of finch, for example, might feed at the top or the bottom of trees, earlier or later in the day, or on the leaves or insects found in the trees. Thus, access to each resource occurs across a dimension ranging from complete utilization of the resource to using only some narrow portion of it.

The sum of these resource dimensions is the fundamental niche space of a species — the resources it could survive on. Species rarely use their full fundamental niche. Competition from other species with overlapping resource needs may lead a population of finches to utilize only parts of its fundamental niche. It may feed in the morning on leaves only at the top of a tree. Its realized niche may represent only a portion of the space defined by its fundamental niche. Niche theory then isolates the central problem of survival. A species can survive only as long as the space defined by its realized niche is sufficiently large that none of the specific resource dimensions it utilizes shrinks to zero. For example, no matter how many mates or nesting places are available, our finch species will not survive if it loses access to food.

To understand how niche theory applies to interest organizations, we need to consider two of its corollaries. First, niche theory makes clear that the primary competitors of one species are other species similar to it — those with overlapping fundamental niches. Raptors acting as predators on one species of finch are not a threat to its survival. Other finch species are the real threat. Only they have the capacity to competitively exclude our first finch species from a resource dimension it depends on, jeopardizing its survival. Second, niche theory suggests that the primary way species with overlapping fundamental niches resolve competition is through **partitioning.** That is, one species will, through a process of **competitive exclusion,** use only a part of a resource — feeding early in the day — while the other utilizes another part of the resource — feeding only in the afternoon. Thus, the hallmarks of niche theory are its emphasis on competition with similar species and resolution of that conflict via partitioning.

Niche theory explains species survival in a competitive and uncertain world with limited resources. Organized interests compete and survive in a world with similarly fixed resources. Virginia Gray and David Lowery draw on the insights of niche theory to understand the maintenance problem of interest organizations.[50] First, we know that organizations must have access to certain resources if they are to survive. While finch species need food, mates, and nesting sites, the resources needed by organized interests include members or sponsors, financial resources, issues to lobby for or against, selective incentives, and access to the policy process. An organization could survive by tapping a range of sponsors, a variety of finances, any number of issues, and so on. These collectively define its fundamental niche — the multidimensional space in which it could survive. But few organizations fully utilize their fundamental niche. Instead, they partition resource dimensions with similar organizations, each seeking distinctive sets of members, financial resources, modes of access, and issues. As James Q. Wilson noted, "The easiest and most prudent maintenance strategy is to develop autonomy — that is, a distinctive area of competence, a clearly demarcated and exclusively served clientele or membership, an undisputed jurisdiction over a function, service, goal, or cause."[51] The critical maintenance task, then, is to insure that resource partitioning does not leave an organization so competitively excluded from access to any one of the resources that it depends on that it cannot survive.

How effective is partitioning? Niche theory suggests that organized interests go to such lengths to find distinct membership bases, finances, and issue agendas that they may not even recognize that they are in competition with other organizations. Gray and Lowery's surveys of state interest organizations provide strong evidence

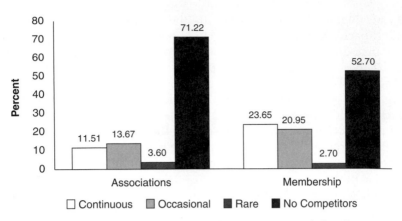

FIGURE 2-5 Perception of Frequency of Competition with Similar Organizations
Source: Virginia Gray and David Lowery, "A Niche Theory of Interest Representation," *Journal of Politics* 58: (1996), p. 186.

of extreme partitioning. They asked leaders of voluntary organizations in six states how frequently they competed with similar organizations for members, funds, contracts, or other resources. As seen in Figure 2-5, strong majorities of both types of voluntary organizations reported that they had no competitors. This lack of recognition is startling in light of other substantial evidence of competition. As we will see in Chapter 3, for example, organization death rates increase when an interest community contains more organizations of a given type. But this lack of recognition suggests just how powerful the partitioning of resources among even similar organizations can be.

Niche theory is abstract, but it explains a great deal about interest organizations. Two organizations dedicated to improving the lot of animals provide an illustration. The American Society for the Prevention of Cruelty to Animals (ASPCA) was founded in 1866. People for the Ethical Treatment of Animals (PETA) was organized in 1980. First, niche theory turns the usual way in which we think about interest organization competition on its head. Typically, we might think that the primary competitors of both the ASPCA and PETA are organizations with animal laboratories, circuses, or food processing plants. While these organizations may contend with the ASPCA or PETA over policy, they cannot threaten the survival of either since they do not rely on a common set of resources. Indeed, alleged mistreatment of animals is a resource both the ASPCA and PETA use to mobilize members. Rather, the primary competitors of the ASPCA and PETA in terms of survival as organizations are each other. If PETA could enroll all animal rights advocates as members, the ASPCA would not survive.

Second, niche theory accounts for the many stark differences between the ASPCA and PETA. Their memberships are markedly different, with the former's typically older and wealthier. They lobby on different issue agendas. PETA espouses a set of issues associated with animal rights, while the ASPCA focuses on animal protection. Their finances differ. PETA depends on membership dues, while the ASPCA receives substantial corporate funding. And they employ different lobbying strategies, with PETA sponsoring a number of highly publicized "stunts" to publicize mistreatment of animals, while the ASPCA employs more conventional influence techniques. This does not mean that they do not at times lobby on the same side of proposed legislation. We will see in Chapter 5 that allies are often useful. But in terms of the critical resources each needs to survive, the ASPCA and PETA have partitioned their overlapping fundamental niches so as to produce two distinct, but so far viable realized niches.

Niche theory is a general tool that can accommodate any of our three perspectives on interest representation. All would find the concepts of resource dimensions, partitioning, and competitive exclusion useful. But they differ sharply by identifying very different sets of critical resources. To Truman and the pluralists, access and finances were minor matters. The American political system was assumed to have a surplus of access points, and finances were of little concern if members were sufficiently concerned about issues. The critical resources to pluralists were members and issues. But Truman was not too concerned about the availability of either. Issues arise naturally from disturbances in society. And members join interest organizations to pursue resolution of those issues. Should the policy problem be solved, the issue, along with members, would fade away. The organization would rightly disappear as well.

Truman recognized, however, that ongoing organizations could face maintenance crises if the issue and member resource dimensions interact in such a way as to undermine group cohesion. That is, an organization may frame issues or policy solutions in such a way that some members may feel threatened. They may believe that the organization is defining an issue too narrowly (or too broadly) or that its tactics are too aggressive (or too passive).[52] Disputes like this can lead to fractious conflict in organizations, even splits into daughter organizations. The founding of Friends of the Earth in 1969 by David Brower, the former executive director of the Sierra Club, is often described in these terms; activists left (or, depending on the account, were exiled from) the older, more conservative organization. But this problem is not limited to membership groups. The Chamber of Commerce, an association of business firms, is severely constrained in selecting issues to lobby on since many regulatory and tax and spending proposals help some of their members while harming others.[53] William P. Browne has similarly argued that the once cohesive farm lobby was shattered by a host of new issues that led to the founding of a number of narrowly focused organizations representing distinct farming interests.[54] To pluralists, then, the central maintenance issue facing voluntary organizations concerns how issues and members interact to influence group cohesion.

To Olson and the transactions school, the only resources that really matter are the selective material incentives organizations use to lure members into joining. In Olson's view, "Only a *separate and 'selective'* incentive will stimulate a rational individual in a latent group to act in a group oriented way."[55] This has two implications for the maintenance problem. First, selective incentives are the key resource dimension for organizational maintenance. At first glance, member dues would seem to constitute a second key resource. But because selective incentives account for joining, membership and finances (e.g., dues) per se are dependent on selective incentives and cannot be considered independent resources. The selective incentives must be provided first to insure that members join and fund interest organizations. And second, the emphasis on selective benefits means that transactions scholars would not see issues as a resource dimension. The issues an organization lobbies on or the collective goods it seeks are not important ultimately to its survival. Rather, Olson argues that "the lobby is . . . a by-product of whatever function [an] organization performs that enables it to have a captive membership."[56] To transactions scholars, then, the only maintenance issue organizations face once mobilized is securing access to an attractive set of material selective incentives.

Neopluralists offer a more variegated view of maintenance. Neopluralists recognize that different kinds of interest organizations depend on very different sets of resources. That is, the fundamental niches of some organizations vary considerably from others. Institutions, for example, need not worry about members. They do need to worry about maintaining a viable enterprise, whether selling cars or running hotels. Lobbying is just one part — and in most cases, a very small part — of what institutions do. The most critical resource dimension for the lobbying function within institutions lies in securing sponsors within the organization. This entails convincing the responsible leaders of the institution that engaging in influence activities will yield returns at least equal to those of the other product lines of the organization. In short, there is no single maintenance problem applicable to all interest organizations. Different types of interest organizations will have distinct maintenance problems depending on the nature of their fundamental niche and the level of competition they face from similar organizations. For some organizations, clearly defined and cohesive issues and/or attractive selective incentives with which to attract members may very well matter, but for others, they may not matter much at all.

Given the importance of survival, organization leaders spend much of their time on maintenance tasks. Heinz, Laumann, Nelson, and Salisbury's survey of Washington lobbying organizations found that 47 percent of the time of business executives who lobby is devoted to nonlobbying duties.[57] This makes sense given that their main interests are producing goods and services for the market. But executives of citizens' organizations, most of which do not produce goods and services, spend fully 44 percent of their time on organizational maintenance. Organization maintenance is clearly important. But what are they spending their time on?

Case histories of voluntary groups indicate that much of the maintenance task includes attention to members and finances. For voluntary organizations, recruiting and retaining members is vital. Voluntary groups do not simply wait for members to arrive at their doors. They seek out and cultivate members. Contrary to the expectations of pluralists, citizens do not join freely or readily. Still, the barriers to joining are not as high as Olson suggested. A number of studies indicate that individuals will join membership groups if asked. But, as seen in Interest Organization Example 2-1, someone

INTEREST ORGANIZATION EXAMPLE 2-1:

I Hear You Knockin'

The North Carolina Public Interest Research Group (NCPIRG) is a grassroots group focusing on environmental, consumer, and government reform issues. It is one of the 35 state PIRGs affiliated with the United States Public Interest Research Group. But state PIRGs select their own issues. In 2002 NCPIRG focused its lobbying efforts on five key issues: recycling, clean air, clean water, a patients' bill of rights, and campaign finance reform. While NCPIRG casts a broad membership net, its core members are activist college students and recent graduates. The state director of NCPIRG, Elizabeth Ouzts, is a 1997 graduate of Yale University.

NCPRIG dues start at $25 for a basic membership. But unlike many membership groups, NCPIRG provides very few selective incentives — only a short newsletter published three times a year. Its recruitment information emphasizes instead collective advocacy benefits. NCPIRG lobbies the North Carolina legislature directly and indirectly through publishing a variety of research reports and preparing legislative scorecards on its key issues. NCPIRG also participates in legal cases raising public policy issues. NCPIRG claims credit for a number of lobbying successes, including passage of the North Carolina health care bill of rights.

The secret of NCPIRG's membership success lies in two tactics. First, NCPIRG recruits aggressively on a personal, door-to-door basis. Two college students knocked on the door of one of the authors and politely and persistently went into their pitch. Second, the pitch was relentlessly negative, emphasizing threats posed by polluting industries' unregulated campaign spending. People respond favorably to being personally asked to join, and threats are always more persuasive than lists of positive accomplishments.

Source: http://www.ncpirg.org

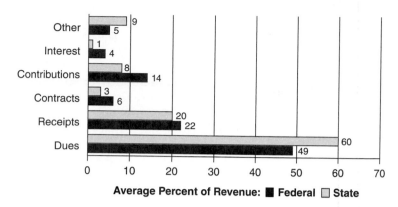

FIGURE 2-6 Average Sources of Revenue of Federal and State Voluntary Organizations

Sources: David C. King and Jack L. Walker, Jr., "The Provision of Benefits by Interest Groups in the United States," *Journal of Politics* (54: 394–426); David Lowery and Virginia Gray, "How Similar are State and National Interest Organizations?" *Comparative State Politics* (18: 1–16, 1996).

has to ask. The success of the North Carolina Public Interest Research Group (NCPIRG) relies on direct, door-to-door solicitations of potential members. In addition to personal contacting, 24 percent of the Washington organizations surveyed by Ken Kollman regularly use direct mailings to potential members.[58] Many potential members are simply unaware of an organization or how the issue it lobbies on influences their lives. Thus, providing basic information is a key part of recruitment efforts.[59] Organizations also recruit new members by subsidizing their joining, charging lower dues to attract new members who are as yet less than fully committed to it and its goals.[60] Members must also be retained after they join. Fully 72 percent of Washington voluntary organizations routinely send letters on their lobbying activities to members to communicate about their ongoing accomplishments, something that would seem unnecessary if only material selective incentives motivate joining.[61]

Raising money is also an ongoing maintenance activity for most interest organizations. Raising money is closely related to membership for many organizations. As seen in Figure 2-6, surveys of national and state voluntary organizations indicate that dues are the primary source of revenue for both: 60 and 49 percent, respectively, but money is raised from other sources. Receipts from the sale of goods and services—20 and 22 percent, respectively—and contributions from patrons — 8 and 14 percent, respectively — are also important sources of revenue. As we have seen, the latter is especially important in the early stages of the lives of voluntary organizations.

Finally, we have seen that niche theory suggests that the major response of most organizations to competition over shared niche space is partitioning so that they have an exclusive set of members, funds, issues, or modes of access to the political process. While many organizations share no resources, those that do try to isolate part of their shared fundamental niches into a realized niche over which they have exclusive access. We have seen that such partitioning is often so severe that organizations no longer recognize that they are competitors. Partitioning should be most extreme on resource dimensions that organizations believe are most vital to their survival. Gray and Lowery's surveys of state voluntary organizations suggest that the resources of members and finances are critical.[62] That is, most organizations believe that they serve an exclusive clientele and receive funding from an exclusive set of financial resources. In contrast, they recognize substantial competition with similar organizations over exercising exclusive control of issues. This suggests that for voluntary organizations, exclusive control of issues is not as important as exclusive access to members and finances.

Exchange Theory

Niche theory suggests that the resources critical to the survival of an organization must be carefully managed. But who is responsible for this management? Who identifies attractive selective benefits? And who selects the issues for which an organization lobbies? Robert Salisbury has developed a model that helps to answer these questions.[63] In Salisbury's **exchange theory**, it is entrepreneurs who do the crucial work of managing an organization's niche. The entrepreneur's efforts are important for both mobilization and maintenance of interest groups. The entrepreneur of an organized interest is much like the entrepreneur of a business. He or she invests in attractive benefits (a product) and offers that package to prospective members in exchange for the cost of membership. Thus, Salisbury identifies a role for entrepreneurs that is functionally different from that of the other group members, with the entrepreneur taking the initiative in promoting exchanges.

Perhaps the most crucial decisions of entrepreneurs concern the benefits that will be offered to potential group members. These may be collective, selective, expressive, or solidary benefits. We have seen that these benefits are important for providing the initial motivation for potential group members to mobilize and form an organization. But they are also important to its continued existence. What makes a group thrive and remain viable depends in large part on the entrepreneur's skill in choosing a package of benefits. Different types of benefits raise different challenges. An organization providing primarily expressive benefits to members may be vulnerable to appeals from other organizations that may draw members away. An expressive benefit is cheap to provide and can easily be offered by a rival organization that claims to "speak" for the cause more effectively or with a truer voice or sense of purpose. In such cases, a resourceful entrepreneur may choose to offer a complementary material or solidary benefit to retain members. A collective benefit can be adequate to offset the cost of joining in some instances. But once the collective benefit is obtained, the entrepreneur must find new goals to keep members from disbanding, as the March of Dimes did so successfully once a polio vaccine was developed by shifting its focus to birth defects. Therefore, the successful maintenance of an organization depends on the resourcefulness of the entrepreneur and the success of the *exchange.*

A successful entrepreneur benefits from the exchange, too, as seen in Interest Organization Example 2-2. Jesse Jackson provides important benefits to the members of Operation PUSH (People United to Serve Humanity), but he receives benefits as well. In general, an entrepreneur may receive an executive salary by which he or she makes a living. And a successfully maintained organization provides the entrepreneur with an official position from which to speak with authority on behalf of the group. In the case of an organization that elects leadership, an additional resource can accrue to the entrepreneur in the form of votes in support of his or her election to the leadership position. The profit that accumulates from a successful exchange can also be invested in additional benefits.

Like niche theory, this is a very simple, general model. The pluralist, transactions, and neopluralist perspectives can each offer an exchange interpretation of organization maintenance. But they differ sharply in terms of specifying what is being exchanged. These

---

INTEREST ORGANIZATION EXAMPLE 2-2:

Jesse Jackson — Entrepreneur

Jesse Jackson has founded two organizations — Operation PUSH (People United to Serve Humanity) in 1971 and the National Rainbow Coalition in 1985, which later merged with Operation PUSH. Operation PUSH pursues economic empowerment and opportunities for minorities. The Rainbow Coalition was founded to focus on political empowerment and public policy issues. The stated mission of the combined organization is to "move the nation and the world toward social, racial, and economic justice." The organization has a broad array of programs to accomplish these goals, including one program working though an associated network of churches to educate members about financial services, credit, home ownership, and mortgages. Another effort involves educating black consumers about products from black owned businesses (such as Baldwin's ice cream and Diamond Sparkle Wax).

Operation PUSH offers members a variety of incentives, including the obvious collective and selective material benefits associated with black empowerment. Operation PUSH offers expressive benefits as well. Jesse Jackson is a knowledgeable leader who is outspoken on policy questions and can argue forcefully about issues such as school vouchers. Solidary benefits are also a part of the package, in the form of demonstrations, conferences, and meetings that bring members together and encourage a spirit of camaraderie. For his part of the exchange, Jesse Jackson as entrepreneur has an opportunity to represent a large membership organization rather than simply himself or an abstract set of ideals. He also has an opportunity to serve in a significant executive position. And, finally, during his presidential bids in 1984 and 1988, the Rainbow Coalition registered several million new voters.

Source: http://www.rainbowpush.org

differences should be evident already from our earlier discussion of mobilization and niche theory. To pluralists, members are provided advocacy on issues they care about in exchange for both the dues members provide to support leaders and opportunities for leaders to advocate issues they may believe in even more intensely than members. To transactions scholars, in contrast, the exchange is quite narrow. Leaders receive support for their status as leaders as well as opportunities to lobby on issues they care about. But the benefits members receive are restricted to material selective incentives. The collective good the leader lobbies for is, from the perspective of the member, a by-product of his or her receipt of material selective benefits.

Neopluralists see the exchange in more varied terms, given variations in the niches of interest organizations. Some organizations depend on members, while others rely on sponsors within an institution. The members of some voluntary organizations are homogenous, but the members of others vary from committed activists to lukewarm supporters. Some organizations have secure finances from one or a few patrons, while others scrimp for every penny. Some organizations face little competition, while others confront many competitors. The collective goods some organizations lobby for are a powerful basis of mobilization, but not for others. These several factors determine the kinds of exchanges interest organization leaders can and need to make to solve the maintenance problem. As James Q. Wilson noted, "How the executive resolves the conflicting demands of member incentives and environmental imperatives will depend in part on his skills and circumstances; it will also depend, however, on the kind of incentives systems he manages and the history and structure of his organization."[64] Thus, there can be no simple, common description of the exchange applicable to all organizations.

This variation matters because it influences how autonomous leaders can be in pursuing collective goods via political activity. The pluralists' assessment of the positive role of organized interests in American politics is premised on the notion that leaders represent the interests of members. If their preferences differ, it is likely to be more on intensity—with leaders more committed—than on substance.[65] Some critics of organized interests, however, suggest that the collective goods leaders lobby for have little relationship to the actual policy preferences of members. Unions, for example, often endorse politicians their members then proceed to toss from office. Leaders of labor unions with memberships based on forced riding in states lacking a right-to-work law and governance rules that insulate leaders from members may have substantial discretion in selecting the issues they lobby on and the stances they take on those issues. The same is true for organizations relying solely on the provision of material selective benefits to induce joining. Lobbying is only a by-product of the exchange for selective incentives. Given variations in the kinds of exchanges leaders make with members, both types of cases are plausible in a neopluralist world. Therefore, control of leaders by members is never assured.

Still, the circumstances in which the leaders of most interest organizations find themselves probably fall somewhere between the poles of pure organizational democracy and unlimited **leadership autonomy.** While no single organization can be described as typical, Lawrence S. Rothenberg's extensive study of Common Cause, a good government organization traditionally concerned about campaign finance and government ethics reforms, illustrates one way in which autonomy is balanced with democratic control. Rothenberg's surveys of rank and file and activist members found that most were broadly satisfied that the leaders of Common Cause represented the views of its members; 89.7 percent of the activists and 86.8 percent of rank and file members agreed that the leaders cared what members think. Yet, against the preferences of both the rank and file and the leaders of Common Cause, activists shifted the issue agenda of the organization in 1982. That is, without prior experience on defense issues, Common Cause became a leading opponent of the proposed MX missile. Rothenberg explains this shift by noting that Common Cause's leaders had to be especially attentive to the preferences of its activist members, those who provided most of its energy and finances.[66] In this case, as likely is true for many organized interests, leaders are neither fully autonomous nor automatically transmit the preferences of members into the political process.

CONCLUSION

This chapter has reviewed several competing explanations of how interest organizations are mobilized and maintained. Mobilization and maintenance are important topics in their own right. For good or for ill, organized interests are important players in American politics.

They are one of the key intermediary institutions that articulate interests in society and represent those interests to public officials. Accounting for the origins and survival of interest organizations is, therefore, essential if we are to understand how the American system of politics operates. But understanding mobilization and maintenance becomes especially important if the manner in which organizations form and survive influences the remaining stages of the influence process. If mobilization and maintenance processes influence the nature of the interest community or condition the influence strategies organizations employ, then explanations of behaviors at these stages of the process must account for how organizations form and survive. For now, such links between the stages of the influence production process remain an open question. But the question ensures that we will return time and again to the topics discussed in this chapter.

KEY TERMS AND CONCEPTS

Mobilization	Subsidization
Disturbance Theory	Patron
Collective Goods	Entrepreneur
Free Riding	Sponsor
Forced Riding	Collective Action
Selective Benefit	Maintenance
By-Product	Niche Theory
Material Benefits	Partitioning
Expressive Benefit	Competitive Exclusion
Solidary Benefits	Exchange Theory
	Leadership Autonomy

QUESTIONS ABOUT YOUR
INTEREST ORGANIZATION

1. Is your interest organization an institution, a membership organization, or an association of institutions? Use the websites of your organization to describe its members or sponsors. Has its membership or sponsors changed recently?

2. What kinds of benefits/incentives does the organization provide its members or sponsors? Using the organization's website, characterize each benefit as either a selective (material, solidary, and expressive benefit) or collective benefit.
3. How does the organization finance itself? Identify its major sources of funding using the organization's website. Have these changed over time?
4. Does the organization compete with similar organizations for funds, members, or control of issues? Do a Web search for similar organizations. How do these organizations differ from yours in terms of membership, finances, or issues?
5. In your view, which of the pluralist, transactions, or neopluralist perspectives best accounts for the mobilization and maintenance behaviors of your organization?

NOTES

1. David Truman, *The Governmental Process* (New York: Alfred A. Knopf, 1951), p. 505.
2. Alexis de Tocqueville, *Democracy in America* (New York: Mentor, 1956), pp. 95–96; For a more recent comparison across nations, see Gabriel Almond and Sidney Verba, *The Civic Culture* (Boston: Little Brown, 1963).
3. Truman, *The Governmental Process*, p. 511.
4. Rachel Carson, *Silent Spring* (Boston: Houghton Mifflin, 1962). Also see Frank R. Baumgartner and Bryan D. Jones, *Agendas and Instability in American Politics* (Chicago: University of Chicago Press, 1993), pp. 83–102.
5. Baumgartner and Jones, *Agendas and Instability in American Politics*, pp. 186–187.
6. Mark A. Smith, *American Business and Political Power* (Chicago: University of Chicago Press, 2000), pp. 78–79; Karen O'Connor and Bryant Scott McFall, "Conservative Interest Group Litigation in the Reagan Era and Beyond," In *The Politics of Interests*, ed. Mark P. Petracca (Boulder, Colorado: Westview Press, 1992): 236–284.
7. Steven J. Rosenstone and John Mark Hansen, *Mobilization, Participation, and Democracy in America* (New York: Macmillan,

1993), p. 80; for a more normative assessment of these issues, see E. E. Schattschneider, *The Semisovereign People* (New York: Holt, Rinehart, and Winston, 1960), p. 33–35.

8. William H. Flanigan and Nancy H. Zingale, *Political Behavior and the American Electorate* (Washington, CQ Press, 1998), p. 16.

9. Robert D. Putnam, *Bowling Alone* (New York: Simon and Schuster, 2000).

10. Mancur Olson, *The Logic of Collective Action* (Cambridge: Harvard University Press, 1965), pp. 5–52.

11. Ibid., pp. 66–97.

12. Ibid., pp. 53–65.

13. Ibid., pp. 132–168.

14. Gerald Marwell and Ruth E. Ames, "Experiments on the Provision of Public Goods. I. Resources, Interest, Group Size, and the Free Rider Problem," *American Journal of Sociology* (85: 1335–1360, 1979); Gerald Marwell and Ruth E. Ames, "Experiments on the Provision of Public Goods. II. Provision Points, Stakes, Experiences, and the Free Rider Problem," *American Journal of Sociology* 85: 926–937 (1980); Gerald Marwell, Pamela E. Oliver, and Ralph Prahl, "Social Networks and Collective Action: A Theory of the Critical Mass III," *American Journal of Sociology* 94: 502–534 (1988); Gerald Marwell and Ruth E. Ames, "Economists Free Ride, Does Anyone Else? Experiments on the Provision of Public Goods IV," *Journal of Public Economics* 15: 295–310 (1981).

15. Robert Salisbury, "An Exchange Theory of Interest Groups," *Midwest Journal of Political Science* 13: 1–32 (1969); Peter B. Clark and James Q. Wilson, "Incentives Systems: A Theory of Organizations," *Administrative Science Quarterly* 6: 129–166 (1961).

16. Both lists include membership groups and associations. Lowery and Gray's analysis indicates that the range of benefits they provide are similar. See David Lowery and Virginia Gray, "How Similar are State and National Interest Organizations?" *Comparative State Politics* 18: 1–16 (1996).

17. David C. King and Jack L. Walker, Jr., "The Provision of Benefits by Interest Groups in the United States," *Journal of Politics* 54: 394–426 (1992). This pattern of finding a strong role for expressive benefits in mobilization is mirrored in Sidney Verba, Kay Lehman

Schlozman, and Henry E. Brady's findings on reasons activists give for participating in voluntary organizations. See *Voice and Equality* (Cambridge: Harvard University Press, 1995), p. 115.

18. Verba, Schlozman, and Brady, *Voice and Equality*, pp. 269–460.

19. Dennis Chong, *Collective Action and the Civil Rights Movement* (Chicago: University of Chicago Press, 1991).

20. Terry M. Moe, *The Organization of Interests* (Chicago: University of Chicago Press, 1980).

21. Verba, Schlozman, and Brady, *Voice and Equality*, pp. 117–119.

22. Moe, *The Organization of Interests*, p. 208.

23. John Mark Hansen, "The Political Economy of Group Membership," *American Political Science Review* 79: 79–96 (1985).

24. Sidney Verba and Norman H. Nie, *Participation in America* (New York: Harper and Row, 1972).

25. Terry M. Moe, "Toward a Broader View of Interest Organizations," *Journal of Politics* (43, 1981), p. 540.

26. Jack L. Walker, Jr., *Mobilizing Interest Groups in America* (Ann Arbor: University of Michigan Press, 1991), p. 79.

27. Thomas Gais, *Improper Influence* (Ann Arbor: University of Michigan Press, 1996).

28. Andrew Rich, "Think Tanks and Advocacy by Experts in the States." Paper presented at the Annual Meeting of the American Political Science Association, San Francisco, August 30–September 2, 2001.

29. Salisbury, "An Exchange Theory of Interest Groups," p. 10.

30. Walker, *Mobilizing Interest Groups in America*, p. 31.

31. Ibid., p. 31.

32. Jeffrey M. Berry, "Building an Effective Lobby." Paper presented at the Annual Meeting of the American Political Science Association, San Francisco, August 30–September 2, 2001.

33. Theda Skocpol, Marshall Ganz, and Ziad Munson, "A Nation of Organizers: The Institutional Origins of Civic Volunteerism in the United States," *American Political Science Review* 94: 527–546 (2000).

34. Walker, *Mobilizing Interest Groups in America*, p. 30.

35. Anthony Nownes and Allan J. Cigler, "Corporate Philanthropy in a Political Fishbowl: Perils and Possibilities," in *Interest Group Politics*, eds. Allan J. Cigler and Burdett A. Loomis (Washington: CQ Press, 1998), p. 71.

36. Rosenstone and Hansen, *Mobilization, Participation, and Democracy in America*.

37. Walker, *Mobilizing Interest Groups in America,* pp. 29–30.
38. Robert Salisbury, "Interest Representation: The Dominance of Institutions," *American Political Science Review* 81: 64–76 (1984); Virginia Gray and David Lowery, "The Institutionalization of State Communities of Organized Interests," *Political Research Quarterly* 54: 265–284 (2001).
39. Salisbury, " Interest Representation: The Dominance of Institutions," p. 74; two scholars have noted social pressures influencing PAC formation in the form of, respectively, interactions arising from service on interlocking boards of directors and the political interests of the founders of firms. See Timothy McKeown, "The Epidemiology of Corporate PAC Formation, 1975–84" *Journal of Economic Behavior and Organization* 24: 153–168 (1994); David M. Hart, "Why Do Some Firms Give? Why Do Some Give a Lot?: High-Tec PACs, 1977–1996," *Journal of Politics* 63: 1230–1249 (2001).
40. Virginia Gray and David Lowery, "Reconceptualizing PAC Formation: It's Not a Collective Action Problem, and It May Be an Arms Race," *American Politics Quarterly* 25: 319–346 (1997); Gais, *Improper Influence.*
41. Specific findings vary, but see Gary J. Andres, "Business Involvement in Campaign Finance: Factors Influencing the Decision to Form a Corporate PAC," *PS.* 18: 156–181 (1985); Kevin B. Grier, Michael C. Munger, and Brian E. Roberts, "The Determinants of Industry Political Activity, 1978–1986," *American Political Science Review* 88: 911–926 (1994); Kevin B. Grier, Michael C. Munger, and Brian E. Roberts, "The Industrial Organization of Corporate Political Participation," *Southern Economic Journal* 57: 727–738 (1991); Craig Humphries, "Corporations, PACs, and the Strategic Link between Contributions and Lobbying Activities," *Western Political Quarterly,* 44: 353–372 (1991); Marick F. Masters, Gerald D. Keim, "Determinants of PAC Participation among Large Corporations," *Journal of Politics* 47: 1158–1173 (1985); McKeown, "The Epidemiology of Corporate PAC Formation, 1975–84;" Hart, "Why Do Some Firms Give? Why Do Some Give a Lot?: High-Tec PACs, 1977–1996."
42. Grier, Munger, and Roberts, "The Industrial Organization of Corporate Political Participation," p. 728.
43. Ann Bartel and Lacy Glenn Thomas, "Predation through Legislation: The Wage and Profit Effects of the Occupational Safety

and Health Administration," *Journal of Law and Economics* 30: 239–264 (1987); Robert W. Crandell, *Controlling Industrial Pollution* (Washington: Brookings Institution, 1983).

44. This does not mean, however, that small states with few manufacturing firms have fewer manufacturing lobby registrations. Large states have so many manufacturing firms that they generate higher numbers of registrations even with a lower rate of participation. This highlights the risks of too readily inferring population traits from evidence about the distribution of traits at the level of individual organizations.

45. The evidence in Figure 2-3, for example, is somewhat confounded by the fact that some of the manufacturing registrations are not individual firms but associations that may have larger memberships in states with more manufacturing firms. Still, this is not too severe a problem given that the overwhelming majority of registrations are individual firms. A more serious problem is that Figure 2-3 does not control for the influence of other variables plausibly associated with decisions to engage in political activity.

46. Frank R. Baumgartner and Beth L. Leech are especially persuasive in arguing that insufficient attention has been given to organizational mobilization. See *Basic Interests* (Princeton: Princeton University Press, 1998), pp. 64–82.

47. James Q. Wilson, *Political Organizations* (New York: Basic Books, 1973), p. 30.

48. Virginia Gray and David Lowery, *The Population Ecology of Interest Representation* (Ann Arbor, Michigan: University of Michigan Press, 1996), p. 125.

49. G. Evelyn Hutchinson, "Concluding Remarks," *Population Studies: Animal Ecology and Demography. Cold Springs Harbor Symposia on Quantitative Biology* 22: 415–427 (1957).

50. Virginia Gray and David Lowery, "A Niche Theory of Interest Representation," *Journal of Politics* (58: 91–111, 1996).

51. Wilson, *Political Organizations*, p. 263.

52. Truman, *The Governmental Process*, pp. 156–187.

53. Mark A. Smith, *American Business and Political Power* (Chicago: University of Chicago, 2000), p. 41; James Q. Wilson, *Political Organizations* (New York: Basic Books, 1973), pp. 143–170.

54. William P. Browne, *Cultivating Congress* (Lawrence: University of Kansas Press, 1988).

55. Olson, *The Logic of Collective Action*, p. 51.

56. Ibid., p. 133.

57. John P. Heinz, O. Laumann, Robert L. Nelson, and Robert Salisbury, *The Hollow Core* (Cambridge: Harvard University Press, 1993), p. 88.

58. Ken Kollman, *Outside Lobbying* (Princeton, Princeton University Press, 1998), p. 35.

59. Paul A. Sabatier and Susan McLaughlin, "Belief Congruence between Interest Group Leaders and Members: An Empirical Analysis of Three Theories and a Suggested Synthesis," *Journal of Politics* 52: 914–935 (1990); Paul A. Sabatier, "Interest Group Membership and Organization: Multiple Theories." In *The Politics of Interests*, ed. Mark P. Petracca (Boulder: Westview Press 1992), pp. 99–129.

60. Lawrence S. Rothenberg, *Linking Citizens to Government* (Cambridge: Cambridge University Press, 1992), pp. 21–24.

61. Kollman, *Outside Lobbying*, p. 35.

62. Gray and Lowery, "A Niche Theory of Interest Representation."

63. Salisbury, "An Exchange Theory of Interest Groups."

64. Wilson, *Political Organizations*, p. 237.

65. Sabatier and McLaughlin, "Belief Congruence between Interest Group Leaders and Members: An Empirical Analysis of Three Theories and a Suggested Synthesis"; Sabatier, "Interest Group Membership and Organization: Multiple Theories."

66. Rothenberg, *Linking Citizens to Government*, pp. 158–189.

CHAPTER 3

Interest Organization Communities

*F*lorida's lobbying community underwent a remarkable transformation during the 1980s and early 1990s. As seen in Figure 3-1, Florida already had a very large lobbying community in 1982. This is certainly true when Florida's population of interest organizations is compared with Minnesota's less crowded and more sedate interest system. With 1,604 organizations registered to lobby in 1982, Florida's community of interest organizations was the largest among the 50 states and more than double Minnesota's 750 registrations. But Florida's population of interest organizations boomed over the next decade to over 3,000 registrations, three times the size of Minnesota's. Equally surprising, a rapid population bust followed this dramatic growth. From 1990 to 1995, the number of organizations registered to lobby in Florida plummeted by nearly a third. What are we to make of this boom and bust cycle? Or, in more general terms, how can we explain the density and diversity of interest organization populations?

Answering these questions requires that we move beyond the mobilization of individual organizations to consider the structure and development of interest organization communities. This is the second stage of the influence production process—the population stage of analysis. This chapter examines two traits of interest communities. First, we examine the size or density of communities of organized interests. Why are some interest communities larger than others? Why do such populations grow or decline over time? Are there limits to the size of interest communities? Second, we will

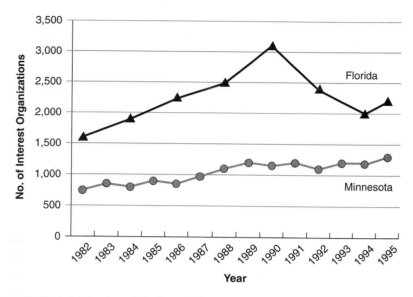

FIGURE 3-1 Number of Registered Organizations in Florida and Minnesota, 1982–1995

Source: Holly Brasher, David Lowery, and Virginia Gray, "State Lobby Registration Data: The Anomalous Case of Florida (and Minnesota too!)," *Legislative Studies Quarterly* 24: 303–314 (1999).

examine the diversity of interest communities. Why are some types of interests better represented before government than others? Are interest communities biased against some types of interests? And, if so, how can we tell? Together, these two sets of questions frame our efforts to understand the dynamics of interest communities.

Before addressing these issues, however, we must consider an antecedent question. Do interest organization communities, as opposed to individual interest organizations, really merit attention? Until very recently interest communities were rarely studied, given a lack of valid data on the size and composition of interest systems, nor were scholars strongly motivated to gather data. They simply did not think that communities per se were especially interesting. If populations are merely sums of mobilization events, then all of the critical action takes place at the mobilization stage of analysis. If we could explain why organizations mobilize in the first place, then we could account for variations in the size and composition of interest communities.

Interest communities have received much more attention over the last decade, however. As noted in Chapter 1, valid federal lobbying registration data have now become available with the implementation of the Lobby Disclosure Act of 1995. Together with data on federal political action committees (PACs), available since the late 1970s, and recent compilations of state lobby registrations, the new federal registration data provide a firm basis for describing the structure of America's interest communities. More importantly, scholars now realize that the processes leading to the mobilization of individual organizations cannot explain much of what happens within interest communities. A distinct set of explanations and models are needed to account for the dynamics of interest communities. Much of this chapter, therefore, is devoted to examining these new explanations and models, often labeled collectively the population ecology approach.

More than any other chapter, this one pays special attention to research on the 50 American states. Quite simply, to explain variations in the size and composition of interest communities, we must examine multiple populations of organized interests. While important research has been conducted on the Washington interest system, it provides but one population of organized interests. It should not be surprising, then, that much of the important research on the second stage of the influence production process has been conducted on the states.

INTEREST COMMUNITY DENSITY

The first set of questions about interest communities concerns their size or **density.** How large are American interest communities? Does their size fluctuate with changes in the economy or politics? Are there limits to their size? Even prior to the newer studies of the population stage of the influence production process, scholars answered these questions in a variety of ways reflecting the pluralist, transactions, and neopluralist perspectives.

Measuring the Density of Interest Communities

As discussed in Chapter 1, defining the boundaries of an interest organization community is difficult. Not all organized interests seek influence in any single venue or use any one set of influence tools. Lacking a census of interest organizations, answering even simple questions about the size of interest communities is difficult. Still, **lobby registration** rolls, and to a lesser extent **PAC registration** lists, provide the most valid tallies of members of interest communities now available. [1] Their validity rests on tapping two major kinds of influence activity employed by interest organizations. With the exception of think tanks and a few organizations working exclusively in the courts or the regulatory process, lobbying and contributing to political campaigns provides the clearest indication that a firm, a professional association, or a citizens' organization has become politically active.

Unfortunately, comprehensive lobby registration lists were not maintained at the national level until the passage of the Lobbying Disclosure Act of 1995.[2] Prior to 1996, efforts to map the national interest community engaged in lobbying Congress relied on a variety of indirect indicators to measure their density. Some of these sources suggested that the interest community was truly huge, with armies of lobbyists swarming the nation's capitol. The *Encyclopedia of Associations*, for example, reported that there were over 20,000 national nonprofit organizations in the United States by the late 1990s.[3] And over 7,400 national associations are headquartered in Washington.[4] But not all or even most of these organizations are politically active, and many other organized interests that are politically active are not on these lists.

The impression of a truly massive interest community was further compounded by what is essentially a form of double counting. Some tallies simply counted reports of lobbying on particular issues without noting that some organizations lobby on many pieces of legislation. Each issue-lobbying event is treated as a distinct organization engaged in lobbying. Other lists of organizations active in Washington counted as separate entries interest organizations, their affiliated PACs, and ad hoc coalitions they might belong to. One such list concluded that well over 15,000 "organizations" were politically active in Washington.[5]

The Lobby Disclosure Act of 1995 provided for a much more valid census of active interests. The act requires that all organizations directly contacting legislators and spending at least $20,500 over a six-month period must register with Congress. Unfortunately, only the 1996 registration data have been thoroughly tallied, making it difficult to assess whether the national interest population is declining, stable, or growing. Still, the 1996 registration data suggest that many earlier estimates of the size of the Washington interest community were overstated. In the first scholarly analysis of this data, Frank R. Baumgartner and Beth L. Leech reported that 5,907 interest organizations lobbied Congress in 1996,[6] with the vast bulk of lobbying activity occurring on just a few issues. Most issues attracted very little lobbying activity.[7] This is roughly a third or less of earlier tallies of the size of the Washington interest system. However, many more organizations surely retain the capacity to become politically active should an issue of concern arise. So, while nearly 6,000 organizations may be lobbying at any time, the lobbying community is a changeable cast of players.

The Federal Election Commission (**FEC**) has gathered PAC registration data since 1978 as a result of the **Federal Election Campaign Act.** We have, therefore, a better sense of how the PAC community has developed over time. We must, however, make an important distinction between connected and nonconnected PACs when considering the FEC data. Connected PACs are associated with other organizations, providing them an alternative or additional means to influence elected officials other than direct lobbying. In contrast, nonconnected PACs are freestanding entities unaffiliated with other organizations. As seen in Figure 3-2, two traits characterize the development of the PAC system. First, PAC numbers grew rapidly from the late 1970s. Nonconnected PACs increased from only 162 in 1979 to 1,053 in 1985. Over the same period, the number of connected PACs registered with the FEC grew from 1,491 to 2,356. The second noteworthy trait, however, is the stability of both PAC populations since 1985. There has been little change in the number of PACs operating at the national level since the mid-1980s.

At the state and local level, some estimates suggest that there are as many as 200,000 organizations actively seeking influence.[8] The data that might be used to test the veracity of these estimates are both more and less comprehensive than that on the Washington interest system. State PAC regulations vary widely, making it exceptionally difficult to compare PAC populations across the states.[9] On the plus side, however, the states have had a fairly uniform set of lobby registration requirements for several decades. And variations in lobbying registration rules have little impact on number of registrations.[10] Thus, we can compare the states with each other and over

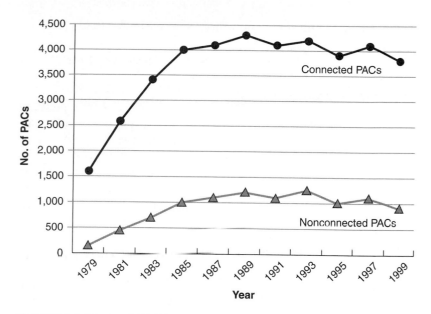

FIGURE 3-2 National PAC Registrations, 1979–1999
Source: Mark J. Rozell and Clyde Wilcox, *Interest Groups in American Campaigns* (Washington: CQ Press, 1999), p. 77; and H. R. Mahood, *Interest Groups in American National Politics* (Upper Saddle River, New Jersey: Prentice Hall, 2000), p. 76.

time. Lobby registrations for 1980 (for only 44 states), 1990, and 1997 are presented in Table 3-1. Total registrations grew remarkably from 1980 to 1990: an increase of 94.85 percent for the 44 states with data for both years. State interest communities continued to grow during the 1990s, but at a much slower pace, growing 18.15 percent overall.

Several features of the density of state interest communities deserve emphasis. First, while many organizations certainly lobby in more than one state, state interest populations are quite distinct. Of the 34,680 registrations reported for 1997, 18,277 (52.99 percent) were registered in only a single state. Many more organizations were registered in only a handful of states.[11] The 34,680 state registrations in 1997 represented political activity on the part of 21,103 distinct organizations. While considerably less than the 200,000 estimate offered by some analysts, this is still four times the number of registrations to lobby Congress in 1996. Thus, the interest communities of the states are, at least collectively, larger than the Washington community.

TABLE 3-1 State Interest Community Demographics, 1980–1997

State	No. of Lobby Registrations 1980	1990	1997	Percent Change 1980–90	1990–97	Survivor from 1990–97	Deaths from 1990–97	New since 1990
Alabama	—	289	515	—		152	137	363
Alaska	219	313	302	42.92	-3.51	120	193	182
Arizona	445	593	976	33.26	64.59	263	330	713
Arkansas	183	231	320	26.23	38.53	85	146	235
California	774	1,348	2,127	74.16	57.79	713	635	1,414
Colorado	360	579	638	60.83	10.19	227	352	411
Connecticut	350	477	636	36.29	33.33	241	236	395
Delaware	174	210	240	20.69	14.29	102	108	138
Florida	872	2,969	1,111	240.48	-62.58	281	2,688	830
Georgia	368	904	906	145.65	0.22	312	592	594
Hawaii	—	196	192	—	-2.04	77	119	115
Idaho	220	263	313	19.55	19.01	142	121	171
Illinois	389	906	1,557	132.90	71.85	401	505	1,156
Indiana	283	438	601	54.77	37.21	243	195	358
Iowa	326	550	438	68.71	-20.36	140	410	298
Kansas	336	518	616	54.17	18.92	250	268	366
Kentucky	241	372	444	54.36	19.35	185	187	259
Louisiana	255	448	650	75.69	45.09	195	253	455
Maine	214	301	322	40.65	6.98	123	178	199
Maryland	279	636	585	127.96	-8.02	205	431	380
Massachusetts	369	673	1,016	82.38	50.97	299	374	717
Michigan	353	1,160	1,042	228.61	-10.17	486	674	556
Minnesota	687	954	1,198	38.86	25.58	497	457	701
Mississippi	140	107	302	-23.57	182.24	55	52	247
Missouri	308	557	1,124	80.84	101.80	252	305	872
Montana	277	345	442	24.55	28.12	178	167	264
Nebraska	274	363	416	32.48	14.60	179	184	237
Nevada	—	826	731	—	-11.50	261	565	470
New Hampshire	149	194	267	30.20	37.63	69	125	198
New Jersey	423	746	869	76.36	16.49	236	510	633
New Mexico	324	466	685	43.83	47.00	239	227	446
New York	452	995	1,160	120.13	16.58	492	503	668
North Carolina	253	479	512	89.33	6.89	213	266	299
North Dakota	285	342	423	20.00	23.68	155	187	268
Ohio	456	945	1,129	107.24	19.47	344	601	785
Oklahoma	197	446	597	126.40	33.86	198	248	399
Oregon	326	636	629	95.09	-1.10	236	400	393
Pennsylvania	705	1,180	1,380	67.38	16.95	490	690	890
Rhode Island	—	233	296	—	27.04	118	115	178
South Carolina	146	221	363	51.37	64.25	127	94	236

(continued)

TABLE 3-1 continued

State	No. of Lobby Registrations 1980	No. of Lobby Registrations 1990	No. of Lobby Registrations 1997	Percent Change 1980–90	Percent Change 1990–97	Survivor from 1990–97	Deaths from 1990–97	New since 1990
South Dakota	207	325	315	57.00	-3.08	161	164	154
Tennessee	227	418	565	84.14	35.17	207	211	358
Texas	782	1,166	2,093	49.10	79.50	505	661	1,588
Utah	—	376	520	—	38.30	145	231	375
Vermont	143	234	388	63.64	65.81	134	100	254
Virginia	320	496	662	55.00	33.47	233	263	429
Washington	434	767	864	76.73	12.65	315	452	549
West Virginia	—	262	308	—	17.56	105	157	203
Wisconsin	303	505	621	66.67	22.97	297	208	324
Wyoming	236	394	274	66.95	-30.46	123	271	151
Total	15,064	29,352	34,680	94.85	18.15	11,806	17,546	22,874

Source: David Lowery and Virginia Gray, "The Expression of Density Dependence in State Communities of Organized Interests," *American Politics Quarterly* 29: 374–391 (2001).
Note: The first three sets of entries are 1980, 1990, and 1997 state lobby registrations of organizations, respectively. The entries in the sixth column are organizations on both lists, while entries in the seventh are those only on the 1990 rolls. The last entries are organizations only on the 1997 rolls.

Second, there is considerable variation in the size and growth rates of state interest populations. As might be expected, larger states typically report more lobbying registrations than smaller states. But close examination of the registration data reported in Table 3-1 indicates that this relationship is not a simple one. Many states of similar size have quite dissimilar interest populations. Further, their growth rates are neither constant over time nor similar to each other over any fixed period. As seen in the fourth and fifth columns of Table 3-1, the interest communities of some states grew rapidly between 1980 and 1990 and between 1990 and 1997, while others grew at a more sedate pace, and a few even experienced population declines. The most extreme case is Florida. Its number of lobby registrations grew 240.48 percent from 1980 to 1990 and then fell by 62.58 percent by 1997.

The third trait concerns stability. The data in the last three columns of Table 3-1 report the changing composition of state interest communities from 1990 to 1997. Looking at a single example indicates the volatility of state interest communities. Arizona's lobbying population grew from 593 in 1990 to 976 in 1997. But this 64.59 percent increase was not solely the result of adding new registrations. Only 263 organizations registered in 1990 (44.35 percent) were still actively lobbying in 1997; fully 330 organizations (55.65 percent) left the lobbying rolls. Of the 976 organizations registered in 1997, 713 (73.05 percent) were not lobbying in 1990. As in the national case, state lobbying communities are highly dynamic, rapidly changing in composition as organizations become politically active or retire from the political influence process.

Explaining Interest Community Density

Why are some interest communities more crowded than others? To David Truman and the pluralists, interest organizations mobilize when like-minded individuals join together on shared concerns about the course of public policy. The interest organization population is simply the sum of these mobilization events. To pluralists, then, explaining the size of the interest community entailed determining the range of interests in society and the range of disturbances motivating mobilization. As societies become more complex in social and economic terms, more discreet or refined sets of interests become salient to citizens. Interest communities should grow to reflect this more complex set of interests in society. Interest organization populations also should expand or contract as disturbances arise in society and are resolved through the political and policy processes of government. Accordingly, all of the interesting action occurs at the mobilization stage of analysis, with mobilization events fully determining the size of the interest community in a process of simple summation. This account of interest community density assumes, however, that the structure of the interest community does not itself influence the likelihood of interest organization mobilizing. That is, the pluralists assumed that the second stage of the influence production process did not feed back to influence the first stage.

The transactions perspective also paid relatively little attention to the dynamics of interest organization populations. Mancur Olson's 1965 book, *The Logic of Collective Action*, rejected the pluralist view that mobilization is natural. Rather, latent organizations with few members but with large stakes should have an easier time overcoming collective action problems. But whether free riding is common or rare, those overcoming it join the interest community. As with the pluralist account, interest system density is merely the sum of mobilization events. The size of the interest system was not expected to feed back to the mobilization stage by modifying the severity of the free rider problem facing latent organizations.

Olson, however, made a number of additional and important assertions in his 1982 book, *The Rise and Decline of Nations*. Olson assumed that interest organizations have passed their most severe challenge to existence by overcoming the collective action problem. Once mobilized, however, they would survive indefinitely.[12] This implies that the size of interest communities is essentially unlimited. As more and more organizations form, the interest community will grow indefinitely. Given the transactions approach assumption that interest organizations are quite powerful in securing benefits from government, the steady accumulation of interest organizations will lead, Olson argued, to a condition he labeled **institutional sclerosis**. The ever-more-crowded interest community will undermine the economy as interest organizations secure ever more special protections from market competition. We will consider the transaction school's institutional sclerosis hypothesis more fully in Chapter 8. Now, however, we must address its core assumption that the size of interest communities is unlimited.

Before doing so, however, we must examine something of an odd convergence of the pluralist and transactions accounts of interest community density. Despite their differences, both traditions assert that the size of the interest system is related to the size of government. To pluralists, a growing government both reflects collective responses to social or economic disturbances and is itself a disturbance that promotes countermobilization. Nearly every textbook on the politics of interest representation repeats this claim.[13] The transactions approach also suggests that the relationship is positive. As more organizations solve the problem of free riding, demands for special interest spending and protective legislation escalates, thereby increasing government size. In this view government growth is more a consequence—much as pigs feeding at a trough—than a cause of the growing size of interest communities.[14]

Both hypotheses are suspect in terms of explaining contemporary variations in the size of interest systems. The pluralist argument is not internally consistent. Once a disturbance is addressed, the issue should become less salient, leading to demobilization. And the transactions interpretation depends on Olson's unverified assumption that interest communities grow in an unchecked manner. In addition, tests of the relationship of state government size and the size of interest systems have failed to find a link.[15] Despite the popularity of these hypotheses in both the pluralist and transaction traditions, we need better explanations.

The alternative favored by some neopluralists relies on insights from research on **population ecology**. Population biologists and organization ecologists explain the density of biological and business organization populations by examining variations in environmental resources.[16] Neopluralists argue that the richness of the supply of resources needed by interest organizations and provided by political environments similarly influences the density of interest communities. Indeed, these resources define a political system's **carrying capacity** for interest organizations, setting limits on their density. Once resources are exhausted, the mobilization of new organizations will be suppressed and/or existing organizations will experience higher death rates, more frequently withdrawing from lobby registration rolls.

The descriptive data reviewed earlier offers preliminary support for the resource hypothesis. In Table 3-1, for example, we saw that a majority of interest organizations registered in the 50 states in 1990 (17,546 of 29,353 registrations) were no longer active by 1997. Contrary to Olson's assumption in *The Rise and Decline of Nations,* many interest organizations do in fact demobilize. The rise and decline of a very prominent example that has been mentioned earlier, the Moral Majority, is discussed further in Interest Organization Example 3-1. The data reported in Figure 3-2 also suggest that national PAC populations stabilized after an initial period of growth, perhaps reaching the national political system's carrying capacity for such organizations. Based on such preliminary observations, neopluralists developed two types of models to assess the impact of environmental resources on the density of interest communities.

One set of models is analogous to those used by organization ecologists studying the density of labor unions, newspapers, breweries, and semiconductor firms.[17] These models do not measure resources directly. Rather, they assume that variation in the availability of resources needed for survival, such as consumers of semiconductors, can be observed over the life cycle of an industry. At first, new organizations may have difficulty finding sufficient resources to survive. When the semiconductor industry began, for

INTEREST ORGANIZATION EXAMPLE 3-1:

Mission Accomplished

The Moral Majority was founded by Reverend Jerry Falwell in 1979 to represent the interests of born-again Christians and other religious conservatives. The organization played a major role in the 1980 presidential election. Reverend Falwell claimed that the Moral Majority registered up to four million new voters prior to the election. Perhaps more importantly, the Moral Majority led the Christian Right into alliance with the Republican Party. Several of those assisting in organization's founding — Paul Weyrich, Richard Viguerie, and Howard Phillips — had long-standing ties to the GOP. Prior to 1980 the votes of conservative Christians were equally divided between the two major parties. The core of Moral Majority's operation was its extensive mailing list of conservative voters. But the Moral Majority also supported subsidiary lobbying, PAC, and litigation organizations. The Moral Majority lobbied for prayer in schools, creationism, and protection of the free enterprise system. Homosexual rights, abortion, and disarmament treaties with the Soviet Union were among the many things it opposed.

By 1989, however, the Moral Majority had exhausted its political appeal to potential members. While it raised $3.5 million in its last year, it was being outorganized by more targeted conservative organizations with less diffuse political agendas. Many of these had split off from the Moral Majority. The organization was also tarnished by scandals surrounding two other televangelists, Jimmy Swaggart and Jim Bakker. As the Moral Majority's Mark Smith noted, "The TV evangelists' scandals hurt us a lot." So, with Reverend Falwell saying that "our mission is accomplished," the Moral Majority closed down its operation on August 31, 1989.

Source: http://www.publiceye.org/research/Group_Watch/Entries-92.htm, visited July 10, 2002.

example, the environment provided few consumers and suppliers. But as the industry developed and resources become more plentiful, founding rates of new companies increased. Then, as the semiconductor niche space was fully exploited as more and more firms joined the population, entry became more difficult. As the environment's carrying capacity is approached, new firms can enter the population only by expropriating the niche space of others, perhaps driving them out of business. This suggests that populations will initially experience slow growth, identified as a period of **legitimation,** during which new kinds of organizations slowly become an accepted mode of business. This is followed by a period of relatively fast growth. The last stage is identified as a period of **density dependence** in which carrying capacities are approached, growth rates slow, and the size of the population stabilizes.

Anthony Nownes has successfully applied this model to mapping the growth of gay and lesbian interest organizations.[18] As seen in Figure 3-3, their population growth from 1950 to 1998 provides striking support for population ecology hypothesis. In the early years, the founding rate of homosexual rights organizations was exceptionally slow, indicating a period of legitimation when few potential members were willing to join. Over time, however, foundings of new organizations increased as potential members become more willing to support gay and lesbian causes. By the 1990s, however, the density dependent growth path suggests that the gay and lesbian niche space became crowded and resources less plentiful. Accordingly, the population of gay and lesbian interest organizations has stabilized.

These results have four implications. First, interest populations are more than the sum of mobilization events. The context in which they form matters as well. Second, the rate at which organizations withdraw from lobbying also matters; we must consider both birth and death rates to explain density. Third, the severity of the problem of collective action is not a constant. Rather, overcoming barriers to free riding can be more difficult during some periods of the life of subpopulations of interest organizations, especially so during initial periods of legitimation and later periods of density dependence. And fourth, the size of a subpopulation of interest organizations is not unlimited. The political system has real, if surely flexible, carrying capacities for interest organizations that are determined by the

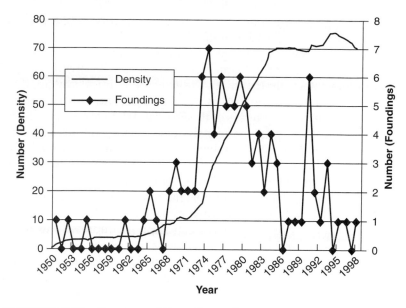

FIGURE 3-3 The Density and Foundings of Homosexual Rights Organizations, 1950–1998

Source: Anthony Nownes, "The Population Ecology of Interest Group Formation," *British Journal of Political Science* (in press).

resources available in the environment needed to support interest representation.

A second set of organization ecology models, used by island biogeographers, has been used to explain variation in the density of state interest communities.[19] These models measure more directly the resources available in the environment. Island biogeographers suggest that three characteristics of the environment are crucial to maintaining biological species. The first is area. As the size of islands increases, more species can be supported because the niche space needed to support viable populations expands. But area operates in a density dependent manner. As available niche space is fully exploited, there will be fewer opportunities to add new species to the biological community. Energy is the second variable; an island of a given size supports more biological species of all types if it is in the tropics than in the arctic. And last, the stability of the environment matters. If a volcano destroys an island's habitat, it must begin accumulating species anew. Together, these factors define the energy, stability, and area **(ESA model)**.

Gray and Lowery have applied the ESA model to understand variations in the size of state interest communities.[20] Barring a major war or other cataclysm that might destroy the political system, they assume that the **stability** term is the least relevant, but they argue that the area and energy terms of the ESA model do apply to state interest communities and provide insight into changes in interest community density. They ask first where interest organizations live — the **area** term of the model. Interest organizations, they argue, live on members and sponsors. It is unlikely, for example, that a state with no manufacturing firms will support manufacturing interest organizations. And the more manufacturing firms it has, the more manufacturing interest organizations it can support, representing more and more specialized concerns of potential members and sponsors. But as with biological species, this relationship is hypothesized to be density dependent. While the membership of existing organizations may increase in states with many manufacturing firms, the growth rate of new interest organizations should slow as the issue niche dimension of concern to the manufacturing sector is fully exploited and thus exhausted as a resource for additional mobilization.

They then ask what organized interests live on — the **energy** term of the ESA model. In answering this question, they rely in part on the pluralist disturbance hypothesis. An interest organization is unlikely to survive if it cannot persuade potential members or sponsors that they have a stake in public policy meriting an expenditure of time, effort, and financial contributions. So, as new issues arise or old issues are aggravated, the environment should provide a more congenial, richer setting for founding interest organizations. There are more issues to exploit in securing members. As we saw in Chapter 2, leaders of institutions also must be given compelling reasons to become involved in politics. For many, as seen in the Microsoft case discussed in Interest Organization Example 3-2, threatened changes in government policy bearing on an institution's interests provide the energy needed to initiate a lobbying campaign.

Issues alone, however, are not the sole energy source. No matter how salient an issue is to potential members or sponsors, few will support an interest organization if there is no chance that the political system will address it. And few satisfied with the status quo will

INTEREST ORGANIZATION EXAMPLE 3-2:

Bill Gates Discovers Politics

Founded in 1975, Microsoft had become by the late 1980s the behemoth of the computer software, services, and Internet industry. Its rapid expansion from a startup to an industry giant was based on its now ubiquitous Windows operating system. By 2001 Microsoft had subsidiary offices in more than 60 countries, employed more than 48,030 employees, and reported net revenues greater than $25 billion. But even as Microsoft became a financial colossus, it remained a political shrimp. Microsoft had no Washington office and contributed little in campaign finance. Microsoft and Bill Gates largely ignored the world of politics.

All of this changed in the mid-1990s as the U.S. Department of Justice became more serious about investigating the company for predatory practices designed to drive competitors out of business. After several years of investigation, the department filed suit in 1998 to break up Microsoft to end its alleged monopoly of the software industry. Microsoft and the Department of Justice then spent several years in negotiation and in court. Microsoft noticed. After opening a Washington office in 1995, by 1998 the firm spent $2.12 million in lobbying, including hiring nine contract lobbying firms. By 2000 expenditures on lobbying increased to $6.36 million with 15 lobbying firms working for Microsoft. From 1994 to the 2000 election cycle, Microsoft's soft money, PAC, and individual employee contributions to political campaigns increased from $109,134 to $4,701,631. Yes, Bill noticed. In September 2001, the Bush justice department announced that it would no longer seek the break up of Microsoft.

Source: David Hart, "High Tech Learns to Play the Washington Game: The Political Education of Bill Gates and Other Nerds." In *Interest Group Politics* 6th ed. Allan J. Cigler and Burdett A. Loomis (Washington, DC: CQ Press), pp. 293–312; http://www.Microsoft.com; http://opensecrtes.org, both visited July 10, 2002

be mobilized unless it is threatened. So the prospect of policy change matters, too. The ESA model, therefore, considers the level of state party competition in tapping the energy available to support interest organization activity. If the out-party has a good chance of becoming the in-party at the next election, then old policies may be overturned and new policies actively considered. So states with competitive party systems should support larger interest communities.

Gray and Lowery found strong support for the ESA model when it was tested with six interest **guilds**—subpopulations of interest organizations concerned with distinct substantive interests—representing agriculture, construction, manufacturing, local government, welfare, and environmental issues.[21] Populations of each guild increased in a density dependent manner with the size of its potential members in the state. States with larger numbers of environmentally concerned citizens, for example, typically support more environmental interest organizations. It is worth emphasizing that this finding is less obvious than it might appear. While we would certainly expect a given environmental interest organization to have more *members* in a state with many environmentalists than in a state with few, it is not obvious that the latter should have more environmental *organizations* per se. The ESA model, however, suggests that this greater organizational representation results from the presence in states with many environmentally active citizens of sufficient numbers to support smaller organizations with very specific issue agendas. In a state with few environmentalists, in contrast, these smaller organizations would not enroll sufficient members to pass the threshold of initial mobilization. But the rate of formation of new organizations eventually slows in a density dependent manner in even the largest states—even if the memberships of existing organizations continue to increase—as more specialized issue agendas are exhausted. And last, populations of the six guilds were also larger in states where the policy stakes of concern to each were larger (e.g., more severe environmental problems) and with higher levels of party competition. Based on these findings, Lowery and Gray conclude that the resources available in the environment matter a great deal.

The key implication of their analysis is perhaps best illustrated, however, not in the individual guild models but in a more general model of the overall size of the state interest communities. That is, Gray and Lowery argue that the size of a state's economy, as

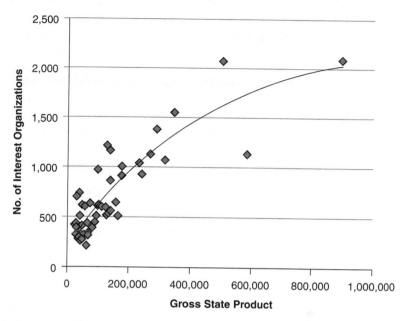

FIGURE 3-4 The Density Dependence of State Interest Communities, 1997
Source: Jennifer Wolak, David Lowery, and Virginia Gray, "California Dreaming: Outliers, Leverage, and Influence in Comparative State Politics, *State Politics and Policy Quarterly* 1: 255–272 (2001).

measured by gross state product (GSP), can serve as a general indicator of the number of potential members or sponsors of all interest organizations, the area concept in the ESA model. States with large economies are likely to have more farms, firms, environmentalists, and every other type of potential member or sponsor of organizations than smaller states. Thus, GSP can serve as a surrogate for the size of the potential sponsor/membership base in a state for all organizations. Their analysis of the relationship between economic size and the density of state interest systems in 1997 is presented in Figure 3-4. Larger states support larger interest communities. But the responsiveness of the size of the entire interest community to GSP declines as states become larger, indicating that the interest community has exhausted viable niche space.

The overall response curve of state interest communities reported in Figure 3-4 may shift upward or downward as political systems become more or less competitive and as political agendas heat up or cool down. Indeed, there is strong evidence that the response curve in the figure shifted upward over the last 20 years due to transfers of many policy responsibilities from the national to state governments and a general increase in the level of party competition in the states.[22] But state-specific variations in resources, the energy term, are possible, too. The extreme case of Florida provides a good example. As reported in Figure 3-1, Florida experienced an exceptional boom in its lobbying population over the 1980s, growing over the decade by 240.48 percent to 2,969 interest lobby registrations, which then collapsed 62.58 percent by 1997. The collapse was even more severe for the lobbyist population than for the organizations they represented; lobbyist registrations fell from 5,798 in 1990 to only 1,897 in 1996. Brasher, Lowery, and Gray (1999) argue that this case is fully interpretable using the ESA model of density. That is, Florida differed from other states only in the severity and breadth of the policy uncertainty it faced. The uncertainties included a chronic and pervasive fiscal crisis where virtually every organization in the state had some stake involved, a fumbling and muddled political response over several legislative sessions that threatened the interests of numerous economic sectors, and an increasingly competitive political party system. Florida's lobbying population skyrocketed, given this extraordinary supply of political energy. The resolution of Florida's fiscal crisis through tax increases and spending cuts then extracted the energy needed to support such a large interest community, leading to catastrophic collapse. The Florida case illustrates just how responsive interest systems are to environmental resources.[23]

The Importance of Interest Community Density

The dynamics of interest organization populations merit attention on their own terms. But the density of interest systems is also important because of its influence on the other stages of the influence production process. We consider how it may change the use of influence tools in later chapters. For now, however, we examine how the density of interest communities influences mobilization and maintenance processes, the topics considered in Chapter 2.

Despite what we have discovered about density dependence and the limited carrying capacity of interest communities, it is not yet clear how the dynamics of interest populations feed back to influence mobilization rates. That is, density dependence might result from one or both of two effects. On the one hand, mobilizing new organizations may be more difficult in crowded interest systems. Once environmental resources are exhausted, a lack of niche space suppresses the founding or birthrate of new interest organizations. Alternatively, density dependence may result entirely from a higher death rate among existing organizations. As political systems approach their carrying capacities for interest organizations, older organizations may be competitively excluded by newer organizations better representing members or sponsors. The enhanced death rate of older organizations frees up niche space for the newly mobilized organizations.

Which of these two mechanisms best accounts for density dependence matters a great deal. First, if density dependence results from higher death rates in crowded interest systems, then the structure of interest populations does not influence the process of mobilization. We can study mobilization only in terms of the issues discussed in Chapter 2. If, however, the density of the interest community itself influences mobilization by suppressing birthrates, then existing explanations of mobilization are likely to be incomplete. Second, the two hypothesized sources of density dependence, birth rates and death rates, have important implications for how well interest communities represent interests in society. If density dependence results solely from the suppression of the birthrate of new organizations, new interests in society might have a difficult time joining the lobbying community. Older, more traditional interests will block their mobilization by exhausting the resources newly mobilized organizations need. But if density dependence is expressed through higher mortality rates in crowded interest systems, the compositions of interest communities will readily turn over as new interests develop in society and old interests lapse in salience.

Gray and Lowery studied this question using the data reported in the last three columns of Table 3-1 on the birth- and death rates of state interest communities from 1990 to 1997. They examined whether the rates of interest organization births and deaths from 1990 to 1997 were related to how crowded the state interest communities were in 1990. They found support for both hypotheses. States with initially dense interest systems experienced both lower birthrates of new organizations and higher death rates among existing organizations. This means that we need to understand the nature of the communities that organizations might join to fully explain mobilization. New organizations find it more difficult to enter crowded interest systems.

INTEREST COMMUNITY DIVERSITY

A second set of questions posed at the population stage of the influence process concerns the **diversity** of interest communities. Are some kinds of interests better represented than others? Has the diversity of interest communities changed over time? How can we explain this variation? And how does the diversity of interest systems influence the political process? The pluralist, transactions, and neopluralist schools answer these questions in very different ways.

Measuring the Diversity of Interest Communities

The concept of interest system diversity is very broad. Interest system density is readily understood as the size of the interest community, even if measuring density is difficult. But diversity is an inherently ambiguous concept, given that interest systems might be diverse with respect to any number of traits — the size or wealth of its interest organizations, the influence tools they typically employ, and so on. But two specific traits stand out in most research.

The first is the diversity of substantive interests represented by interest organizations. Many critics of the politics of interest representation argue that traditional business interests are heavily overrepresented in both national and state interest systems relative to organizations claiming to represent the public interest.[24] To such critics, the dominance of business interests constitutes strong evidence that American interest communities are heavily biased. While we will consider the issue of bias more fully at the end of this chapter, there is little doubt that business interests are very heavily represented before both national and state governments.

Frank R. Baumgartner and Beth L. Leech analyzed the diversity of the national interest community with registration data gathered as a result of the **Lobby Disclosure Act of 1995**.[25] As seen in Figure 3-5, individual business firms (e.g., Anheuser-Busch Companies, RJ Reynolds Tobacco Company, or MCI Telecommunications) comprised 43 percent of all organizations registered to lobby Congress,

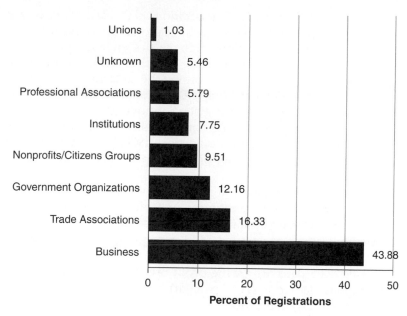

FIGURE 3-5 The Substantive Diversity of the Washington Lobbying Community, 1996
Source: Frank R. Baumgartner and Beth L. Leech, "Interest Niches and Policy Bandwagons: Patterns of Interest Group Involvement in National Politics," *Journal of Politics* 63: 1199 (2001).

while trade associations (e.g., American Automobile Manufacturers Association, Soft Drink Association, or National Association of Independent Business) contributed an additional 16 percent. In contrast, unions (e.g., the AFL-CIO, or American Federation of Teachers) constituted only one percent and nonprofit and citizens' organizations (e.g., Sierra Club or NAACP) only nine percent of the organizations lobbying Congress. This pattern of business dominance of the national interest system is fully consistent with other studies conducted over the last four decades using less systematic data. While directly comparable data across time are not available, many observers conclude that business dominance is now greater than ever.[26] Business dominance is also evident in PAC registrations. In 1999, 82.14 percent of all affiliated PACs represented trade associations or corporations.[27]

A few students of the Washington interest system, however, have argued that nonprofits and citizens interest organizations, which comprised only 9.51 percent of registrations in the Baumgartner and Leech census reported in Figure 3-5, have grown in relative terms recently. Jack L. Walker and Jeffrey M. Berry, as seen in Chapter 2, suggest that patrons and sponsors have been very creative in recent decades in finding means of overcoming the collective action problem facing citizens' organizations.[28] Unfortunately, the lack of systematic data on national lobby registrations over time makes it very difficult to test this assertion. Although it is clear that lobbying by citizens' organizations has increased since 1970, it is not at all clear that they have grown at a faster or slower pace than other kinds of organizations.

Similar patterns are evident in the states. State registration data for 1980, 1990, and 1997 are reported in Table 3-2. Ignoring interest organizations whose substantive interest could not be identified, profit organizations constituted 73.81 percent of lobby registrations in 1997. This proportion hardly changed from 1980 (73.61 percent) and 1990 (72.05 percent). Of the profit organizations, health (13.08 percent), manufacturing (11.65 percent), and banking (6.86 percent) interests were especially heavily represented. In contrast, not-for profit organizations comprised just more than a quarter of all state lobby registrations.[29] Environmental (1.99 percent), good government (1.42 percent), and religious (0.66 percent) organizations constitute only tiny proportions of state interest communities.

At the state level, the availability of registration data across time allows us to test directly Walker and Berry's hypothesis that the pace of mobilization by citizens' organizations has increased sufficiently that they now comprise a larger and growing relative share of interest communities. Of the not-for-profit interest organizations reported in Table 3-2, those representing good government, civil rights, environmental, and women's interests perhaps best reflect the Walker and Berry definition of citizens' organizations. Comparing their numbers of registrations in 1980 in column one with those reported for 1997 in column three indicates that their numbers have indeed increased over time. The number of good government organizations grew from 188 in 1980 to 482 in 1997, with similar patterns of growth reported for civil rights (102 to 222), environmental (319 to 676), and women's interest organizations (220 to 360).

As seen in the right-hand columns of the table, however, this increase in registrations by citizens' organizations has not changed their relative share of the lobbying community. Good government

TABLE 3-2 The Composition of State Interest Communities, 1980, 1990, and 1997

Interest Guild	Number of Organizations			Percent of All Organizations		
	1980	1990	1997	1980	1990	1997
Profit Organizations						
Communications	280	705	1,265	1.89	2.40	3.66
Manufacturing	1,066	3,326	3,964	7.18	11.34	11.46
Health	1,230	2,993	4,452	8.28	10.20	12.88
Legal	223	717	783	1.50	2.44	2.26
Banking	874	1,584	2,336	5.88	5.40	6.76
Business Services	843	1,004	1,979	5.68	3.42	5.72
Small Business	1,047	2,863	2,357	7.05	9.76	6.82
Insurance	917	1,630	1,928	6.17	5.56	5.58
Agriculture	449	718	798	3.02	2.45	2.31
Utility	620	1,149	1,097	4.17	3.92	3.17
Transportation	648	1,033	1,047	4.36	3.52	3.03
Natural Resources	914	1,106	1,401	6.15	3.77	4.05
Construction	843	1,079	1,184	5.68	3.68	3.42
Hotel	441	437	529	2.97	1.49	1.53
Subtotal	10,395	20,344	25,120	69.99	69.34	72.65
Not-for-Profit Organizations						
Welfare	350	977	1,301	2.36	3.33	3.76
Intergovernmental Relations	494	1,536	1,564	3.33	5.23	4.52
Police/Fire	250	500	689	1.68	1.70	1.99
Good Government	188	415	482	1.27	1.41	1.39
Sport	449	1,049	1,080	3.02	3.58	3.12
Civil Rights	102	156	222	0.69	0.53	0.64
Education	945	1,686	2,035	6.36	5.75	5.89
Environment	319	593	676	2.15	2.02	1.96
Religion	108	239	226	0.73	0.81	0.65
Women	220	360	306	1.48	1.23	0.89
Military	77	152	95	0.52	0.52	0.27
Tax	226	230	239	1.52	0.78	0.69
Subtotal	3,727	7,893	8,915	25.09	26.90	25.78
Unknown	731	1,104	540	4.92	3.76	1.56
Total Percent	14,853	29,341	34,575	100.00	100.00	100.00

Source: Virginia Gray and David Lowery, "The Institutionalization of State Communities of Organized Interests," *Political Research Quarterly* 54: 268 (2001).

interest organizations comprised 1.27 percent of state lobby registrations in 1980, a proportion that increased to only 1.39 percent by 1997.
And the proportion of organizations representing civil rights, environmental, and women's interests actually fell from 1980 to 1990: 0.69
to 0.64 percent, 2.15 to 1.96 percent, and 1.48 to 0.89 percent, respectively. So, while state lobby registrations by citizens' organizations
have certainly grown in number, their pace has not exceeded the
growth rates of for-profit organizations.

While the substantive diversity of the interest organizations lobbying government has attracted the lion's share of attention, diversity in terms of organizational *form* has also been studied. As
discussed in Chapter 2, membership groups, associations, and institutions differ in a number of ways. Unfortunately, little systematic
data are available on representation by organization forms at the national level. Robert Salisbury, however, has used a number of quali-
tative indicators to conclude that the proportion of the Washington
lobbying community comprised of institutions has grown markedly
in recent decades.[30]

This impression is fully supported by evidence from the states
reported in Figure 3-6. Institutions — organizations without members, like General Motors or the University of North Carolina —
comprised only 39.55 percent of state lobby registrations in 1980.
By 1990 that proportion increased to 49.02 percent, and by 1997 it
grew to 57.81 percent. Institutions, not associations and membership
organizations, now dominate state interest communities. But it is
worth noting that the institutional mode of interest representation
occurs in both profit and not-for-profit sectors. While 61.27 percent
of all profit interest organizations registered in 1997 were freestanding institutions, fully 45.93 percent of not-for-profit organizations
were institutions. In particular, school districts and local governments were among the fastest-growing guilds. So, even as the distribution of substantive interests in the states has remained stable for
some time, participation by institutions has grown considerably.

Explaining the Diversity of Interest Communities

As with density, political scientists are not satisfied simply to describe the diversity of interest systems. We also try to explain why
observed patterns of diversity develop and change and why some
interest communities are more diverse than others. To a pluralist like

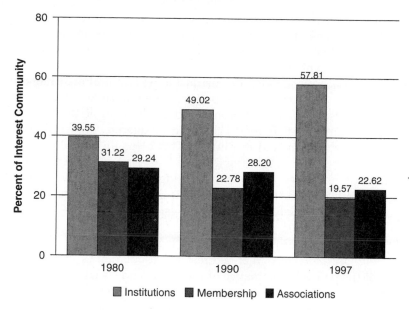

FIGURE 3-6 The Form of Diversity of State Interest Communities, 1980, 1990, and 1997

Source: Virginia Gray and David Lowery, "The Institutionalization of State Communities of Organized Interests," *Political Research Quarterly* 54: 271 (2001).

Truman, interest community diversity was not especially puzzling. If interest organizations form naturally from the cooperative activity of like-minded people, then all salient interests will be represented in the interest community. The key term here, of course, is *salient*. If their interests are not threatened by government policy or a proposed change in policy, individuals will not bother engaging in political activity. But if a policy disturbance occurs or is threatened, then latent interests will become represented via organized political activity. Thus, the organized interest community will only selectively represent the full range of interests in society. As John P. Heinz and his colleagues noted in *The Hollow Core*, "One of the salient characteristics of the policy-making system is that most of the potential participants are, at least at any given time, inactive and largely indifferent."[31] If this is true, then the diversity of the community of organized interests more likely reflects the pattern of ongoing policy disturbances than the unobserved distribution of salient and nonsalient interests in society. From this perspective explaining variations in interest community diversity across time or space entails mapping how the public policy agenda changes. The composition of the interest community should change as old issues fade and new issues are added to the policy agendas.

To transactions school proponents, interest community diversity is more than a reflection of the political agenda. As we will see in later chapters, scholars in the transactions school argue that organizations do far more than reflect the political agenda. They influence its content, direction, and resolution. This turns the pluralist argument on its head by suggesting that we must first examine the composition of the interest community to understand the policy agendas of public officials. The principal task of transactions scholars, then, is to explain why some types of interests, especially business interests, are better represented than others.

They offer two arguments. First, E. E. Schattschneider argued in *The Semisovereign People* that interest representation is merely one facet of the political dominance of economic and social elites. Those with more resources, connections, and better-formed conceptions of self-interest are more likely to be represented, irrespective of the political forum. This class-based explanation is captured by Schattschneider's often cited statement that "the flaw in the pluralist heaven is that the heavenly chorus sings with a strong upper-class accent."[32] Class-based views of American politics, although popular through much of the 1960s and 1970s, have faded due to lack of evidence that traditional economic interests work in anything like a coordinated fashion.[33] Transactions scholars, most notably, Kay Schlozman and John Tierney, now explain the dominance of traditional economic organizations by their advantages in mobilization.[34] As discussed in Chapter 2, Olson suggests that small groups with large stakes in the policy process have greater incentives to overcome the costs of organizing than larger latent groups with smaller individual stakes. If this is true, then traditional economic interests will be significantly overrepresented within interest communities.

Neopluralists find both explanations to be incomplete. Starting with the transactions school's mobilization explanation, the many solutions to the collective action problem examined in Chapter 2 suggest that its impact on the composition of the interest community may not be as telling as suggested by Schlozman and Tierney. Moreover, if problems of free riding influence membership organizations, their primary effect likely will be in reducing their average size, not their numbers. Membership organizations may have fewer members than they might in the absence of collective action problems, but many will still have sufficient numbers to mobilize.

Further, while business interests are heavily represented in the interest communities of all 50 states, there is considerable variation in degree. The data in Table 3-2 indicate that the balance between profit and not-for-profit interest sectors has hardly changed since 1980, with the former comprising 72 to 73 percent of state interest communities. But this is an average. Some states have much higher relative rates of participation by not-for-profit organizations than others.[35] Only 14.04 percent of New Jersey's lobby registrations in 1997 represented not-for-profit interests. But they comprised fully 37.52 percent of New Mexico's interest system. Problems of free riding, then, do not seem to be a constant bearing equally on the mobilization of not-for-profit organizations across all states. Problems of collective action, therefore, cannot fully explain why some states have relatively greater numbers of organizations representing business. While the concept of collective action is one of the most important theoretical insights about interest representation of the post-war period, it is not sufficiently powerful to account for either the general pattern of dominance of traditional economic interests or its variation.

To explain diversity from the neopluralist perspective we can once again draw on organization ecology models. Neopluralists do not disagree with the pluralist argument that the composition of the interest community better reflects the range of issues on political agendas than the distribution of interests—both latent and organized—in society. The ESA model of interest community density suggests that the number of organizations reg-istered to lobby is highly responsive to the threats and opportuni-ties associated with policy agendas. This is the "energy" term of the model as reflected in measures of both the policy concerns of interest guilds and the competitiveness of the two major political parties. Thus, unlike the trans-actions approach, neopluralists share the pluralists' premise that political agendas influence the composition of interest communities.

Neopluralists, however, go further to suggest that the "area" term of the ESA model of interest system density also has a significant impact on the diversity of interest communities. Research on the ESA model suggests that numbers of interest organizations grow as numbers of potential members increase, but at a declining rate reflecting density dependence. More to the point, the several interest guilds respond differently to the availability of potential members depending on their unique economies of scale of organization and the homogeneity of their members' interests. For organizations such as the NAACP, where members have relatively **homogeneous interests,** membership can grow quite large without the organization fragmenting into smaller daughter organizations representing narrower issue agendas. In contrast, business firms often have complex or **heterogeneous interests** with some firms opposing the policy goals of others.[36] As the number of potential members of a business interest organization grows, it will be more likely, therefore, to fragment into daughter organizations better representing the specific, narrower concerns of its members.

While this distinction may seem subtle, it has important implications for explaining variations in the diversity of interest systems. This is illustrated in the simple, stylized model presented in Figure 3-7. We assume that all 50 states are identical in all respects except the size of their economies. That is, each state's economy is divided evenly between but two types of economic activity—a manufacturing sector and an agriculture sector. A state with a GSP of size four will have four times the number of manufacturing firms and four times the agricultural establishments of states with a GSP of size one. But in relative terms, the distribution of interests in society is the same in all states—one-half concerned about manufacturing and the other half attentive to agriculture issues. Accordingly, the interest organization community will have but two guilds representing manufacturing and agriculture interests. The solid and dashed lines in the figure chart the responsiveness of the number of organizations in each guild to changes in GSP. The points on the two lines indicate the number of interest organizations of each type a state is expected to support on its lobby registration rolls at a given economic size.

With a fixed distribution of interests in society, the figure suggests that the composition of state interest systems will differ markedly as economies increase in size. At an economy of size one, agriculture organizations dominate the interest community with 23 (62.16 percent) lobby registrations. Manufacturing, by contrast, is represented by only 14 (37.84 percent) organizations. This pattern is reversed, however, when state economies grow to size four. Manufacturing interests are now the largest guild in the interest community with

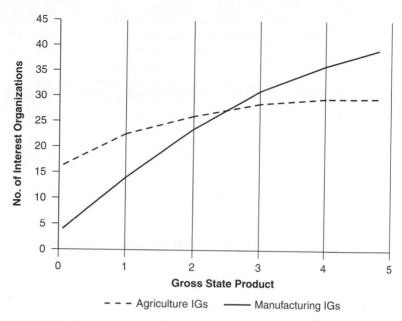

FIGURE 3-7 Composition of Hypothetical Interest Community across Economic Size Range
Source: Compiled by authors.

36 (57.14 percent) organizations. And the agriculture sector is represented by only 27 (42.86 percent) organizations. The point of our simple model is that this relative change in interest system diversity does not arise from change in the distribution of interests in society. Our simple model has held these constant. Rather, the changing composition of interest communities results from the different levels of responsiveness and density dependence of the two guilds to numbers of potential members as economies increase in size. This suggests that the composition of interest communities is only loosely linked to the distribution of interests in society.

Our simple model is not the real world. But Gray and Lowery report that the several interest guilds in the states vary considerably in their responsiveness to economic growth and its associated increase in the number of potential organization members.[37] Some guilds—public utilities, transportation, good government, and welfare interests—increase in size only slowly as the size of economies increase. They are also highly density dependent since their growth rates flatten as economies grow. But other guilds, especially those with large numbers of institutions capable of lobbying on their own behalf, such as manufacturing firms, banks, school districts, and local governments, continue generating new lobby registrations as economies grow, if at a slower pace. As the economic size of a state increases, therefore, its interest community will be composed, all other things equal, of a higher proportion of the latter kinds of organizations.

This may also account for why institutions came to dominate state interest communities since 1980. The growth rate of interest guilds with few institutions slowed as they approached states' carrying capacities for organizations representing their substantive interests. That is, these guilds exhibit a high level of density dependence. But guilds with large numbers of institutions among their potential ranks — banking, manufacturing, local government, and education — are far less density dependent. As a result, those interest guilds comprise a larger proportion of state interest communities as economies grow. But this effect is achieved because of the higher proportion of the institutional form of organization found in less density dependent guilds. As a result, the proportion of institutions, as opposed to membership organizations and associations, will also increase with economic size.[38]

To neopluralists, then, the diversity of interest communities cannot be fully explained by referring to mobilization processes operating only at the organization level or to the greater resources of traditional economic interests. While these factors surely matter, the size of the interest system matters, too. Because carrying capacities vary across interest guilds, the composition of the interest community will change in complex ways as states grow in size.

Interest Community Bias

Research on interest system diversity can seem quite abstract. But at its heart is a critical question about **bias.** To the transactions school, the heavy representation of business interests constitutes a smoking gun indicating that the American political system is biased in favor of elite interests. As Schattschneider argued so forcefully in *The Semisovereign People,* "The system is skewed, loaded, and unbalanced in favor of a fraction of a minority."[39] This assertion has been echoed by numerous analysts of American democracy over the last four decades.[40] Given its resonance over time, we must take Schattschneider's criticism seriously.

Two critical premises underlie the transactions school's claim that bias exists and is problematic. The first is that representation within the interest community can be understood in the same manner as individual voting.[41] Under the one-person, one-vote norm, all opting to vote are assured an equal voice in elections. When applied to interest communities, this assumption implies that organized interests and the guilds they are part of should have an equal influence in determining policy, with absent or unorganized interests having no influence at all. By this standard, interest communities obviously provide a poor representation of interests in society. The heavy registrations by traditional economic organizations clearly misrepresent the balance of interests in society.

Pluralists and neopluralists reject the one-person–one-vote analogy. Only citizens with salient interests — those threatened by proposed policies or seeking solutions to new problems amenable to government solution — are likely to undertake the costs of organizing for political action. Thus, the absence of organizations representing a given interest may simply mean that it is so secure from threat that those supporting it need not bother influencing policy makers. In this regard, Arthur T. Denzau and Michael C. Munger have argued that members of Congress are so motivated by the pursuit of reelection that they will rarely vote against the interests of their constituents on issues those constituents care about.[42] These interests will be well defended within Congress whether or not they are represented by interest organizations. In effect, they have a vote.

Given this view, pluralists are not alarmed by business dominance of interest systems. Indeed, some scholars have suggested that business dominance of lobby registrations provides better evidence of the weakness of traditional economic interests than of strength. As Robert Salisbury has suggested, "The descent on Washington of so many hundreds of associations, institutions, and their agents does not mean that these private interests have acquired greater sway or even a more articulate voice in the shaping of national policy. In many ways, the opposite is true."[43] From this perspective, the numerical dominance of traditional economic interests is not an expression of excessive power, but arises from the heightened level of threats posed to them because elected officials are so highly responsive to constituents.

Neopluralists would argue further that all interest organizations are not equal nor equally representative of the societies from which they spring. Unlike the one-person–one-vote standard, a membership organization with thousands of members across the country, like the American Association of Retired Persons, will represent a wider range of interests in society than one with but a handful of members. Similarly, a business firm like Golden Age Fisheries, which lobbies only the Alaska legislature, is unlikely to represent the range of societal interests as Anheuser-Busch, which lobbies in Washington and 49 of 50 state legislatures. It is difficult to compare an individual to an individual interest organization. Further, we have seen that interest system diversity is related to economic size in very complex ways; interest system diversity may change as economies grow, even if there is no change in relative distributions of interests in society. Given this it is simply not clear what an unbiased system would look like. For both reasons, neopluralists join pluralists in rejecting the claim that simple counts of lobby registrations can say much about bias in a political system.

The second premise of the transaction school's bias hypothesis is that presence on lobby rolls actually results in influence. If organized interests strongly influence the agendas that policy makers consider and adopt, then evidence that interest systems only poorly represent the distribution of interests in society threatens democratic government. But if pluralists and neopluralists are correct in arguing that the composition of interest systems is responsive to the political agendas of policy makers and that the influence of interest organizations is limited and contingent, then evidence that traditional economic interests dominate lobby rolls is less problematic. It simply would not matter very much in terms of meaningful political outcomes. We cannot resolve these questions here. Indeed, these are the issues we consider in the next four chapters. But we shall return to the issue of bias in the Chapter 8 when we consider the broader implications of interest representation for democratic politics.

CONCLUSION

We have seen that American interest communities are crowded and growing, if not nearly as much or as fast as some suggest. If there is a single critical message to be drawn from the density models we have examined in this chapter, it is that an organization's prospects for survival within these communities depends greatly on how many other organizations with similar policy goals are already members of the community. If an interest community's size approaches its political system's carrying capacity, the life prospects of both new and long-standing members of the community may be compromised. Our analysis of interest system diversity echoes earlier works highlighting the strong representation of traditional economic interests within American politics. But contrary to the claims of those heralding the advocacy explosion among citizens' organizations, this pattern of dominance has changed little in recent decades. Instead, the dominance of the institutional form of organization is the most notable change occurring among interest communities. But perhaps the most important message to be drawn from our analysis of diversity is that the composition of interest communities is only loosely related to the distribution of interests in society. While organized interests are ultimately derived from society, the dynamic or emergent properties of interest systems have a profound impact on how well or how poorly the latter represent the former.

KEY TERMS AND CONCEPTS

Density	ESA Model
Lobby Registrations	Stability
PAC Registrations	Area
FEC	Energy
Federal Election Campaign Act	Guild
Institutional Sclerosis	Diversity
Population Ecology	Lobby Disclosure Act of 1995
Carrying Capacity	Homogeneous Interests
Legitimation	Heterogeneous Interests
Density Dependence	Bias

QUESTIONS ABOUT YOUR
INTEREST ORGANIZATION

1. How many interest communities does your organization participate in? Use lobby and PAC registrations to identify the governments your organization seeks to influence.

2. How long has your interest organization been a member of the national or state communities of interest organizations? Employ registration data to determine whether your organization has been active for only a short time or maintains a continuous lobbying presence.
3. How crowded or dense are the interest communities in which your interest organization participates? Examine national and/or state lobby and PAC registrations to determine the overall size of the interest communities in which your organization operates.
4. Does your interest guild have a relatively new presence within interest communities? Use lobby and PAC registration data to determine whether your organization's guild is in the legitimation, growth, or density dependent stage of development.
5. How diverse are the interest communities in which your interest organization operates? Does the interest guild of which your organization is a member comprise a large or small share of the interest communities in which your organization participates?

NOTES

1. Virginia Gray and David Lowery, *The Population Ecology of Interest Representation* (Ann Arbor, Michigan: University of Michigan Press, 1996); Virginia Gray and David Lowery, "Reconceptualizing PAC Formation: It's Not a Collective Action Problem, and It May Be an Arms Race," *American Politics Quarterly* 25: 319–346 (1997); Thomas Gais, *Improper Influence* (Ann Arbor, Michigan: University of Michigan Press, 1996), p. 77.
2. Frank R. Baumgartner and Beth L. Leech, "Interest Niches and Policy Bandwagons Patterns of Interest Group Involvement in National Politics," *Journal of Politics* 63: 1191–1213 (2001).
3. Ronald J. Hrebenar, *Interest Group Politics in America* 3rd ed. (Armonk, New York: M. E. Sharpe, 1997), p. 14.
4. Ibid., p. 15.
5. See, for example, Anthony Nownes, *Pressure and Power* (Boston: Houghton Mifflin Company, 2001), pp. 24, 29.
6. Baumgartner and Leech, "Interest Niches and Policy Bandwagons: Patterns of Interest Group Involvement in National Politics," p. 1196.

7. Baumgartner and Leech, "Interest Niches and Policy Bandwagons: Patterns of Interest Group Involvement in National Politics," p. 1200.
8. Nownes, *Pressure and Power*, p. 24.
9. See Clive Thomas and Ronald Hrebenar (1991) "Political Action Committees in the American States: Some Preliminary Findings." Paper Presented at the Annual Meeting of the American Political Science Association, Washington, DC: August 29–September 1, 1991.
10. David Lowery and Virginia Gray, "How Some Rules Just Don't Matter: The Regulation of Lobbyists," *Public Choice* 91: 139–147 (1997); "Do Lobbying Regulations Influence Lobbying Registrations?" *Social Science Quarterly* 75: 382–384 (1994).
11. Jennifer Wolak, Adam J. Newmark, Todd McNoldy, David Lowery, and Virginia Gray, "Much of Politics Is Still Local: Multi-State Lobbying before State Legislators," *Legislative Studies Quarterly* 27: 527–555 (2002).
12. Mancur Olson, Jr., *The Rise and Decline of Nations* (New Haven: Yale University, 1982).
13. Nownes, *Pressure and Power*, pp. 34–35; Mahood, *Interest Groups in American National Politics*, pp. 20–23; Allan J. Cigler and Burdett A. Loomis, *Interest Group Politics*, 3rd ed. (Washington: CQ Press, 1998), pp. 11–17.
14. William C. Mitchell and Michael C. Munger, "Economic Models of Interest Groups," *American Journal of Political Science* 35: 512–546 (1991).
15. Gray and Lowery, *The Population Ecology of Interest Representation*, pp. 137–158.
16. Leslie A. Real and James H. Brown, *Foundations of Modern Ecology* (Chicago: University of Chicago Press, 1991) and Glenn R. Carroll and Michael T. Hannan, *The Demography of Corporations and Industries* (Princeton: Princeton University Press, 2000).
17. Carroll and Hannan, *The Demography of Corporations and Industries*, pp. 213–238.
18. Anthony Nownes, "The Population Ecology of Interest Group Formation," *British Journal of Political Science* (in press).
19. E. O. Wilson, *The Diversity of Life* (Cambridge: Harvard University Press, 1992), pp. 180–205.

20. Gray and Lowery, *The Population Ecology of Interest Representation*, pp. 137–158.

21. David Lowery and Virginia Gray, "The Population Ecology of Gucci Gulch, or the Natural Regulation of Interest Group Numbers in the American States," *American Journal of Political Science* 39: 1–29 (1995).

22. Jennifer Wolak, David Lowery, and Virginia Gray, "California Dreaming: Outliers, Leverage, and Influence in Comparative State Political Analysis," *State Politics and Policy Quarterly* 1: 255–272 (2001).

23. Holly Brasher, David Lowery, and Virginia Gray, "State Lobby Registration Data: The Anomalous Case of Florida (and Minnesota too!)," *Legislative Studies Quarterly* 24: 303–314 (1999).

24. See, for example, Kay Lehman Schlozman and John T. Tierney, *Organized Interests and American Democracy* (New York: Harper and Row, 1986).

25. Baumgartner and Leech, "Interest Niches and Policy Bandwagons: Patterns of Interest Group Involvement in National Politics," p. 1199.

26. Frank R. Baumgartner and Beth L. Leech, *Basic Interests* (Princeton: Princeton University Press, 1998) p. 5; Schlozman and Tierney, *Organized Interests and American Democracy*, p. 87.

27. Mark J. Rozell and Clyde Wilcox, *Interest Groups in American Campaigns* (Washington: CQ Press, 1999), p. 77.

28. Jack L. Walker, Jr., *Mobilizing Interest Groups in America* (Ann Arbor, Michigan: University of Michigan Press, 1991); Jeffrey M. Berry, *The New Liberalism* (Washington: Brookings Institution Press, 1999).

29. This distinction is rough; many profit organizations are included in the not-for-profit sector.

30. Robert Salisbury, "Interest Representation: The Dominance of Institutions," *American Political Science Review* 81: 64–76 (1984).

31. John P. Heinz, O. Laumann, Robert L. Nelson, and Robert Salisbury, *The Hollow Core* (Cambridge: Harvard University Press, 1993), p. 392.

32. E. E. Schattschneider, *The Semisovereign People* (New York: Holt, Rinehart, and Winston, 1960), pp. 34–35.

33. Heinz, Laumann, Nelson, and Salisbury, *The Hollow Core*, p. 377.

34. Baumgartner and Leech, *Basic Interests,* pp. 115–118; Schlozman and Tierney, *Organized Interests and American Democracy,* p. 130.
35. Authors' data.
36. Mark A. Smith, *American Business and Political Power* (Chicago: University of Chicago, 2000), p. 41; James Q. Wilson, *Political Organizations* (New York: Basic Books, 1973), pp. 143–170.
37. David Lowery and Virginia Gray, "Representational Concentration and Interest Community Size: A Population Ecology Interpretation," *Political Research Quarterly* 51: 919–944 (1998).
38. Gray and Lowery, "The Institutionalization of State Communities of Organized Interests," *Political Research Quarterly* 54: 265–284 (2001).
39. Schattschneider, *The Semisovereign People,* p. 35.
40. For more recent interpretations, see Elizabeth Drew, *The Corruption of American Politics* (Woodstock: New York: The Overlook Press, 1999); Darrell M. West, *Checkbook Democracy* (Boston: Northeastern University Press, 2000).
41. Key Lehman Scholozman, "What Accent the Heavenly Chorus? Political Equality and the American Pressure System," *Journal of Politics* 46: (1984), pp. 1009–1011.
42. Arthur T. Denzau and Michael C. Munger, "Legislators and Interest Groups: How Unorganized Interests Get Represented," *American Political Science Review* 80: 89–106 (1986).
43. Robert Salisbury, "The Paradox of Interest in Washington: More Groups, Less Clout." In *The New American Political System* 2nd ed., ed. Anthony S. King (Washington: American Enterprise Institute, 1990) p. 228.

CHAPTER 4

Organized Interests and the Public

Organizations become interest organizations when their concerns intersect with public policy. When this occurs, organized interests try to shape public policy in a manner more favorable to their preferences. These efforts constitute the third stage of the influence production process identified in Chapter 1. Attempts to influence public policy come in many forms and may occur throughout the policy process. We often associate interest organization influence with legislative politics, but substantial efforts to influence public policy occur even before issues are discussed in the legislative, executive, and judicial branches of government. Organized interests routinely lobby both mass and elite publics to influence their opinions and choices. Those efforts are the focus of this chapter. In the next chapter we will consider the familiar topic of legislative lobbying and also see in the following chapters that influence does not stop with the passage of a law. As we will see in Chapters 6 and 7, many organized interests also try to influence the executive branch's implementation of laws and their interpretation by the courts. However, the appropriate place to begin to understand interest organization influence is with the efforts of interests to influence the public's choices and the context and content of those choices.

In the spring of 2002, for example, the National Organization for the Reform of Marijuana Laws (NORML) launched a $500,000 media campaign in New York City designed to alter how the public views the use of marijuana and the enforcement of laws regulating its use.[1] The campaign included ads in the *New York Times*, posters on buses and kiosks throughout the city, and radio spots. The print ads prominently featured a picture of newly elected Republican mayor Michael Bloomberg and his response to a reporter's question about whether he had ever smoked pot. The mayor's response: "You bet I did. And I enjoyed it." While the ads discussed the legalization of marijuana in very general terms, no specific laws or proposed laws were mentioned. Rather, the ad campaign was designed to influence how the public perceives legal efforts to restrict the use of marijuana. Why was NORML "lobbying" the public rather than the politicians who actually propose and vote on marijuana laws?

We try to answer this question in this chapter while considering how organized interests influence the public. We will examine three broad ways through which interest organizations try to influence mass and/or elite publics along with more detailed examples of each of these three means of influence. The first is through influencing the *context* within which citizens make choices about public policies. Organized interests try to frame issues so that the public will hold more favorable views about the organizations' positions. Second, interest organizations also lobby the public through influencing the *content* of the choices placed before citizens in our democratic political system. And third, organized interests try to influence the actual *choices* of citizens.

INFLUENCING CHOICE CONTEXT

Before legislation is formally considered, the issue it addresses must make it onto the national agenda. Clearly, how an issue is framed — identifying and characterizing the problem and proposing candidate policy solutions — can in the long run have a significant impact on the fate of legislation. **Framing** an issue has several stages. The first is simply defining a condition as a problem in need of a public policy solution. Some conditions may not be widely perceived to be appropriate for a governmental solution. The challenge in such cases would be to redefine the condition as a problem that could be, and should be, solved by public policy. Liberal and conservative ideology often shapes how problems are defined. Conservatives tend to favor private-sector solutions, while liberals are often more likely to argue that a problem warrants a public-sector solution.[2] For example, homelessness may be attributed either to the shortcomings of individuals or a to problem arising from the deinstitutionalization of the mentally ill or a lack of affordable housing. If framed in the former manner, no public policy solution may be warranted. But if framed in the latter manner, policy solutions may involve government subsidized housing, mental health care, or economic aid from federal or state government.[3]

Once an issue is defined as a policy problem, how it is framed may influence the support or opposition faced by a proposed solution.[4] In the 1980s, for example, tax reform was put on the political agenda by President Reagan who initially framed reform as an opportunity to reduce the size and scope of the federal government.[5] But that is not the only frame in which tax reform might be considered. Citizens for Tax Justice (CTJ), an organization that drew much of its inspiration from Ralph Nader's Public Citizen, took the lead in publicizing the distorted nature of corporate tax breaks. CTJ, headed by Robert McIntyre, researched corporate tax abuses at length. Some of the more outrageous findings—for example, that a woman in Milwaukee raising three children paid more taxes than Boeing, General Electric, DuPont, and Texaco combined—helped characterize tax reform as an issue of fairness. The "fairness" frame opened the door for legislators from both parties—especially Bill Bradley, Dick Gephardt, and other Democrats—to support tax reform. The way in which the issue was framed was an important part of why the Reagan Administration was successful in its 1986 effort to change tax policy.[6]

This does not mean, however, that organized interests can easily or often reframe issues to their liking. In a study exploring the framing process, Frank Baumgartner and his colleagues identified a number of factors that may limit an interest organization's ability to frame policy issues. Often, an organized interest's efforts to exert influence involve an existing policy that has been on the agenda for some time. In such cases, opportunities for framing may be limited because opponents and proponents line up in predictable ways using familiar arguments. The expertise of an established policy community in Washington or state capitols may also make an issue less susceptible to reframing. Framing efforts can also be limited by the sheer difficulty of attracting public attention, especially from those who are not already concerned about an issue. Young voters, for example, may well avoid messages about Medicare policy. Finally, the public policy agenda is very crowded. Because of fierce competition for agenda space and public attention, placing a new issue on the table or reframing an old issue is not always possible.[7]

Despite these difficulties, many organized interests try to influence the policy process at its earliest stage—identifying problems, framing the problem, and then offering solutions that fit the frame. If an organization takes the lead in identifying and discussing a problem, it can shape public perceptions of the issue and legislators' responses to it. Organized interests frame issues using a variety of means. Most interest organizations, for example, routinely conduct research on policy issues. This research is often presented to the media to highlight the organization's take on the issue. Three means of framing—issue advocacy, think tanks, and media lobbying—have become especially important lately and warrant attention as specific ways in which interest organizations shape perceptions of issues.

Issue Advocacy

One powerful tool available to interest organizations is **issue advocacy**. Issue advocacy often takes the form of a television ad, but it can also include direct mail sent to citizens or advertisements on radio or in print media. Issue advocacy may communicate virtually any message. Specifically, as long as the communication does not include the words "vote for," "elect," "defeat," or "support" the candidacy of a specific federal candidate, the ad is not subject to the same federal regulations governing candidates' campaign ads. This means that issue advocacy can be funded from virtually any source. Contributions are unlimited and need not be disclosed. It is easy to understand why issue advocacy has become an appealing tool for interest organizations.

Lobbying the public through issue advertising occurs throughout the public policy process. The NORML ad featuring Mayor Michael Bloomberg discussed in the introduction of this chapter illustrates the use of issue ads at a very early stage of the policy process. In such cases, the general public is the target and the organization's efforts are, at best, part of a long-term strategy. But issue ads are also used during elections to frame how voters perceive key issues that may be part of an ongoing campaign, although they may not take the additional step of urging votes to support one candidate or another. One such effort is discussed in Interest Organization

Example 4-1. The United Seniors Association (USA) has close ties to the Republican Party. In the 2002 election, USA ran issue ads that, while never urging viewers to vote Republican, were designed to blunt Democrats' efforts to mobilize senior citizens by suggesting that their party would better protect the Social Security and Medicare programs.

Framing via issue advertising even occurs during the latest stages of the policy process. While the public may still be addressed by these efforts, such late-stage framing is more often targeted at political elites who are still considering specific proposals. In these instances, however, the preferences of the general public may still be a large part of the message aimed toward legislators and executives. That is, the organized interest will try to provide a palatable frame for politicians with which to sell what may be unpopular policies to their constituents.

The debate over the Homeland Security Act, which was signed into law by President Bush on November 25, 2002, illustrates well such late-stage attempts at framing. Initially proposed by Democrats and opposed by the president and Congressional Republicans, the GOP eventually embraced the idea of a new Department of Homeland Security. But many Democrats opposed President Bush's version of the bill. The core of the dispute concerned the rights of the 170,000 employees of the new department to join a union. Both sides attempted to frame the dispute in terms designed to win public support. To the president and his GOP colleagues, rescinding the collective bargaining rights of public employees was essential for national security. The President argued that he needed the ability to hire and fire employees in order to sharpen our nation's defenses against terrorism. Because labor unions comprise a strong element of the Democratic Party coalition it is not surprising that many Democrats opposed President Bush's version of the bill. Even as the Senate neared a final vote on the Homeland Security Act, public employee unions attempted to reframe the debate using issue ads in order to recast public employees from potential obstructions to national security to the frontline heroes in the fight against terrorism. These efforts are discussed in Interest Organization Example 4-2. This example also illustrates that not all efforts to reframe issues are successful. The Senate passed the president's version of the Homeland Security Act.

INTEREST ORGANIZATION EXAMPLE 4-1:

Organized Interests Say the Darndest Things!

Founded in 1991, the United Seniors Association (USA) claims to be a nonpartisan grassroots organization representing the interests of senior citizens through the efforts of a million and half members. It has, however, very strong ties to the Republican Party. USA president Charles Jarvis worked for the Reagan and the first Bush administrations, and many of its board mem-bers and staff were previously employed as GOP lobbyists or worked for conservative organizations. USA relies heavily on selective benefits—discounts on prescription drugs, hearing aids, phone service, and hotels—to attract members. USA's press releases routinely claim that the American Association of Retired Persons misrepresents the interests of seniors, defend the privatization of Social Security, support the elimination of the estate tax and the marriage tax penalty, and oppose both campaign finance reform and the Democratic Party's efforts to provide prescription drug coverage to senior citizens through the Medicare program.

While USA contributed $11,000 in PAC funds in the 2002 election cycle (all to Republicans), its primary efforts are devoted to running issue ads. In the 2002 election, for example, USA spent more than $20 million in print, television, and radio ads. The Center for Responsive Politics reported that the Pharmaceutical Research and Manufacturers Association provided some of this money. Several USA ads featured television host Art Linkletter, creator of "Kids Say the Darndest Things." In an ad titled "2002 Stop Scaring Seniors Now," Mr. Linkletter observes that "politicians say the darndest things. Each time our elections roll around, we see politicians frightening senior voters with scare tactics about Social Security and Medicare. Don't let dishonest politicians manipulate your vote."

Sources: http://www.opensecrets.org/payback; http://unitedseniors.org, visited December 2, 2002.

INTEREST ORGANIZATION EXAMPLE 4-2:

Heroes or Obstructions to National Security?

The American Federation of Government Employees (AFGE) is a labor union representing 600,000 employees working for the federal and District of Columbia governments. Headquartered in Washington DC, AFGE was founded in 1932 and has been affiliated with the AFL-CIO since then. The Department of Defense, the Department of Veterans Affairs, the Social Security Administration, and the Department of Justice employ AFGE's highest concentrations of members. In addition to negotiating working conditions with federal officials, AFGE routinely lobbies the Congress and the executive branch on issues influencing public employees. AFGE also contributes to political campaigns through its PAC. In the 2002 election cycle, these contributions approached half a million dollars, with 93 percent going to Democrats.

AFGE opposed President Bush's version of the Homeland Security Department, given its restrictions on employee bargaining rights. But arguments about bargaining rights seem weak in the face of strong claims about national security. AFGE, therefore, linked public employees to national defense in a positive manner, pointing out that many of those who rushed to defend the nation following the 9-11 attack were union members. AFGE ran several print ads highlighting the patriotism of its members. A *Washington Post* ad, for example, pictured Federal Emergency Management Agency employee Denise Dukes, who spent four weeks working 12-hour days at ground zero, saying, "Union members aren't obstacles to homeland security. We ARE homeland security." Another AFGE ad pictured "two sweet-looking" kids wrapped in the American flag and accusing the Bush administration of 'an all-out assault on federal employees.'"

Source: http://www.afge.org, http://www.opensecrets.org, visited December 2, 2002.

Think Tanks

We have seen that most interest organizations conduct research on the policy issues that concern them. But some interest organizations — think tanks — specialize in research as an important means of framing issues and the solutions proposed to address them. Think tanks are independent, nonprofit, public policy research organizations. The analysis of think tanks is typically produced using social science research methods borrowed from academia. Indeed, think tanks are often characterized as colleges without students. The perceived neutrality and rigor of the research produced by think tanks has traditionally lent them an especially influential role in the policy process. Changes in the nature of think tanks, however, have led them to be perceived as less neutral more recently. An evolution in the mission and the practices of think tanks has occurred that has made them appear far more ideological and partisan. Andrew Rich and Kent Weaver chart this transition and the rise of these new **advocacy tanks.**[8]

The earliest think tanks, such as the Russell Sage Foundation, founded in 1907, and the Brookings Institution, created in 1927, focused on producing knowledge and information that would solve social and economic problems. They deliberately avoided affiliation with political parties and they employed academically trained researchers.[9] The academic disciplines of sociology, political science, planning, and public administration were becoming established fields of inquiry, and there was a growing confidence that their methods could identify solutions to public problems.[10] By the 1960s more sophisticated ideas about economics had gained currency with policy makers, and the research of think tanks began to reflect economic principles and methods.[11] Nearly all of the first generation of think tanks assumed that public policy could be used in a constructive manner to solve social problems.

By the end of the 1960s, however, the belief that well-designed public policy could readily solve social problems was coming into question. Big government and public solutions for problems such as unemployment, poverty, and inflation were increasingly perceived by some to be ineffective. This prompted the establishment of new think tanks with a conservative outlook and a strong preference for smaller government. In 1973 the Heritage Foundation was established with the help of Joseph Coors, the chairman of the Colorado Brewing Company. Edward H. Crane founded the Cato Institute in 1977. The Heritage Foundation, the Cato Institute, and other think tanks began to pursue an overtly conservative agenda.[12] Indeed, the goal of the Heritage Foundation was to replace the New Deal coalition that had dominated American policy for decades.[13] In response the 1980s saw the founding of several think tanks that represented a more assertive liberal perspective, including the Center on Budget and Policy Priorities and the Economic Policy Institute. These new advocacy tanks justify presenting findings with either a liberal or conservative bias by arguing that policy research cannot avoid some sort of bias. They even make a virtue of the fact that their bias is clearly stated.[14] At the same time, however, the research of the newer advocacy organizations continues to have at least some of the aura of neutrality associated with the earlier generation of think tanks.

Not only has the nature of the analysis produced by these think tanks changed, their approach to influencing the policy making process has evolved as well. First, the newer advocacy tanks try to be responsive to legislative policy agendas in order to have a more timely influence on policy debates. Rather than presenting analysis and commentary in book form, as the Brookings Institution has traditionally done, the new advocacy tanks produce shorter and more accessible issue briefs that can be faxed to members of Congress or posted on the organization's Web page. Even the venerable Brookings Institution and the American Enterprise Institute have adopted this format in order to maintain their influence in policy debates.[15] An additional development has been the specialization of think tanks on particular issues. The Center for Nonproliferation Studies is the largest nongovernmental organization devoted to combating the spread of weapons of mass destruction. The Committee for the Study of the American Electorate focuses on issues of citizen engagement. These specialized think tanks survive in a narrower niche by developing reputations for expertise in a particular policy area.

Media Lobbying

The media provide another avenue to communicate the messages of organized interests. Free media—when members of the media choose, for their own purposes, to communicate the views of an interest organization—complement the paid media of issue advocacy. It also complements the efforts of advocacy tanks by providing a vehicle for communicating their research findings. One study of the media found that organized interests constituted 14.4 percent of all sourced stories.[16] The study defined news sources as those whose statements or actions were reported, such as the president, the opposition party, policy experts, media commentators, and judges. Given the number of possible alternative sources, interest organizations featured relatively prominently in news coverage, as prominently as the president's opposition party.

Some interest organizations are more successful in lobbying through the media than others. The researchers also found that the frequency with which different types of organizations were represented in media coverage corresponded more closely with the resources they possess than with how representative they were of the working population. At the same time, certain organizations received disproportionate coverage, such the AFL-CIO, the NAACP, the U.S. Chamber of Commerce, and General Motors. The authors of the study concluded that "the media seem to seize upon a few prominent individuals or groups to speak for broad sets of interests, such as the AFL-CIO for organized labor and Ralph Nader for consumers."[17] These organizations were viewed as authoritative and legitimate sources for points of view equal to major government officials. The study also found that different types of organizations received coverage on different types of issues. For example, they found that business interests were most often associated with stories about economic issues. In contrast, citizens' organizations were more often associated with coverage of civil rights.[18]

The *source* of information has a strong influence on how it is received by citizens. News commentary and communication by journalists has a substantial influence on public opinion, as does the information provided by policy experts.[19] Messages attributed directly to interest organization sources have somewhat less credibility and less influence on public opinion. Thus, organized interests have a strong incentive to get their less credible messages communicated through more credible and influential news sources. When the views of organized interests are expressed indirectly through the media, it enhances their opportunity to shape public opinion.[20] Some organized interests go to considerable lengths to lobby the media. One recent study describes the efforts of organized interests to

influence the views of journalists by placing advertisements in journalism periodicals, such as the *American Journalism Review,* that are
read by the journalists who shape the content of news and commentary. These ads, which are growing in number, have been labeled
advertorials because they appear in the style and format of editori-
als.[21] In short, the media itself—and indirectly the public—are lobbying targets.

INFLUENCING CHOICE CONTENT

Not only do interest organizations shape the context in which citizens make choices, they also try to influence the range of choices
placed before citizens. Perhaps the most important choice made by
citizens in a democracy is how to vote in an election. We will later
examine how organized interests lobby directly on these choices.
But perhaps even more importantly, organized interests can powerfully influence the menu of choices presented to the electorate. Organized interests influence the content of citizens' choices in three
ways. They actively participate in the nomination process via candidate recruitment, funding, and training. They are also active participants in the internal politics of political parties. And last, interest
organizations provide financial donations to political parties.

Candidate Recruitment and Training

Competition between candidates for elective office is the hallmark of
democratic politics. Interest organizations play an important role in
determining who these candidates are. Simply put, organized interests often provide the early funding that is crucial to starting an election campaign. That is, they often provide funds for candidates
during nomination campaigns. Political party contributions are also
important to candidates, but parties often reserve their funds for
the winning nominee. Parties prefer to let the candidates compete
in the primary and then fund the winner of the nomination contest.
This avoids the bitterness or division that might arise if the party
supported a candidate who did not ultimately win the nomination.
This is not a minor problem. Generally, political parties do not have
sufficient control over primary elections to guarantee the nomination

of preselected or favored candidates. Backing a loser in a primary election may well mean that the winner feels that he or she owes little to the party.

In many cases, then, candidates must rely on their own resources during nomination contests. This means that interest organization support and involvement can be pivotal at this stage of the election process. Indeed, interest organizations and the financial resources and endorsements they provide are often vital at the nomination stage because their support may well determine if a candidacy is even viable. The ability to raise money is often considered the best measure of a qualified and capable congressional candidate. Thus, support by organized interests is a key political asset of a candidate.[22] Also, candidates who receive funding early during campaigns — seed money — are much more likely to raise money later on. Particularly for challengers in campaigns against incumbents, the early contributions and endorsements from organized interests are important assets for the candidate's prospects later in the campaign.[23]

Not only do interest organizations fund candidates in the early stages of elections, they may also be involved in initially encouraging candidates to enter a race. One study comparing the role of political parties to that of interest organizations in recruiting women candidates for office found that the latter played a much stronger role.[24] Specifically, while the Democratic Party was less aggressive than the Republican Party in recruiting female candidates for office, more female Democrats appeared on final election ballots because women's organizations associated with the Democratic Party were very successful in recruiting women. Groups such as the Women's Campaign Fund, EMILY'S LIST (an acronym for Early Money Is Like Yeast), the National Organization for Women, and the National Women's Political Caucus are heavily involved in recruiting and supporting women as political candidates.

Recruitment often entails more than securing a "yes" from a prospective candidate. Many interest organizations provide training for candidates using videos, campaign seminars, and other forms of advice on both campaign techniques and policy issues. Novice candidates, especially, value these resources. For example, an antigun-control candidate who is recruited to run for office by the NRA may have thought a great deal about problems with proposed gun control legislation. But he or she may not have thought about how the NRA's

position should be framed for larger audiences not inclined to oppose all restrictions on firearms. Further, elections are rarely about
one issue. The recruited candidate may have given little prior
thought to tax, education, environmental, and other policies that
will surely become part of a campaign. Finally, the novice candidate
simply may know little about the nuts and bolts of running an
effective political campaign. In short, organized interests offer new
candidates access to vital resources they need to win such as information on how to handle issues as they arise in the campaign. At the
same time, the training tools organized interests provide to candidates offer an important opportunity to communicate the organization's views on a host of issues.

The vital role of interest organizations in the recruitment, funding, and training of political candidates is understandable, given the
distinct goals of political parties and interest organizations. The goal
of parties is to win. Parties generally try to avoid becoming too involved in primary battles, but hope that the strongest candidates
will emerge from these contests. Interest organization support is one
important measure of the strength of a candidate. But this often allows organized interests to shape the choices political parties present to the electorate. Organized interests, in contrast to parties, are
more focused on specific policy and political goals. For women's organizations, for example, one important objective is simply having
more female candidates on election ballots and in office. This is true
of almost any organization that recruits and funds political candidates, such as the National Federation of Independent Businesses
and the NRA. The NFIB wants to elect more candidates who have a
small business background. The NRA seeks to elect candidates who
will advocate the rights of gun enthusiasts. But by allowing organized interests a strong role in the nomination process, parties always run a risk of allowing supportive organizations to define party
stands on issues.

Interest Organizations and Parties

Interest organizations employ a "retail" influence strategy when they
recruit and support candidates for office. That is, they try to influence the policies of political parties one candidate at a time and in
doing so influence the available choices. But organized interests also
employ a "wholesale" influence strategy by working within party

organizations day-to-day. The active involvement of the Christian Right with state Republican Party organizations provides the most recognized recent example of this. Christian organizations emerged rapidly as a political force in the 1980s as religious conservatives were politicized, especially in the South.[25] They championed prolife and socially conservative candidates and mobilized supporters to vote Republican. The Christian Right also worked to enshrine many of its favored positions in party platforms as the Republican Party's official policy stance. The involvement of the Christian Right was welcomed as Republicans sought to overturn Democratic one-party dominance in Southern politics. The successes of the Christian Right organizations led many observers to conclude that they had captured Republican Party organizations in the South during the 1980s and 1990s in much the same way that many thought labor unions had captured some state Democratic Party organizations in the 1950s and 1960s. Such capture may not be in the long-term interest of the party if it leads to adoption of party platforms and positions that are viewed as more extreme than the general electorate's.

What, however, does such capture really mean? Generally, it entails members of an organized interest gaining control of the machinery of party organizations—the state and county committees that conduct their routine business. One early study, for example, assessed the influence of the Christian Right by considering two factors—the percentage of members of the state GOP central committee that supported the issue agenda of Christian conservatives and the percentage of those on the committees who were members of Christian Right organizations.[26] A more recent study using the same criteria found that, while still strong, the influence of the Religious Right in southern state Republican Party organizations was less pervasive in 2000 than in 1994. At the same time, however, the influence of Christian conservatives in Republican Party politics has increased nationwide.[27] This significant influence in party politics has allowed Christian conservatives to influence the choices offered to voters.

Still capture is far from inevitable. While many members of party committees are also members of interest organizations, not all are, and in many cases, more than one interest organization may seek to influence party organizations. In many states, for example, Democratic Party organizations must balance the sometimes conflicting policy preferences of labor unions, environmentalists, and racial minorities.[28]

The wholesale and retail influence strategies often merge in states that select candidates for office, not through primary elections, but through party caucuses. Relying on caucuses can render a party very vulnerable to interest organization influence. Like many states, Colorado uses party caucuses, often no larger than neighborhood gatherings, to select party officers and members of party committees. But Colorado also employs caucuses to nominate party candidates for office. Because of a drop-off in attendance since the 1980s, only one percent or so of registered voters may attend caucuses. Given low attendance, an interest organization can easily pack a caucus and ensure that its favored candidates win. As former Republican state representative Bill Kaufman explained, "It's so easy for a small group to take over the caucuses, it's not even funny."[29] Colorado officials placed a referendum, Amendment 29, on the ballot in 2002 to change the way the state's parties select candidates by requiring a minimum number of signatures for nomination rather than solely the support of those attending party caucuses. Opponents of the referendum argued that Amendment 29 would take away an important reason for grassroots political gatherings and would discourage local candidates from running for office.[30] Amendment 29 did not pass. Thus, Colorado's nomination process remains vulnerable to capture by committed interest organizations. More generally, the party machinery—local and state party committees— of most states provides a key opportunity for organized interests to capture on a wholesale basis the platforms of political parties.

Soft Money

Active involvement with primary campaigns and party organizations is an important way in which interest organizations shape choice content. Money, not surprisingly, is also an avenue for shaping the policy choices political parties present to voters. The funds that organized interests provide to political parties have received a great deal of scrutiny and attention in recent years. As we will see in Chapter 8, such contributions were a significant target of the reforms adopted in the Bipartisan Campaign Finance Reform Act (BCFRA) of 2002.

Much of the financial support that organized interests have provided to political parties in recent elections is in the form of soft money contributions. **Hard money** contributions by individuals and political actions committees (PACs) to candidates and parties are those funds used specifically to advocate the election or defeat of a political candidate. Hard money contributions by PACs are limited to relatively small amounts: $5,000 per election before 2002 and $10,000 after the passage of the MacCain-Feingold measure. And state and federal law restrict the sources of hard money contributions to candidates. Corporations, for example, cannot contribute hard money directly to candidates in federal elections. They may, however, establish affiliated PACs to channel funds to candidates. **Soft money** contributions to political parties, in contrast, are intended for use in developing the party rather than supporting the election (or defeat) of specific candidates. That is, soft money contributions are used for voter registration and get-out-the-vote efforts, for political advertising promoting the party generally, and other types of party building efforts. Prior to the passage of the BCFRA there were no limits on the amounts of soft money that could be contributed, nor was the source of soft money funds restricted. Corporations, for example, could directly contribute soft money to political parties, while they could make hard money contributions to federal candidates only through affiliated political action committees.

As the cost of campaigns increased during the 1990s and parties confronted hard money limits, the uses of soft money expanded beyond what many considered legitimate bounds. By the 1990s soft money was extensively used by political parties for advertising campaigns that were almost indistinguishable from those that directly advocated the election of specific federal candidates. Political parties, just like interest organizations, found that they could engage in issue advocacy so long as the "magic" express advocacy words of "vote for" or "vote against" were avoided. As soft money was applied to new uses, political parties became adept at finding contributors among major interest organizations. Figure 4-1 highlights the growth of soft money receipts between 1992 and 2000 relative to hard money receipts. While the Republican Party raised more soft money than did Democrats in the 2000 election cycle, soft money comprised a much larger proportion of the total funds contributed to Democrats. Both organized interests and political parties saw important advantages to relying more heavily on soft money. Soft money appeals to interest organizations because they can contribute

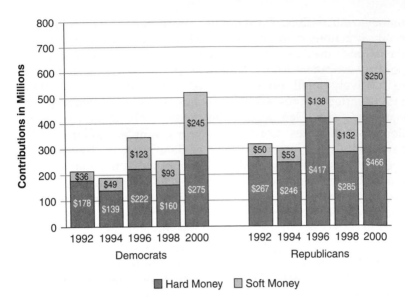

FIGURE 4-1 Soft and Hard Money Contributions to Political Parties by Party and Election Cycle, 1992–2000
Source: http://www.opensecrets.org, visited October 15, 2000.

very substantial amounts of money to a political party — enough to be noticed. Soft money is appealing to political parties because larger contributions allow for more efficient fundraising.

Soft money has become important in nonelection settings as well. The parties' national conventions provide a good example. During its 2000 national convention, for example, the Republicans developed a pecking order for soft money donors. Donors who contributed $50,000 received a limited edition Philadelphia 2000 lapel pin and six commemorative golf shirts. For $100,000, donors received a VIP golf outing, a reservation at a choice hotel, and the right to host a reception for a state delegation, which typically included the state's governor and its congressional delegation. For a million dollars, contributors won an exclusive dinner with important GOP players in Washington and face time with the presidential nominee. These large contributions were controversial because many of the donating companies had issues pending before the federal government. The list of contributors included Philip Morris, AT&T, Lockheed Martin, Ernst & Young, General Motors, Microsoft, Hewlett-Packard, and Enron. Bell Atlantic contributed about three million dollars to the Philadelphia convention and won the contract to build the convention's $4.5 million telecommunications network. The *St. Petersburg Times* reported that the contract enabled Bell Atlantic to lay miles of fiber-optic cable across Philadelphia and compete for new business after the convention ended.[31] Comcast Corporation, a cable company, was also a major corporate sponsor of the convention. Its president was a convention co-chair, and many of its employees volunteered to work at the event. The company hosted a reception for the congressman who championed the 1996 Telecommunications Act, which greatly benefited the cable industry.[32] Such conflicts of interest did not pass without notice. Common Cause's Don Simon noted that "conventions have become free-for-all, soft-money orgies where you have all this corporate money flooding in."[33]

The Bipartisan Campaign Finance Reform Act of 2002 largely bans such soft money contributions to political parties. We will see in later chapters, however, that the fate of the act is still uncertain pending the implementation of rules adopted by the Federal Election Commission and court decisions on its constitutionality. But if the past is any guide, restricting large soft money contributions will be very difficult. Indeed, reforms adopted in the 1970s provided public financing for conventions in order to prevent just the sort of influence buying that many think now takes place. But the Federal Election Commission later allowed corporations to make contributions to local party host committees, which now provide the bulk of the financing for conventions. As was the case with soft money and party building, host committees are only supposed to spend soft money contributions on economic development associated with convention activities. But most of the host committee's expenses, including paying for the convention site, clearly benefit the major political parties. In short, restricting the role of money as a wholesale means of influencing political parties must be an ongoing task, given the powerful incentives of both political parties and organized interests.

INFLUENCING CITIZENS' CHOICES

Once the issue context is established and parties select candidates to present to the electorate, many organized interests turn to influencing the voting choices of the public. This entails communicating the candidates' issue positions to voters, contributing money and other resources to candidates, and sometimes spending money independently to influence the outcome of an election. The logic of these efforts is straightforward. If organized interests are successful in promoting the candidacies of those supporting their policy positions, later lobbying efforts on behalf of those positions are far more likely to be successful or at least afforded a hearing.

Campaign Information

Interest organizations communicate information in a clear and unambiguous way to the public and to their own members through **ratings** and **endorsements**. National organizations such as the AFL-CIO, the Americans for Democratic Action, and the U.S. Chamber of Commerce routinely rate legislators by how they have voted on key legislation. In 2001, for example, the Chamber of Commerce used votes on tax relief, ergonomics rules, and international trade legislation among other issues to score legislators' performance. Legislators who support the Chamber's position on at least 70 percent of votes important to the Chamber's agenda receive the annual "Spirit of Enterprise Award."[34] Even at the state level, the ratings of organized interest are now commonly used to communicate voting records. In 2002 a report in the *Boston Globe* on the contest for president of the Massachusetts Senate was accompanied by a full complement of ratings by organized interests. One candidate, Senate Majority Whip Robert Travaglini, had earned a zero percent rating from Citizens for Limited Taxation, an 83 percent rating from the Massachusetts Audubon Society, and an F from the Gun Owners Action League. These scores provide clear, concrete assessments of legislator ideology and issue positions, allowing voters to make informed decisions.[35] Interest organizations rate legislator voting records in an effort both to reap the rewards of an informed electorate and, perhaps more importantly, to remind legislators that their actions are closely monitored.

The available evidence on voting behavior suggests that these efforts have considerable payoff. In 1988, for example, voters in California faced a number of complex issues on the ballot concerning reform of the insurance industry. Based on the results of an exit poll, Arthur Lupia concluded that voters who were uninformed about the technical issues, but who could correctly identify the position of the insurance industry on an initiative, were more likely to vote like other similar but better-informed voters than those who could not identify the industry's position.[36] This finding suggests that at least some voters used industry endorsements to overcome their lack of information about the issues. Endorsements by labor unions have been found to affect voting behavior by union members in a number of different studies.[37]

If voters rely on endorsements, then candidates and parties should have a strong incentive to compete for them. In their efforts to compete, we should expect candidates to announce issue positions that appeal to the leadership of endorsing organizations. There is solid anecdotal evidence that candidates do so. Both George Herbert Walker Bush and Bob Dole changed their positions on abortion in their campaigns for the Republican presidential nomination in 1992 in an effort to win the endorsement of the Christian Coalition. More recently, the AFL-CIO required congressional candidates to oppose fast-track trade legislation to win its support.[38] The NRA regularly requires that candidates issue public statements and respond to NRA questionnaires with the "right" answers — those revealing a sympathetic stance on gun-control issues — in order to receive its support. The National Organization for Women supports only those candidates who favor unrestricted abortion rights.[39] Not only will endorsements draw votes, but a correct issue position can also draw the kinds of campaign contributions discussed earlier.[40]

Voter guides are similar to endorsements and the ratings of interest organizations, although they do not explicitly favor one candidate over another. Churches and other nonprofit groups are allowed to distribute **voter guides** only if they are unbiased, wide-ranging, and do not track the organization's known position on issues.[41] Still, voter guides are often designed in ways that make it more than clear whom the organization supports. The Christian Coalition is one of the largest and best known organizations using voters' guides. The Coalition distributed nearly 30 million voter guides that scored legislators' records for the 1994 congressional races; another 45 million were distributed during the 1996 presidential race.[42] The guides or scorecards typically list candidates' votes in Congress or their stated positions on issues important to the organization distributing the guide, such as school choice vouchers, abortion, welfare reform, or term limits. They may also include candidate responses to the organization's questionnaires. Some have criticized guides for being oversimplified, often reducing complex issues to sound-bite style communications.[43] It is difficult to know what degree of influence voters' guides have. A study of voters' guides in the Georgia state legislature primary did not find evidence of increased voter support for the candidates and positions promoted.[44]

Campaign Labor

Although the campaign contributions of organized interests receive the bulk of media and scholarly attention, they contribute to political campaigns and party politics in many non-monetary ways. Political candidates especially value the campaign labor provided by organized interests. While television ads have become the major way in which candidates communicate to voters, older campaign activities have not disappeared, especially in state and local elections. Knocking on doors, placing yard signs, stuffing envelopes, manning phone banks, and driving voters to the polls require labor. Membership organizations often provide that labor.

Groups whose members directly participate in campaigns are a small percentage of all interest organizations.[45] However, their participation in political campaign is often important. The 2002 Minnesota race for Paul Wellstone's Senate seat was extremely close both before and after his death. Both the Democratic Farmer Labor Party (Minnesota's Democratic Party) and the state Republican Party relied on the labor of allied interest organizations to mobilize voters. Former Vice President Walter Mondale inherited a grassroots network of 15,000 volunteers, many linked with membership groups endorsing Democratic candidates. On election day, members of the groups associated with the campaign held signs and offered voters rides to the polls. Steve Rosenthal, director of the AFL-CIO's $15 million get-out-the-vote drive, noted that in 2000 79 percent of Minnesota's 650,000 members of union households voted. They represented 17.7 percent of eligible state voters, but cast 30 percent of the votes.[46] Members of organizations supporting Republican Norm Coleman, for their part, made thousands of phone calls to encourage potentially sympathetic voters to go to the polls. Businesses also worked to offset the strong labor union support provided to Mr. Mondale by emailing candidate report cards to workers and stuffing them in the envelopes with employees' paychecks.[47]

Campaign Money

We have already seen how money can influence the context and content of the choices placed before citizens. But money is also a means by which interest organizations shape how citizens decide among the choices presented to them. One of the most durable findings in studies of congressional elections is that money matters, especially for challengers. Incumbents have well established avenues for communicating with constituents. In effect, voters already know most of what matters to them about their incumbent member of Congress.[48] Challengers, on the other hand, must spend money to convince an electorate that is unfamiliar with them to take a risk. Incumbents are usually able to raise more money than challengers by a good margin. This advantage is telling. In 2002, in over 95 percent of House races and 76 percent of Senate races, the candidate who spent the most won. Given that money matters and incumbents are very good at raising money, it is not surprising that there is such a high rate of reelection for members of Congress. As pundit Jeff Greenfield observed, "I think the incumbency rate over the last several elections is roughly 98 percent, which exceeds the Soviet Politburo . . . You get free frank mail, you get on television for free, people give you money because you cast votes in committee, and therefore you can outspend your opponent. It's tough to lose."[49] In the following section, we discuss the regulation of political money and examine three types of funds used by organized interests in campaigns: PAC contributions, issue advocacy, and independent expenditures.

The regulation of campaign contributions in U.S. federal elections changed dramatically in the 1970s as a result of a series of Watergate-inspired reforms and has continued to change in the decades since. The Federal Election Campaign Act (FECA) became law in 1971 and was amended in important ways in 1974. As amended, the FECA sharply limited and regulated campaign contributions and spending. It also established the Federal Election Commission (FEC) as the agency in charge of enforcing the regulations. The new regime did not last long.

The Supreme Court's 1976 *Buckley* v. *Valeo* decision modified the campaign-finance system established by 1974 in significant ways. This decision had far reaching implications by imposing a Constitutional test on the FECA reforms. The Court struck down several of the act's key provisions. First, it rejected its limitations on spending by candidates for Congress, arguing that they constituted an abridgment of First Amendment protections of free speech. It also struck down restrictions on candidates' contributing to their own campaigns, arguing that a contribution to one's own campaign did not represent the same type of potentially corrupting influence as contributions that candidates might receive from organizations and other individuals. But the Court upheld restrictions on spending for *presidential* campaigns, reasoning that the compelling national interest of avoiding corruption or its appearance justified the costs of restricting free speech. The reforms established public funding for presidential campaigns. The Court reasoned that, because the limitations on spending in presidential elections were linked to voluntarily accepting public funding, restrictions on spending could stand at the presidential level.

In short, the first decade of reform resulted in the following regulations governing the funding of campaigns: (1) Contributions to federal candidates and parties in any election were limited to $1,000 from individuals and $5,000 from PACs; (2) cash contributions and coordinated expenditures from political parties to candidates were limited; (3) full disclosure of campaign contributions was required for individual, PAC, and party contributions; and (4) partial public funding of presidential campaigns was established.

Political Action Committees   Under the new campaign finance regime, **political action committees** (PACs) became an important part of the campaign finance process. PACs became the legal way for organized interests, such as membership groups, associations, and institutions, to legitimately contribute funds to their preferred candidates and parties. PACs are subject to contribution limits, as noted earlier, and must report their receipts and spending to the FEC. Still, as seen in Figure 3-2, the number of **connected PACs**—those affiliated with interest organizations—and **nonconnected PACs**—those not associated with a parent organization—grew rapidly after 1974. While their individual contributions to a given candidate were limited to $5,000 per election, PACs collectively came to control a much larger portion of all campaign funds than parties.[50] By the 1980s interest organizations and their associated PACs became major players in the campaign finance system. Winning Senate candidates now

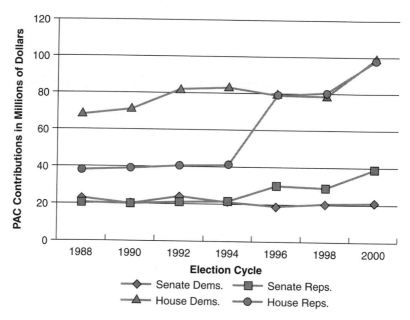

FIGURE 4-2 PAC Contributions to Congressional Candidates by Party and Chamber, 1988–2000 Election Cycles
Source: http://www.fec.gov, visited October 15, 2000.

raise about a quarter of their funds from PACs. For House winners the figure is 45 percent.

Certain patterns in PAC giving have become well established over the last two decades. First, PAC contributions go disproportionately to members of the majority party. Simply put, members of the majority party have much greater control over the policy agenda organized interests care about. Figure 4-2 clearly illustrates this pattern. The shift in PAC contributions from Democratic to Republican House members after the 1994 election, which led to GOP control of Congress, is clearly evident. The increased contributions to Republican senators after the 1994 election are not as dramatic, but a shift is evident for the upper chamber as well. Second, PAC contributions go disproportionately to party and committee leaders of Congress. In 2002 Speaker of the House Dennis Hastert received $1.3 million in PAC contributions ($1.1 million from business PACs). In contrast, Republican Todd Akin of Missouri received only $205,964 in PAC

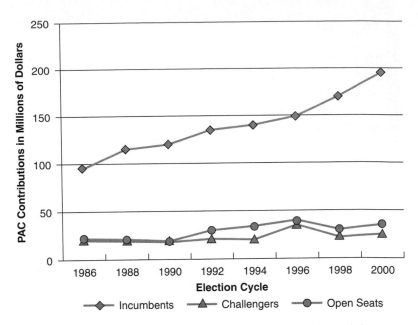

FIGURE 4-3 PAC Contributions by Type of Congressional Candidates,
1986–2000 Election Cycles
Source: http://www.fec.gov, visited October 15, 2000.

contributions. Third, incumbents also receive a much larger share of
PAC contributions. Figure 4-3 shows a large gap between incumbents and non-incumbents' PAC receipts in 1986, a gap that has only
grown larger in more recent years. Interest organizations contribute
to incumbents because there is a strong likelihood that they will
win reelection. Finally, candidates in close races receive more PAC
contributions. Gary Jacobson found that in 1990 more than 72 percent of total PAC contributions went to the top 10 percent of House
challengers.[51]

Patterns in PAC contributions are driven not only by the traits of
the recipient. They are also determined by the characteristics of the
contributing PAC. For example, PACs differ systematically in how
they allocate funds between incumbents and challengers. Corporate
PACs gave only 7.3 percent of their total contributions to challengers
in recent elections. In contrast, PACs associated with labor unions
typically give far more money to challengers.

Together, these two sets of patterns of PAC giving tell us a great deal about the goals of the organized interests supporting PACs. By more often than not contributing to incumbents, legislative leaders, and members of the majority party, most interest organizations, but especially those representing business interests, typically pursue what scholars have labeled an **access strategy** or legislative strategy. In other words, they contribute to candidates more often for the purpose of securing access to them once they are in office than to further their election chances. Still, some PACs pursue an **electoral strategy** or ideological strategy. Under this strategy, contributions are based on the candidate's ideological or policy compatibility with the interest organization's goals. With an access strategy, interest organizations work with whoever is in office. With an electoral strategy, organizations try to influence who the office holders are. While PACs linked to larger interest organizations commonly pursue an access strategy, nonconnected PACs, which often represent more ideologically charged interests, contribute heavily to challengers in a manner consistent with the electoral strategy.

Soft Money and Issue Advocacy   The campaign finance system changed further during the 1980s. Most importantly, parties and organized interests exploited the soft money loophole in the Federal Election Campaign Act. Only those party-building efforts that directly benefit federal candidates, such as a get-out-the-vote-drive for a congressional candidate, are subject to the limitations and disclosure requirements of FECA. We have seen, however, that politicians soon recognized that the line between party building and campaigns is fuzzy. The increasing pressure to provide funding for candidates gave politicians a strong incentive to further blur the fraying distinction between hard and soft money. As a result, political parties began using soft money in increasingly liberal ways. The loophole appealed to organized interests as well because it allowed for much larger, unlimited, and undisclosed contributions. Table 4-1 shows the top 15 soft money donors during the 2002 election. While the GOP raised more soft money overall, Democrats were very dependent on fewer but larger contributions.

Soft money is still used for the party building activities envisioned in FECA, but it is also used to fund candidates' campaign ads that meet the legal requirements to be considered issue advocacy

TABLE 4-1 The Top 15 Soft Money Contributors in 2002

Organization	Total	Democrats	Republicans
Saban Entertainment	$10,800,000	$10,800,000	—
Newsweb Corporation	6,890,000	6,890,000	—
Shangri-La Entertainment	6,525,000	6,525,000	—
American Federation of State, County, and Municipal Employees	6,071,500	6,071,000	500
Service Employees International Union	4,029,739	3,988,117	41,622
Carpenters & Joiners Union	3,518,709	3,498,709	20,000
Communications Workers of America	3,473,000	3,473,000	—
Propel	3,288,786	3,288,786	—
Freddie Mac	2,875,615	1,200,000	1,675,615
Pharmaceutical Researchers & Manufacturers of America	2,679,787	115,500	2,564,287
American Federation of Teachers	2,567,000	2,557,000	10,000
Philip Morris	2,409,909	378,388	2,031,521
Williams & Bailey	2,261,400	2,261,400	—
Microsoft Corporation	2,218,751	626,000	1,592,251
AT&T	2,038,471	870,250	1,168,221

Source: http://www.opensecrets.org, visited December 5, 2002.

rather than electoral activity. They may not say the magic words "vote for" or "vote against," but these ads clearly further the interests of particular candidates. Both parties and organized interests use such election-oriented issue advocacy. In some 2002 congressional contests, such as those in Arkansas and South Dakota, the Democratic Senatorial Campaign Committee, heavily funded by soft money, transferred more money to help the campaigns than the candidates raised on their own. Such soft money funded issue advocacy spending allows parties to rapidly transfer money to close races near to election day. In mid-October of 2002, the largest transfers by the Democratic committee were to the Senate races in Minnesota ($7.2 million), Missouri ($6.6 million), and South Dakota ($6.3 million). The National Republican Senatorial Committee transferred the most to Missouri ($5.7 million), Minnesota ($4.8 million), and South Dakota ($3.9 million).[52] All were close, tight races.

Not all of the funds used by organized interests to influence voting choices are channeled through the political parties. By the same stage of the 2002 congressional campaign, groups affiliated with the large pharmaceutical companies were estimated to have spent more than $12 million. The Council for Better Government, under the direction of its president John Altevogt, a Republican activist from Kansas, spent close to a million dollars on radio and television ads aimed at black and Hispanic voters across the country. One ad stated, "Don't buy the Democrat line. Killing unborn babies is not the way to help those in poverty."[53] In sum, both parties and interest organizations wage expensive and extensive issue advocacy campaigns that often resemble the candidates' own campaign advertising. Indeed, parties and interest organizations spend more than the candidates in some political campaigns.

Independent Expenditures   Sometimes, the efforts of organized interests go beyond the often thinly cloaked campaign activities associated with issue advocacy. **Independent expenditures** are similar to issue advocacy. Both often entail the use of issue ads during political campaigns, and, as with issue advocacy, both interest organizations and political parties engage in independent expenditures. Unlike issue advocacy, however, independent expenditures must be funded with regulated, limited, and reported hard money contributions. But these costs come with a modest advantage. Campaign ads funded by independent expenditures may expressly advocate the election or defeat of a candidate. They may use the magic words "vote for" or "vote against." Moreover, a PAC may contribute only $5,000 (now $10,000) to a candidate's campaign in any election. Given the decisions of the Supreme Court, that same PAC may independently spend an unlimited amount to support the election of the candidate. Importantly, however, such expenditures must be made entirely independently from the candidate and the candidate's campaign organization and must be funded by hard dollars.

Independent expenditures were not always a major part of American political campaigns. Just as the campaign finance system changed as the uses of soft money expanded, it was modified further as the legal foundation of independent expenditures was established. During Ronald Reagan's 1980 and 1984 presidential campaigns, a number of conservative organizations engaged in independent spending in support of his candidacy. A 1985 Supreme Court case challenged the legality of these expenditures by two groups: the National Conservative Political Action Committee and the Fund for a Conservative Majority. The Fund for a Conservative Majority ran the memorable and influential "Morning in America" television ad, which extolled Reagan's role in restoring America's optimism.[54] The Supreme Court rejected this challenge, as well as an earlier one brought by Common Cause and the FEC. The Court's decision followed the freedom of speech principle articulated in *Buckley* v. *Valeo* and found no compelling interest in restricting political speech by imposing the same type of spending limits on independent expenditures that govern the funding of presidential campaigns.[55]

The Bush campaign in 1988 was also supported by independent expenditures. The infamous Willie Horton ad, sponsored by the National Security Political Action Committee, is an especially noteworthy example of ads funded by independent expenditures. A legal challenge in this case questioned whether these expenditures were truly independent from the campaign of the then Vice President Bush. In spite of some evidence that they were not, the FEC concluded that there was insufficient evidence of coordination to suggest illegal behavior.[56] These court victories established that independent expenditures were a legal means for organized interests to spend unlimited amounts in making their case to voters about the merits of candidates.

The campaign activities of U.S. Term Limits (USTL) provides a more recent example of independent expenditures. In 2002 USTL focused on the U.S. House candidate for Ohio's 12th district, Pat Tiberi. In USTL's view, candidate Tiberi was an appropriate target for opposition spending because he served in the state senate for 17 uninterrupted years and left only when forced out by a new Ohio law that limited the terms of state legislators. The Washington-based USTL planned a six-figure attack on the candidate, in part because he refused to sign a pledge to limit his tenure in Congress unless all other members were also term limited. The race between Tiberi and opponent Gene Watts, who had signed the pledge to serve no more than four terms in the House, was chosen to "send some messages round the country."[57] In the previous election cycle, USTL had spent a formidable $11.5 million on independent advertising in key House campaigns to pursue further its goal of instituting term limits at all levels of government. In some ways, USTL's ad attack campaign differed from most independent expenditures. As seen in Figure 4-4, and despite complaints about attack ads from outside interests, independent expenditures by PACs more often than not support rather than oppose candidates.

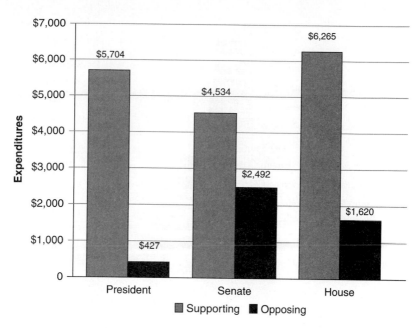

FIGURE 4-4 Independent Expenditures by 163 PACs in the 2000 Election Cycle, in Thousands
Source: http://fec.gov, visited October 14, 2002

As noted earlier, not all candidates enjoy the "help" they receive from even supportive independent expenditures. The issues raised by organizations using independent expenditures may differ from those candidates may wish to emphasize. The organized interests participating in electoral politics have varied agendas, including helping candidates, pushing legislation, and furthering their own policy goals. These objectives are not always compatible with the candidates'. The authors of one recent study noted that "some groups indicated they would continue to push their agendas through ads even if tracking polls showed that they were hurting the candidate they presumably were trying to help," adding that "other contests showed that despite a candidate's request that an interest group not join the campaign, the outside campaign went ahead."[58]

The Impact of Contributions on Elections   How effective is political money? The answer very much depends on its purpose. If political money is intended to change who sits within legislative chambers or

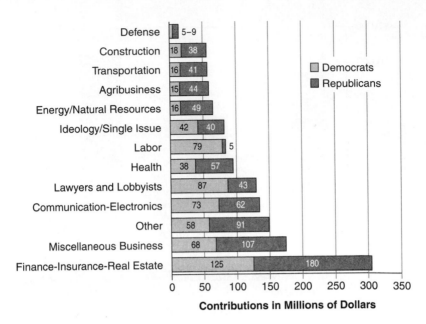

FIGURE 4-5 PAC, Soft Money, and Individual Contributions by Sector and Party, 1999–2000
Source: http://www.opensecrets.org/overview, visited October 15, 2002.

in executive offices in order to alter the ideological balance of government, it may have little impact. Most organized interests pursue an access strategy in contributing to legislators. This means that most interest organization money is contributed to incumbents, thereby blunting its partisan and ideological impacts. This is readily seen in Figure 4-5, which lists the total political contributions of all types from 13 economic sectors during the 1999–2000 election cycle. Overall, Republicans raised more money than Democrats. A few sectors—energy and natural resources for Republicans and labor for Democrats—are strongly committed to one party or another, suggesting that they follow an electoral strategy. But most of the economic sectors do not put all of their eggs in one partisan basket. They give to both parties; or, more specifically, they give to incumbents, which means that they give to both parties. Thus, the critical election impact of interest organization money is to reinforce incumbency. With interest organization money, individual incumbents are more likely to stay in office. Once established, incumbent majority parties are more likely to remain in power.

If most interest organizations do not work resolutely to change who is in office, why do they give such large sums of money to political candidates? In truth, much of the money interest organizations bring to politics is less about shaping citizens' choices in elections than working with whoever wins once they are in office. Indeed, the safest strategy for many interest organizations is to contribute to both candidates. The importance of this strategy is evident in Table 4-2, which lists the top five overall contributors, counting all types of contributions, including those from individuals listed by their employer, to the 2000 presidential candidates. Two facts are worth noting. Interest organizations tend to bet on potential winners. George Bush and Al Gore received far more contributions than did minor party candidates. Second, with the exception of contributions from employees of the USDA, the largest contributors to both major parties include finance and accounting firms. Indeed, Ernst & Young, while the largest contributor to Al Gore, was the fourth largest donor to George Bush and actually gave the Texas governor a bit more than they sent to the vice president. Do these contributions actually buy access and influence? These are issues we consider in the next two chapters.

Money in Initiative Campaigns   Finally, interest organization money can influence voters' choices in initiative and referendum campaigns. That is, 26 states have direct legislation in the form of initiatives and referendums. In two-fifths of the states, citizens may submit constitutional or statutory proposals to the voters and their votes are binding. Direct legislation is interesting for a number of reasons. First, it provides an exceptionally clean test of the influence of interest organization money on voter choices. Voters determine whether referendum proposals become law. This means that organized interests supporting or opposing these proposals must lobby voters directly. Later access to political elites counts, therefore, for little. Votes on ballot initiatives are also uncomplicated by party labels.

Second, expectations about direct legislation clearly pit the pluralist and transactions school interpretations of the politics of interest organizations against each other. For pluralists, direct legislation provides the most immediate means for translating public preferences

TABLE 4-2 Five Major Contributors to Presidential Candidates, 2000

George W. Bush *(Republican)*	MBNA Corp.	$240,675
	Vinson & Elkins	202,850
	Credit Suisse First Boston	191,400
	Ernst & Young	179,949
	Anderson Worldwide	145,650
Al Gore *(Democrat)*	Ernst & Young	134,925
	Citigroup Inc.	111,750
	Viacom Inc.	105,175
	U.S. Department of Agriculture	102,466
	Goldman Sachs Group	95,750
Patrick J. Buchanan *(Reform)*	Milliken & Co.	64,250
	NASA	8,500
	Electrospace System Inc.	7,000
	Naval Surface Warfare Center	7,000
	RMC Industries	7,000
Ralph Nader *(Green)*	Jack H. Olender & Associates	$6,500
	University of California	6,400
	Kayline Enterprises	5,000
	University of Illinois	4,500
	ESRI	4,000
Harry Browne *(Libertarian)*	Susquehanna International Corporation	11,500
	Microsoft Corporation	9,975
	IBM Corporation	8,550
	Northwest Airlines	4,000
	LH Thompson Company	3,800

Note: Sums include funds from sponsored PACs and individuals with employer of individual contributors cited for the contribution.
Source: http://www.opensecrets.org, visited October 14, 2002.

into policy. Indeed, the progressives of the early 20th century who promoted direct democracy believed that the initiative and referendum were necessary to avoid the corruption of state legislatures by special interests. Transactions scholars would lead us to expect that organized interests would find some way to hijack direct legislation for their own purposes. There are good reasons to take the transactions school hypothesis seriously. An entire industry has grown around the initiative process. Highly specialized companies assist any organization or individual interested in sponsoring an initiative. Some firms gather the required number of signatures, while specialized law firms draft the language of the initiative proposal in the appropriate way. Still other firms conduct campaigns in support of or opposition to the ballot measures. The initiative industry can provide significant advantage to a moneyed interest over ordinary citizens who might wish to use the initiative process to further their policy goals. Journalist David Broder reports that it can cost between one and two million dollars to qualify an initiative for the ballot, including the signature-gathering process, drafting the initiative, and sponsoring a campaign.[59] Critics like Broder argue that the initiative and referendum process has been so subverted by wealthy interest organizations that they can readily manipulate the public into supporting incredibly narrow, self-interested policy proposals.

Fortunately, scholarly analyses of the initiative process and referendum voting has not supported Broder's dire predictions. Todd Donovan and Shaun Bowler analyzed several different kinds of direct democracy campaigns.[60] In some, narrow interests—often business interests—supported one side of the referendum, while interest organizations representing broader constituencies—often citizens groups—supported the other side. In such contests, Donovan and Bowler's analysis found that the narrow, well-heeled interests had a very low rate of success. Similarly, Elizabeth Gerber's extensive analysis of 168 direct legislation campaigns in eight states found that even well-financed campaigns by such narrow interests as the insurance industry and tobacco companies have little impact on voters' decisions.[61] In contrast, citizens' groups with broad-based support have been very successful in translating their preferences into law through the use of direct legislation. In short, money is not everything.

CONCLUSION

When Americans think about interest organizations, they commonly envision crowds of well-heeled lobbyists buttonholing legislators in the halls of Congress. We have seen, however, that organized interests spend much of their time lobbying citizens. Organized interests work hard to frame the issues citizens consider and how they consider them. The information, labor, and money that organized interests bring to politics influence both the choices citizens have and, perhaps, how they select among them. These two images of lobbying — the inside lobbying of political elites and the outside lobbying of the public — are, of course, related. As we will see in the next chapter, legislators do not easily dismiss the views of their constituents when voting on the issues organized interests care about. Influencing those constituents is often the very best, most sure way to influence the decisions of political elites.

Is this good for democracy? Our three broad perspectives on the politics of interest representation offer sharply divergent answers. To pluralists, lobbying the public is an essential part of democratic politics. Issues do not appear in a void. Someone must bring them to the public's attention, frame them in understandable and persuasive ways, and link them to electoral choices in a manner that has policy consequences. Transactions scholars would in many ways agree, but they also suggest that the public is easily misled. Money, especially, may be used not so much to frame issues as to manipulate public perceptions of them in ways beneficial to very special interests. Neopluralists, based on the very mixed evidence we have reviewed about the effectiveness of efforts to lobby the public, opt for a middle ground. While they view the preferences of the public as fairly resilient, voters may on some occasions be misled, not fully considering their stakes in an issue. Moreover, the machinations of organized interests may not always present voters with meaningful choices on key issues. At times, the flood of interest organization money may even lead voters to vote against their interests. In the neopluralist view, then, specific regulations may well be needed to curb specific abuses of interest organization influence. And it is clear that such reform efforts must be ongoing as organized interests — and politicians — discover and exploit opportunities for playing the influence game. The most recent of such efforts, the Bipartisan Campaign Finance Reform Act, is discussed in Chapter 8.

KEY TERMS AND CONCEPTS

Framing
Issue Advocacy
Think Tanks
Advocacy Tanks
Advertorials
Recruitment
Hard Money
Soft Money
Ratings

Endorsements
Voter Guides
Buckley v. *Valeo*
Political Action Committee
Connected PACs
Nonconnected PACs
Access Strategy
Electoral Strategy
Independent Expenditures

QUESTIONS ABOUT YOUR
INTEREST ORGANIZATION

1. Does your organization sponsor a political action committee? When was it founded? What is its fundraising history?
2. If your organization sponsors a PAC, does it pursue an access or electoral strategy? How many state and federal candidates received funds from the PAC in the last election cycle?
3. Has your organization sponsored issues or used independent expenditures in campaigns? If so, what were they about? How extensive is your organization's reliance on this activity?
4. Does your organization conduct original research? If so, on what? How are the results of this research distributed?
5. Has your organization made soft money contributions to political parties in recent election cycles? If so, to whom and how much?
6. Given all of the evidence, would you say that your interest organization is affiliated with one of the major political parties?

NOTES

1. The NORML Foundation, "Join the Campaign: 'It's NORML to Smoke Pot,' http://www.norml.org/index.cfm?Group_ID=5229.
2. James T. Patterson, *America's Struggle Against Poverty, 1900–1980,* (Cambridge, MA: Chatham House Publishers, 2000), p. 81.
3. David A. Rochefort and Roger W. Cobb, "Framing and Claiming the Homelessness Problem," *New England Journal of Public Policy* 8: 49–65 (1992).

4. E. E. Schattschneider, *The Semisovereign People* (New York: Holt, Rinehart, and Winston, 1960), p. 68.

5. Gary Mucciaroni, "Problem Definition and Special Interest Politics in Tax Policy and Agriculture." In *The Politics of Problem Definition: Shaping the Policy Agenda*, David A. Rochefort and Roger W. Cobb, eds. (Lawrence, KS: University Press of Kansas, 1994), pp. 118–119.

6. Ibid., p. 125

7. Beth L. Leech, Frank R. Baumgartner, Jeffrey M. Berry, Marie Hojnacki, and David C. Kimball, "Organized Interests and Issue Definition in Policy Debates." In *Interest Group Politics*, 6th ed. Allen J. Cigler and Burdett A. Loomis, eds. (2002), pp. 285–287.

8. Andrew Rich and R. Kent Weaver, "Advocates and Analysts: Think Tanks and the Politicization of Expertise." In *Interest Group Politics*, 5th ed. Allan J. Cigler and Burdett A. Loomis, eds. (Washington, DC: CQ Press, 1998), p. 241.

9. Ibid., p. 237.

10. Dietrich Rueschemeyer and Theda Skocpol, *Social Knowledge and the Origins of Modern Social Policies* (Princeton, NJ: Princeton University Press, 1996).

11. Rich and Weaver, "Advocates and Analysts," p. 239.

12. R. Kent Weaver, "The Changing World of Think Tanks," *PS: Political Science and Politics* 22: 563–578 (1989).

13. Lee Edward, *The Power of Ideas* (Ottawa, IL: Jameson Books, 1997), p. 32.

14. Rich and Weaver, "Advocates and Analysts," p. 242.

15. Paul Starobin, "Rethinking Brookings," *National Journal*, 1875–1879 (July 22, 1995).

16. Lucig H. Danielian and Benjamin I. Page, "The Heavenly Chorus: Interest Group Voices on TV News," *American Journal of Political Science* 38: 1062 (1994).

17. Ibid., p. 1069.

18. Ibid., p. 1070.

19. Benjamin I. Page, Robert Y. Shapiro, and Glenn R. Dempsey, "What Moves Public Opinion?" *American Political Science Review*, 81: 31 (1987).

20. Ibid., p. 30.

21. Clyde Brown and Herbert Waltzer, "Lobbying the Press: 'Talk to the People Who Talk to America.'" In *Interest Group Politics*,

Allan J. Cigler and Burdett A. Loomis, eds. (Washington, DC: CQ Press), pp. 249–275.

22. L. Sandy Maisel, Walter J. Stone, and Cherie Maestas, "Reassessing the Definition of Quality Candidates," Colby College, Typescript (1999). Jon R. Bond, Cary Covington, and Richard Fleisher, "Explaining Challenger Quality in Congressional Elections," *Journal of Politics* 47: 510–529; (1985). Peverill Squire, "Challengers in U.S. Senate Elections," *Legislative Studies Quarterly* 14: 531–547 (1989).

23. Robert Biersack, Paul S. Herrnson, and Clyde Wilcox, "Seeds for Success: Early Money in Congressional Elections," *Legislative Studies Quarterly* 18: 535–551 (1993).

24. Rosalyn Cooperman, "Party Organizations and the Recruitment of Women Candidates to the U.S. House since the 'Year of the Woman,'" Vanderbilt University, Typescript (2000).

25. Ibid.

26. John Persinos, "Has the Christian Right Taken Over the Republican Party?" *Campaigns & Elections* 15: 20–24 (September 1994).

27. Ibid.

28. Gregory A. Pettis and Thad Beyle, "The Christian Right, the South, and State Politics," *SouthNow* 3: 9 (June 2002).

29. Denise L. Baer and Julie A. Dolan, "Intimate Connections: Political Interests and Group Activity in State and Local Parties," *American Review of Politics* 15: 257–289 (1994).

30. Kirk Mitchell, "Caucus Overhaul Lauded, Panned for Power Shift," *Denver Post* (October 15, 2002), p. A10.

31. Ibid.

32. David Karp and Bill Adair, "GOP Money Men Get Ready to Roll," *St. Petersburg Times* (December 8, 2002), p. 1A.

33. Ibid.

34. Ibid.

35. United States Chamber of Commerce, "U.S. Chamber Recognizes Pro-Business Lawmakers—Senators, Representatives Receive Annual Award," http://www.uschamber.com/press/releases/2002/march/02-45.htm, January 8, 2003.

36. Frank Phillips, "Travaglini Said to Have Votes to Lead Senate," *Boston Globe* (October 21, 2002), p. A1.

37. Arthur Lupia, "Busy Voters, Agenda Control, and the Power of Information," *American Political Science Review* 86: 390–403 (1992).

38. Arthur Kornhauser, Harold L. Sheppard, and Albert J. Mayer, *When Labor Votes: A Study of Auto Workers* (New York: University Books, 1956); Michael H. LeRoy, "The 1988 Elections: Re-Emergence of the Labor Bloc Vote?" *Labor Studies Journal* 15: 5–32 (1990).

39. Gene M. Grossman and Elhanan Helpman, "Protection for Sale," *American Economic Review* 84: 833–850 (1994).

40. Gene M. Grossman and Elhanan Helpman, "Competing for Endorsements," Princeton, Typescript (1996).

41. Rob Boston, "Cardinal Bevilacqua's Voter Guide Scheme Sparks Protest," *Church and State* (May 1999).

42. Robert Booth Fowler and Allen D. Hertzke, *Religion and Politics in America: Faith, Culture, and Strategic Choices* (Boulder, CO: Westview Press, 1995).

43. Ibid.

44. Dale McConkey and John C. Hickman, "Deus Ex Voter Guide: The Effect of the Christian Coalition on State Primaries," *Comparative State Politics* 18: 13–21 (1997).

45. Ken Kollman, *Outside Lobbying* (Princeton: Princeton University Press, 1998), p. 35.

46. Greg Gordon and Tom Ford, "Voter Turnout Efforts Hit Peak; Interest Groups Across the Spectrum Work to Energize Their Partisans," *Minneapolis Star Tribune* (November 5, 2002), p. 16A.

47. Ibid.

48. Gary C. Jacobson, "The Effects of Campaign Spending in House Elections: New Evidence for Old Arguments," *American Journal of Political Science* 34: 334–335 (1990).

49. "America Votes 2002: Real Votes Are Way to Go," *CNN Live Event/Special* (November 5, 2002).

50. Frank J. Sorauf, *Inside Campaign Finance* (New Haven: Yale University Press, 1992).

51. Gary C. Jacobson, "The Misallocation of Resources in House Campaigns." In *Congress Reconsidered,* 5th ed. Lawrence C. Dodd, ed. (Boulder, CO: Westview Press 1993).

52. Richard A. Oppel, Jr., "Democratic Committee Outspent Candidates in Some Races," *New York Times* (November 4, 2002), p. A20.

53. Ibid.

54. Darrel M. West, *Checkbook Democracy* (Boston: Northeastern University Press, 2000), pp. 23–24.

55. Ibid., pp. 21–22.
56. Ibid., pp. 31–35.
57. John Gizzi, "Will Paul Jacob Strike Again?" *Human Events* 55: 20 (1999).
58. David Magleby and Marianne Holt, "The Long Shadow of Soft Money and Issue Advocacy Ads," *Campaigns and Elections* (May 1999).
59. David Broder, *Democracy Derailed* (New York: Harcourt, Inc., 2000), p. 69.
60. Todd Donovan and Shaun Bowler, "Contending Players and Strategies: Opposition Advantages in Initiative Elections." In *Citizens as Legislators*, Shaun Bowler, Todd Donovan, and Caroline J. Tolbert, eds. (Columbus: Ohio State University Press, 1998).
61. Elisabeth R. Gerber, *The Populist Paradox* (Princeton, NJ: Princeton University Press, 1999).

CHAPTER 5

Organized Interests and the Legislature

O n July 25, 2002, a bill adopting sweeping reforms in government oversight of major corporations and the accounting industry rolled through Congress. The vote in the House was 423 to 3. In the Senate the vote was 99 to zero. Among other provisions, the bill imposed stiff new penalties for corporate fraud and document shredding. It outlawed personal loans of company funds to corporate officers and prohibited accounting firms from providing consulting services to firms they audit. The bill also established a new independent board to oversee the accounting industry.[1] Spurred on by a series of scandals involving some of the country's largest corporations—Enron, Arthur Andersen, WorldCom, Global Crossing, Xerox, and others—and falling stock markets, Congress overcame furious lobbying by the financial services industry and other business lobbies. Only days before passage of the reform measure, the House Republican leadership was searching for ways to delay a vote until the bill could be watered down in a less heated political environment.[2] Their failure is all the more striking since Arthur Levitt, Jr., President Clinton's head of the Securities and Exchange Commission (SEC) was severely rebuffed by Congress when he proposed many of the same reforms in previous years.[3]

The transactions and pluralist interpretations of the politics of interest representation have a difficult time explaining this about-face. The transactions school assumes that politics are about money, with legislation purchased like any other commodity. Why were the corporations that so readily influenced legislators in prior years so easily routed in July of 2002? Pluralists, in contrast, suggest that it is difficult for interest organizations to persuade legislators to vote against constituents' interests. So why were corporate lobbyists so successful in opposing reform prior to 2001? Neither perspective explains the *change* in policy. Neopluralists, however, suggest that it all depends on context. The intervening scandals and the collapse of stock prices altered the effectiveness of the tools organized interests use to secure influence.

This chapter explores how organized interests seek influence in the legislative arena. We first consider the complex stages of the legislative process. Each offers opportunities and challenges for interest organizations as they try to shape legislation. We then review the many tools organized interests employ to influence legislators. Next, we consider how interest organizations select among the influence tools available to them. We will see that the nature of issues legislators consider constrains the kinds of influence tools organized interests can employ. Along the way, we will return to the corporate and accounting reform bill to assess the plausibility of the pluralist, transactions, and neopluralist interpretations of influence in the legislative process.

INFLUENCE AND THE STAGES OF LEGISLATION

We all too often consider only legislators' final votes on a bill in teasing out the influence organized interests exert on the legislative process. But the process is complex. Seen broadly, it even includes the effects discussed in the previous chapter. That is, even before a bill is introduced, someone must define the problem it addresses. As we have noted, many organized interests, especially think tanks, devote considerable time to framing issues for both the general public and political elites so as to prepare for later action within legislative bodies. But once an issue takes its place on the public agenda, a bill must be introduced, delegated to committee, hearings held, and committee action taken before the proposed legislation is subject to a final floor vote. There is also a later stage after the floor vote when a measure is considered in conference committee. In short, the legislative process includes several distinct stages. Considering only final votes, then, neglects numerous other opportunities for interest organizations to shape both the ultimate outcome and the content of legislation. We will see that neopluralists have expanded the study of legislative influence to include all of these stages of the process. They therefore provide a more nuanced understanding of influence in the legislature.

Introducing Legislation

Only members of Congress introduce legislation. And though some states provide opportunities for citizens to introduce bills for legislative consideration, state legislators introduce most bills. So interest organizations must find an ally in the legislature. The most likely allies, of course, are the legislators that organized interests have supported in their electoral campaigns. But PAC contributions per se have little relationship with introducing bills, and more than gratitude motivates legislators. Most legislators are policy entrepreneurs who actively look for issues on which to work.[4] Specializing on an issue is one way to establish a strong reputation as a productive legislator. And introducing legislation that constituents strongly favor can also benefit a legislator. So, if organized interests need allies, legislators in turn need the ideas, issues, and drafts of legislation that interest organizations can provide. Organized interests have an opportunity to exercise influence if they can find a sympathetic legislator to author legislation favorable to them, but they may also succeed by authoring legislation themselves that the legislator then introduces. Indeed, for decades professional associations have proposed drafts of legislation for consideration by state legislatures.

A recent example of a successful link between an organized interest and legislators sympathetic to its concerns is the Leave No Child Behind Act. The Children's Defense Fund (CDF) authored the draft legislation that included provisions for the protection and improvement of children's health and education and many aspects of the welfare of children. The bill was introduced by the CDF's ally Christopher Dodd (D-CT) in the Senate and by ally Representative George Miller (D-CA) in the House. They were sympathetic to the goals of the CDF and were willing to introduce the legislation. In return, the CDF provided the two legislators a potent issue to pursue and an opportunity to claim credit with constituents and colleagues.

The Committee Stage

Voting occurs not only when legislation is considered on the floor; it is also part of the committee process. Most bills in legislatures are considered first in committee and require the support of a majority of committee members to be reported to the floor. But voting is only the final element of the committee process. Importantly, committees establish the *content* of legislation. Therefore, the committee stage can hold significant appeal for organized interests. That is, it is a natural convergence of the interests of constituents, legislators, and advocacy organizations because legislators often seek assignments to those committees that have jurisdiction over policy that is relevant to their constituents or to their own policy interests. A member of Congress whose state or district includes a city that is a financial center will often seek an assignment to the Financial Services Committee in the House, or Banking, Housing, and Urban Affairs in the Senate. A member whose state or district represents oil and gas interests will seek service on Energy Committee and Commerce Committee in the House or Senate. Because of constituency considerations, these legislators are likely to be supportive of the concerns of the banking or oil and gas interests. The preferences that members of Congress express in choosing committee assignments make it more likely that members of the committee will be receptive to the interest organizations concerned with its issues.[5]

Finding energetic allies on a committee provides important benefits for interest organizations. The most important lies in finding a **champion** for one's cause. Even legislators who might otherwise be sympathetic to a cause have far too many demands on their time to work vigorously on behalf of all of their potential friends. Senator Ted Kennedy is highly sympathetic to a number of liberal causes, but he does not have the time to work on all of them equally as vigorously. So, committee lobbying is often about mobilizing sympathetic allies to become more fully engaged in promoting — or sometimes derailing — a bill or an amendment. Indeed, Richard Hall and Frank Wayman suggest that this is the real goal of campaign contributions. If interest organizations receive something in exchange for a campaign contribution, it is a legislator's *time* and *effort* rather than his or her *vote*.[6] If interest organization support influences the level of a legislator's participation in committee meetings, then money and other forms of campaign support may influence how vigorously that interest is represented.

What does this effort provide the interest organization? Having an energetic ally on the committee as legislation is drafted can be worth far more than votes in committee or on the floor. One legislator's vote is useless unless there are enough other votes to form a majority, but it requires only one ally to author a narrow amendment on behalf of an organized interest. When legislation involves complex or technical issues that are of little interest to the general public, a legislative ally may have opportunities to modify a bill in order to favor an interest organization.[7] On highly technical or obscure issues, the input of lobbyists also can be useful for a committee member by providing confirmation that he or she has understood the potential consequences of the legislation. A large percentage of congressional business considered in committee is low-visibility, highly technical work that provides such opportunities for influence.

It is also more *efficient* for an organization to try to influence legislation in committee. At the committee stage, a smaller number of legislators can have a larger impact on the character of the final legislation. The product of the committee's effort is also likely to make it all the way through the legislative process if it survives the committee process. Amending a measure on the floor is difficult and often prohibited by procedures in the U.S. House. Thus, organized interests often seek influence at the committee stage where a smaller investment may yield a large return.[8]

Champions on important or relevant committees are also important because they may be willing to lobby fellow legislators on behalf of the interest organization. This is, in effect, a two-stage lobbying process. If an interest organization finds a receptive member of the legislature, he or she may, in turn, be willing to persuade fellow members to support the position of the interest organization. Such indirect lobbying is common. Beth Leech and Frank Baumgartner found in their survey of interest organizations with offices in Washington, DC, that 67 percent reported that they lobbied indirectly by asking their allies in Congress to lobby other members.[9] A direct lobbying effort by a member of Congress aimed at another member of Congress can be very effective. But if influence is exercised *indirectly* through fellow members of legislatures, it will be difficult to find a simple link between money and votes.

Ultimately, however, most legislatures require a positive committee vote on most bills before they can reach the floor, so, beyond their champion, whom do organized interests lobby? Two sorts of legislators receive the lion's share of attention. First, all other things equal, interest organizations are far more likely to lobby committee members who are already more sympathetic than their foes or undecided members. Second, if a member on the relevant committee is not already an ally, he or she may still be lobbied if the organization has a strong presence in the district. Lobbyists representing labor unions, for example, will lobby legislators from districts with many union members. Given the importance of constituents' views, a strong presence in the district makes even potential opponents lobbying targets of an interest organization.[10] In either case, because the target legislators have reasons to be sympathetic, most lobbying probably entails little or no "pressure." If an organization represents a popular cause that plays well with constituents, the legislator may benefit from an opportunity to use the technical and political information provided by it.

Voting Decisions

To become law, a bill must pass in a full legislative chamber. Floor deliberations vary across state and national legislatures and across chambers within legislatures. Deliberations on the floor of the House and Senate of Congress differ significantly. In the House, the **Rules Committee** — strongly guided by House majority party leadership — establishes the rules governing floor debate for each bill. The rules associated with a bill can and do vary greatly. They vary in the time allowed for debate, whether or not amendments may be added, how many amendments may be considered, and the order in which the amendments are considered. And amendments that are not germane or relevant to the legislation being considered may not be introduced at any time in House deliberations. This highly structured process gives the majority party leadership in the House a strong influence on this stage of the process. It also sharply limits opportunities for organized interests to influence the outcome. Lobbyists wishing to exercise influence on floor deliberations must work with the leadership and with members of the Rules Committee if they are to create an advantage for themselves on the floor vote.

Each senator, in contrast, has opportunities to influence the floor debate. Deliberation typically is not limited in length, nor is there a limitation on who may speak. Any senator may offer amendments and it is not necessary that the amendment be relevant to the issue at hand. It is therefore less important for lobbying efforts on floor deliberations in the Senate to focus on chamber leadership. However, one common element for lobbying at the floor stage for both the House and Senate is that the majority of members of each chamber must support a measure in order for it to succeed. This requires lobbying a larger number of members than must be contacted at the policy formulation or committee stage of the process.

Because it is the most visible stage of the legislative process, many political scientists examine floor voting for evidence of the influence of organized interests. A rather large number of studies examine how patterns of lobbying, and campaign contributions especially, are related to the distribution of final votes in legislatures. We will examine some of these studies in more detail later. For now, though, we must emphasize the difficulty of uncovering such relationships. Any attempt to exercise influence on the part of organized interests is mitigated by other factors that powerfully influence the voting decisions of members of legislatures. In many cases, these forces work together to influence legislators' votes, making it difficult to untangle their separate effects.

The most important of these forces is constituency. Particularly for members of legislatures that are reelected every two years, attention to constituent preferences is vital to electoral success. Research on the relationship between lobbying, campaign contributions, and members' votes strongly suggests that the efforts of organized interests are mitigated by legislators' concern for constituents' preferences. Arthur Denzau and Michael Munger, for example, have examined the nature of the relationship between constituent preferences and campaign contributions. The "supply price" for policy — what an interest organization must pay in the form of campaign contributions to obtain their desired response from a legislator — increases when the policy is unpopular with voters. So an interest organization's contribution in an effort to "purchase" policy from a legislator must be balanced against the preferences of his or her constituents. Contributions fund campaigns and they can pay for political ads to offset an unpopular vote, and better funded candidates receive more votes; but if a legislator's vote on a bill is sufficiently unpopular, he or she may experience a net loss in votes. The votes gained with campaign money provided by an interest organization may not be enough to offset those lost due to taking an unpopular stand on the bill. At the opposite extreme, if the interest organization seeks a policy that is *consistent* with what most constituents prefer, then the cost of a policy may go to zero.[11] No contribution or lobbying may be required to gain a favorable vote from the legislator.

This has two implications for lobbying and campaign contributions. The first concerns the rational allocation of interest organizations' efforts. If the price for policy is cheaper when a policy desired by the interest organization is acceptable to constituents, then the same level of effort will buy more when lobbying legislators with supportive constituents. Because interest organizations prefer to use their resources efficiently, they will be more inclined to approach such legislators. They will, all other things equal, lobby their friends. Legislators are simply less responsive to interest organizations that seek policy that is inconsistent with district preferences. In this way, the "unorganized" voters in districts are more likely to influence legislators' votes than are organized interests. But all things are not always equal. When the distribution of aye and nay votes in a legislature is expected to be very close, interest organizations must seek votes from those whose districts incline them to be opponents.[12] In such cases, the **supply price of policy** escalates as real pressure is required to switch a legislator's vote.

The second implication concerns salience, or how attentive voters are to a legislative outcome. Constituents matter when constituents have firm and uniform preferences on an issue. But in many cases, legislators vote on proposals of limited concern to voters or on issues that are so highly technical that their implications are unclear or ambiguous. In other cases, a legislator's constituents may be very divided on a proposal. There may, for example, be as many voters in a district employed by export-oriented businesses as by import-oriented firms. In this kind of situation, the legislator may be relatively free to select which set of constituents will determine his or her vote on a free trade bill. When voters don't care or are divided, a legislator is less constrained by their preferences. Thus, organized interests may exercise more influence.

Political party is also a significant element of a member's voting decision. Parties have a strong influence on legislators' careers in Congress and some state legislatures. The party caucus in Congress controls committee assignments, and a member's committee assignment is a vital part of how well he or she can serve constituents. This is particularly true in the U.S. House where committees are such an important part of the legislative process. Party influence over a member's committee assignment gives it leverage in gaining members'

compliance. Parties in Congress also have an extensive whip system that allows them to pressure members to vote in a way that is
consistent with the position of party leadership. Whips conduct
head counts and try to persuade recalcitrant members to vote with
the party. But parties rarely pressure members for support when the
party's position would put them in jeopardy with constituents. In
the end, it is more important for the party that a member stays in office than how he or she votes on a given bill. But barring extreme
conflicts of interest, the party may bring pressure to bear on members to vote the party line—pressure that can be more telling than
that of interest organizations.

Legislators' voting decisions are also influenced by their own
preferences. Members have their own ideology, priorities, and be-
liefs about policy. The ideology of members is often consistent with
their district's ideology and with their party's position. But in some
cases and for some issues, members have their own strong preferences. Interest organizations may not have much influence when
their preferred positions are inconsistent with the legislator's personal convictions. At the same time, interest organizations often contribute to members sharing their ideological orientation. Vote choices
may therefore *appear* to be influenced by campaign contributions or
lobbying, but the choice is actually the one the member would have
made even without a campaign contribution from, or lobbying by,
the interest organization.

This point was well highlighted in two influential studies of
campaign contributions by tobacco companies to U.S. senators. In the
first, Stephen Moore et al. concluded that contributions were the pivotal force in defeating two bills—one that would have raised the
price of tobacco products in military commissaries and another that
would have eliminated tax breaks for tobacco companies with the
additional revenue directed toward antismoking campaigns.[13] The
study failed to account for the legislator's ideology, considering only
the party of the senator, the presence of the tobacco industry in the
senator's state, and tobacco PAC contributions. When the legislator's ideology was included in the model in a replication study by
John R. Wright, the estimated influence of tobacco industry campaign contributions declined markedly. Indeed, the results indicated
that the tobacco PAC contributions were not sufficient to change
the outcome.[14]

While legislators are loath to admit it,[15] the positions of governors and presidents are also a factor in members' decisions about how to vote on a measure. An executive appeals to members of his or her own party to support measures that are part of the executive's legislative agenda. Executives also appeal to members of either party by providing jobs, grants, or contracts for those members' state or district. Executives can urge cooperation from members of executive agencies to accommodate legislators, make campaign appearances to support a member's reelection efforts, and allow the member a role in nominating judges. Through obligation or coercion, then, the position and preferences of executives can weigh heavily in determining a legislator's vote.

Other members of the legislature and legislative staff also influence members' votes. Given the scope and complexity of the issues considered by modern legislatures, members cannot claim expertise in all policy areas. They specialize in some and then rely on their fellow members' expertise or the expertise of congressional staff for advice on how to vote on others. Finally, members of Congress rely on the voting cues of members of their state delegation. An issue may have implications for the state as a whole. Voting in these cases can cross party lines as members from the state delegation vote together in the interests of the state. For all of these reasons, getting one member to lobby another can be a very effective lobbying strategy to counter other influences.

After the Vote

A lobbyist's job is not done when a legislature chamber adopts a measure. First, all discrepancies between the two chambers' versions of a bill must be reconciled in a conference committee. Such differences are common since two chambers can differ ideologically, may have somewhat different constituencies, and may represent a different mix of champions arrayed for and against a bill. But conference committees lend interest organizations another opportunity to take advantage of the special strengths of the committee setting for pursuing influence. Again, a single champion can make all the difference, so interest organizations often lobby legislative leaders to appoint conference committee members supportive of their positions. Also, some—but not all—conference committees work outside the glare of publicity falling on floor votes. This will advantage organized interests with positions running counter to constituents' opinions. Once a bill is passed by a legislature, it may still be vetoed by most governors and the president. Indeed, some governors can veto portions of bills with a line-item veto. Failure by interest organizations opposed to a bill in a legislature can be transformed into a victory by securing the ear of the executive, an issue we consider in the next chapter. For organizations supportive of the legislation, vetoes return the issue to the legislature, but with an increased burden. They must now find the additional votes to override the veto, but for those who prefer the status quo, an executive veto is promising because it is difficult to override.

MEANS OF INFLUENCING THE LEGISLATURE

The legislative process is complex. To fully understand the influence of organized interests, we need to consider all stages of the process. But we must also consider how variations in resources influence what interest organizations can do. The three most important types of resources are information, votes, and money. Not all organizations have equal access to each, and each provides unique opportunities for influence. But it is also important to recognize that all three resources are used in the same fundamental way. Success in exerting influence often depends on providing a legislator with something he or she needs. In other words, an exchange takes place.[16] Organized interests provide something of value to the legislator in order to secure something in return. Many critical assessments of the corrupting influence of money often overemphasize this one resource and ignore the others. In this exchange information and votes are as much a currency as, and perhaps a more important currency than, money.

Information

Information plays an important role in the influence process. Indeed, pluralists like Raymond Bauer, Ithiel de Sola Pool, and Lewis Dexter thought that information was far and away the most important resource of lobbyists.[17] Interest organizations use information both with allies and with undecided members and opponents. Indeed, information has many different uses. Information and the persuasion accompanying it can redefine a problem so that it finds a firm place on the public policy agenda. It can persuade legislators to become champions of the organization's cause. These champions can then use information to persuade fellow legislators. The information provided by an interest organization can be used as talking points in floor debate or in committee deliberations. Especially important, information provided by organized interests helps legislators fine-tune legislation so that it effectively addresses their concerns. And finally, information is vital when interest organizations attempt to directly persuade undecided members or opponents as the time of a final vote nears. While interest organizations present many forms of information, two broad types address somewhat different needs of legislators. Members need to know both the policy and the political consequences of their actions.

Policy information includes background data on the issue and data on the technical workings of proposed legislation. Background research identifies for a legislator the nature of a problem and its magnitude. Such policy information also tells legislators how the problem might be addressed by legislation and whether it should be so addressed. But policy information also includes technical analyses of the consequences of legislation. These several types of policy information enable legislators to know how well a proposed policy will work or whether it is necessary. Good research on a policy question can be a powerful resource for interest organizations. As we saw in Chapter 4, think tanks play a special role in framing public policy issues in the prelegislative stage of the policy process. Their analyses are also used by allied organizations in legislative deliberations. But, as seen in the boxes highlighting specific interest organizations scattered throughout this book, many interest organizations have their own staff and resources to conduct original research. Others assemble and collate research from universities and government agencies. Presenting research, from whatever source, is a very common practice.

Political information ultimately concerns the electoral consequences of a member's vote on legislation. It too comes in many forms. For legislative entrepreneurs looking for issues with good political traction, background data on a policy problem can be viewed in a distinctly political light. Political information includes intelligence on how constituents will receive a particular action, what public opinion is in the district, or how strongly members of the interest organization feel about the decision. Political information can also be linked to the other two currencies in the legislative process—votes and money. For an interest organization with a large membership base or significant financial resources, political information about how a decision will be received by the organization or its members can be an important consideration in the member's decision. If the members of an organization oppose a legislator's prospective vote, its leadership can let legislators know that their actions will be communicated to the membership of the organization with possible consequences in terms of electoral support. An organization may also threaten to withhold campaign funds as a consequence of a vote. With this type of information, the member of Congress can weigh the benefits and risks of a vote.

While information is presented to legislators in a variety of ways, two forums are especially important—**testimony** at committee hearings and **direct contacts** between legislators and lobbyists. According to Ken Kollman's survey of Washington interest organizations, providing testimony at hearings is a common form of participation.[18] Indeed, he reports that *all* of the organizations in his study testified at hearings at least occasionally. This finding echoes an earlier study by Schlozman and Tierney, who reported that 99 percent of Washington lobbyists testified at hearings as part of their lobbying efforts.[19] The prevalence of testifying suggests that interest organizations find it particularly useful. But testifying does more than influence votes. Testifying provides information in a very public forum that signals members of voluntary associations that their leaders are fighting the good fight. Many voluntary groups post their testimony on their websites as an additional signal to members of their advocacy activities.

In view of the exchange framework, of course, testifying at hearings is not only useful for the interest organization, but also for members of the committee.[20] Invitations to testify may result from a genuine need on the part of committee members to acquire information. When this is the case, interest organizations representing a variety of perspectives are invited to testify. Hearings may also be designed to provide information confirming the opinion of the chair or the members who hold the majority opinion.[21] In such cases, testimony is requested selectively and those organizations that represent the chair's perspective are more likely to be invited to testify. In other cases, the chair of a committee lacking jurisdiction over an issue may be interested in claiming it.[22] It may be a popular issue or one that will play well with the public. As chairman of the Judiciary Committee's Administrative Practices Subcommittee in the Senate, Edward Kennedy held a number of hearings on the issue of deregulation of the airlines. By emphasizing the deregulation aspect of the aviation issue, he succeeded in moving jurisdiction for oversight of the Civil Aeronautics Board from the Commerce Committee's Subcommittee on Aviation to his own committee.[23] In cases such as this, the chair will invite interest organizations that share his or her particular perspective. If a committee can then claim expertise in the technical details or the most recent developments for an issue, it will bolster its claim to jurisdiction.[24] Whether the hearing is a genuine quest for information, a public relations promotion of the chair's views, or a ploy to claim jurisdiction, it is a valuable opportunity for exercising influence. Testifying provides a chance to join the debate at a highly visible stage of the process. In sum, hearings serve the interests of both legislators and the interest organizations that testify.

Nearly all organized interests testify at hearings, but given time constraints and the preferences of committee chairs, only a fraction of the organizations that lobby on a particular bill may provide public testimony on it. Also, many organizations may not want to testify publicly. The information they provide legislators may concern narrow electoral calculations that neither the organization nor legislators want to bandy about in public, or the organization may represent an unpopular position on a bill. Given these incentives, it seems as if citizens' organizations are especially advantaged when it comes to testifying. Jeffrey Berry analyzed testimony in all 1991 Congressional hearings on social and economic policies receiving at least some press attention.[25] As seen in Figure 5-1, citizens' groups comprised 31.8 percent of all testimonies on these bills. This rate of participation far outstrips their proportion of the total population of Washington lobbying organizations of 9.5 percent, as seen in Figure 3-5.

Direct contacting entails making a personal, one-on-one case to a legislator about an organization's position on a bill. Direct contacts with legislators and legislative staff are almost certainly the most important means by which organized interests present information. Indeed, the term *lobbying* is often taken as synonymous with such direct contacts. Kollman's survey of Washington organizations found

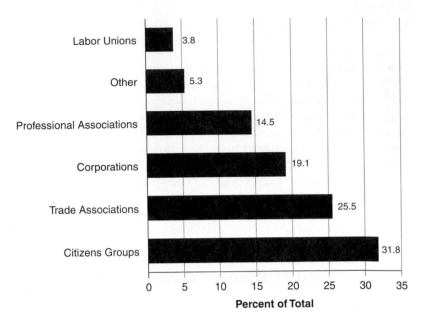

FIGURE 5-1 Percent of Organizations Testifying in Congressional Hearings by Sector, 1999 (n=922)
Source: Jeffrey M. Berry, *The New Liberalism* (Washington, DC: Brookings Institution, 1999), p. 20.

that 96 percent regularly contacted legislators directly. Only four percent said they did so occasionally, and none indicated that they never lobbied directly.[26]

In-house lobbyists and leaders of interest organizations engage in direct lobbying; but since securing access to legislators is more readily attained when there is a prior, long-standing relationship between the lobbyist and a legislator, direct contacting is the primary arena in which **contract lobbying** firms operate. Traditional economic interests, especially, often employ contract lobbying firms to represent their interests. Microsoft, for example, spent $6,360,000 lobbying in Washington in 2000 using 15 different contract lobbying firms. The recent clients of a major Washington lobbying firm, Barbour, Griffith, and Rogers, are listed in Table 5-1. Contract lobbying firms, long established in Washington, are now also common in the states.

TABLE 5-1 Barbour, Griffith & Rogers, Inc.

THE FIRM

Barbour, Griffith & Rogers, Inc. (BGR) is a quintessential Washington contract lobbying firm. While many firms have close ties to both major political parties, BGR has very strong ties to the Republican Party. Haley Barbour, Ronald Reagan's Director of the White House Office of Political Affairs, founded the firm in 1991. During the 1990s, Mr. Barbour served two terms as Chair of the Republican National Committee. Lanny Griffith was President George H. W. Bush's Special Assistant for Intergovernmental Affairs and later served as Assistant Secretary of Education. More recently Mr. Griffith was national chairman of the Bush/Cheney Entertainment Task Force, which coordinated many inaugural events. In the first Bush administration, Ed Rogers served as Deputy Assistant to the President and Executive Assistant to the White House Chief of Staff. Earlier, he was Senior Deputy to Bush-Quayle Campaign Manager Lee Atwater and worked in the Reagan White House Office of Political Affairs. BGR primarily represents clients to Congress and the federal executive branch. BGR also provides lobbying services in the American states and internationally.

ITS CLIENTS

The following retained BGR in 2000 with the expenditures that year listed in parentheses: Air Transport Assn. ($320,000), Alliance for Quality Nursing Home Care ($360,000), American Financial Services Assn. ($0), American Maritime Congress ($80,000), Amgen Inc. ($120,000), Artists Coalition ($20,000), Assn. of Oil Pipe Lines ($60,000), Avioimpex ($80,000), Bay Harbor Management ($660,000), BellSouth Corporation ($180,000), Better World Fund ($270,000), Broadcast Music, Inc. ($260,000), Camp, Dresser & McKee ($70,000), Canadian National Railway ($400,000), CBS Corporation ($40,000), Citizens for Jobs and the Economy ($40,000), DaimlerChrysler ($200,000), Delta Airlines ($60,000), FM Watch ($560,000), Glaxo Wellcome, Inc. ($120,000), Home Insurance Federation of America ($100,000), Institute of Scrap Recycling Industries ($110,000), International Telecoms Satellite Organzation ($220,000), Lockheed Martin ($240,000), Lyondell Petrochemical ($120,000), Makedonski Telekomunikacii ($160,000), Massachusetts Mutual Life Insurance ($260,000), Microsoft Corporation ($540,000), Moet Hennessy Louis Vuitton SA ($80,000), National Geographic Society ($50,000), New England Development ($120,000), Oxygenated Fuels Assn. ($200,000), Philip Morris ($100,000), Professional Benefit Trust ($320,000), Qwest Communications ($160,000), RJR Nabisco ($200,000), Southern Company ($200,000), Illinois State Board of Education ($440,000), State Street Bank and Trust ($240,000), Tulane University ($160,000), GCG Partners ($0), Unitedhealth Group ($320,000), University of Mississippi ($80,000), University of Mississippi Medical Center ($80,000), University of Southern Mississippi ($70,000), US Telecom Assn. ($200,000), US Tobacco Company ($0), Vektra Corporation of Montenegro ($0), Winterthur Swiss Insurance ($240,000), Yazoo County Port Commission ($0)

Source: http://www.opensecrets.org, visited July 20, 2002.

Given the importance of personal relationships in directly contacting legislators, former staffers and legislators often follow their legislative tenure with careers as lobbyists. Former members of Congress are considered the most valuable commodity a Washington lobbying firm can have. In his first year as a lobbyist, for example, former House Appropriations Committee chair Bob Livingston (R-LA) collected over a million dollars in lobbying fees.[27] Lobbying firms are willing to pay seven-figure salaries to retain well-connected former members of Congress as lobbyists. In 1999, 129 former members of Congress were active as lobbyists: 66 Democrats, 62 Republicans, and one independent.[28] But former legislators are not the only government officials who move on to lucrative careers as contract lobbyists. As seen in Table 5-1, former members of the executive branch — in this case, former officials with close ties to GOP presidents — also attract many clients in their second careers. Currently, while rules vary at the state level, members of Congress and federal executive branch officials are required to wait a year before they may actively lobby former colleagues. In 1999, there was a five-year interim period for federal executive branch officials, but this has since been reduced to one year. In spite of the delay however, former officials are often hired by lobbying firms as consultants immediately after leaving government service, then begin lobbying once the "cooling off" period is over.[29]

Whether the lobbyist works directly for an interest organization or represents clients on behalf of a lobbying firm, **credibility** is the key to direct contacts. Credibility has several sources. One is a reputation for honesty and reliability. Jerry Giovaniello, chief lobbyist for the National Association of Realtors (NAR), put it this way: "The way you do it is, over the years you earn his or her trust just by giving straight information, giving it to them in a very succinct manner and also, what I do, is give them the other side, too."[30] Legislators need to know that they can trust the information they receive. Credibility based on trust is especially important for traditional economic interests that cannot readily ground their information on a higher moral plane. A transportation company cannot easily claim altruistic goals. Although patriotism and the virtues of free enterprise are readily invoked, corporations are concerned about profits. But lobbyists working for profit-oriented interests can provide accurate and reliable information. Dealing in a straightforward manner with members and their staffs is simply a way in which organized interests enhance the likelihood that the information they provide legislators will be heard, understood, and perhaps influence their decisions.

Another source of credibility lies in a reputation for **expertise** on an issue. Organizations with a long history of activity on a complex issue are more likely to be viewed as credible sources than a newcomer just joining the lobbying fray. Some think tanks, especially, develop solid reputations based on expertise and sustained attention to an issue. Credibility based on expertise is vital for organizations lacking access to other kinds of resources, especially money. For some organizations, such as a foreign interest that is legally prohibited from making campaign contributions, money is simply not available as a tool for influence. For many citizens' organizations, principles prohibit reliance on money as a source of influence. For example, Common Cause lobbies on government reform issues, most importantly campaign finance reform. Making campaign contributions runs against the principles of the organization.

Principled stands, however, are also an important source of credibility. Common Cause is a nonpartisan organization and maintains good working relationships with both Republicans and Democrats. It also relies heavily on small contributions and dues from individual members and limits contributions from labor unions and corporations to under $100 per year, and it does not accept money from foundations or government grants. It thereby distances itself from "corrupting" sources of influence. Common Cause's central concern is accountability from government. It is a principled goal and therefore one that is difficult for lawmakers to reject. Those who do oppose the specific goals of Common Cause, such as Senator Mitch McConnell (R-KY) or Representative Dick Armey (R-TX), must choose an equally principled position to justify their opposition. As we will see in Chapter 8, the opposition argument for campaign finance reform is based primarily on the notion that limiting campaign contributions restricts another important principle—free speech. But Common Cause, by representing goals that many Americans agree with, has a high level of credibility on campaign finance reform because of its principled stand. Principled stands, however, are not immutable. Credibility—and, thus, influence—can be lost if an interest organization is viewed as violating its own principles, as illustrated by Interest Organization Example 5-1. Stung by sexual scandals involving priests, the Catholic Church found it more difficult to lobby on a number of issues on which it previously exercised considerable influence.

INTEREST ORGANIZATION EXAMPLE 5-1:

The Value of Reputation

The Catholic Church lobbies Congress and many state legislatures on a variety of issues. The Church is a leader among Christian organizations opposed to liberal abortion and birth-control policies. And it is a reliable ally of liberals on many social issues. The Church's influence was especially strong in the northeastern states with large Catholic populations. As the *Washington Post*'s Michael Powell reported, "Church officials in this region are accustomed to respectful hearings in state-houses, and exerting broad influence."

In 2001 and 2002, the Church was rocked by a series of sex scandals involving priests and young boys. The scandal severely damaged the Church's lobbying reputation. With an aggressive lobbying effort by the Church, bills in four states requiring priests to disclose to police confessional reports of child sexual abuse were beaten back. But other bills requiring the Church to forward reports of sexual abuse to authorities passed easily. And the scandal spilled over to undermine the Church's credibility on its traditional issues. The president of the Catholic League of America noted, "We've seen an erosion of the church's moral authority in statehouses." A Democratic lobbyist in New York agreed, noting, "You would immediately go to the Church on social, justice, and labor issues in the past but they no longer have the same credibility." Perhaps most telling of all, Powell reported that "Cardinal Law traditionally attends the (Massachusetts) governor's state-of-the-state address, and finds himself surrounded by a press of legislators seeking a handshake. But this year, when he stepped into the chambers to listen to Governor Jane Swift, he found himself ostracized."

Source: Michael Post, "Sex Scandal Erodes Catholic Clout," http://www.msnbc.com/news/776732.asp, visited July 6, 2002.

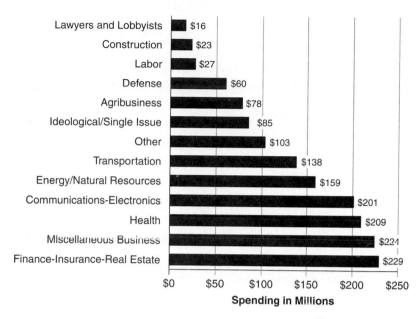

FIGURE 5-2 Congressional Direct Lobbying Expenditures by Sector, 2000
Source: http://www.opensecrets.org/lobbyists/index.asp, visited July 5, 2002.

Overall, traditional economic interests spend the most on direct contacting, much of it by hiring contract lobbyists with long-standing contacts with the legislature. As seen in Figure 5-2, spending on direct lobbying of Congress and federal executive officials (excluding campaign spending, grassroots lobbying, and legal fees) exceeded $1.5 billion in 2000. Ideological and single-issue organizations, including most citizens' organizations, accounted for only $85 million or 5.48 percent of this total. And despite complaints about the power of trial lawyers and labor unions, they accounted for only 1.03 and 1.74 percent of the total, respectively.

How important is direct contacting? One of the best answers was provided by John R. Wright's comparison of the relative influence of campaign contributions and lobbying on congressional committee votes.[31] Wright defined lobbying contacts broadly to include testifying at a committee hearing, generating grassroots letters and phone calls, and meeting personally with representatives and their staffs. These avenues of influence involve the communication of both political and policy information. Wright found that voting decisions were more strongly related to the number of lobbying contacts than to campaign contributions. Campaign contributions did predict interest organization's *lobbying* efforts fairly well. That is, contributions may prepare the ground for a lobbying contract, but it was the lobbying itself that mattered.

VOTES

Contrary to popular notions of influence, legislators do not consistently accommodate big money interests at the expense of their constituents. The analysis of Denzau and Munger makes clear why this is so. Any electoral advantage a legislator receives from a campaign contribution from an interest organization must be offset against the votes lost if he or she votes against constituents' preferences. Elected officials care a great deal about votes, and, because of this, some interest organizations have ready access to a critical resource legislators need. The importance of a **district presence** for organized interests cannot be overstated. Any interest organization has a much better chance of gaining access to a legislator if it can claim a strong presence in the district, such as a headquarters, a plant, or a large number of group members. In the mind of a legislator, such organizations do not represent a narrow policy interest but his or her constituents. This link is so strong that it is often tied to direct contacts with legislators. As Jerry Giovaniello of the NAR noted when discussing direct lobbying, "The thing that works best always is a face-to-face meeting with constituents who actually vote for [members]. And more importantly [the constituents] can tell them how a certain piece of legislation will affect them in their community. That's by far the best way to do it."[32] But whether or not they join lobbyists in direct meetings with legislators, the influence of constituents is paramount.

Those organizations that have a strong district presence in a large number of districts are uniquely advantaged. The National Rifle Association (NRA) is one such group. The NRA claims 4.3 million members nationwide and it maximizes the political impact of this large base. The NRA mobilizes its members in several ways. It assigns election volunteer coordinators to register pro-gun voters to enhance their electoral strength. The coordinators arrange for NRA members to work on the campaigns of politicians who support the NRA. The NRA also encourages members to write their local newspapers and elected representatives in support of the NRA's political positions. The organization includes on its website specific guidelines instructing members how to write such letters. Members are also urged to call and email elected officials. In addition to these efforts, the NRA includes political preference charts in its publications, telling NRA members which candidates in the election support their interests. These mobilization tactics combine to give the NRA a unique strength in American politics. With an annual budget of $168 million, the NRA can afford to spend a great deal, but its real advantage lies in its strength at the grassroots level. Particularly in rural congressional districts, the NRA's endorsement can have an impact on election results. The NRA has a significant influence on Senate races in western states with smaller populations. The combination of high membership in the NRA in these states and the small number of people voting can make the NRA's endorsement a critical factor in deciding an election.[33]

The American Association of Retired Persons (AARP) is also a vast membership group that can boast a significant presence in many congressional districts. It has over 34.3 million members — about half the size of the population of U.S. citizens over 50.[34] Not only is it a large organization, but it can claim that a large percentage of *potential* members are members of the organization. Each American is sent an invitation to join AARP on his or her 50th birthday, with the AARP mailing 9 million of these letters per month.[35] As a result, the AARP is second in size only to the Catholic Church among nonprofit organizations.[36] It is also ranked by *Fortune* magazine as one of the top two most influential groups in Washington, DC, second only to the NRA.[37] Because of the AARP's large number of members and their dispersion throughout the country, electoral consequences need not be explicitly stated for members of Congress to know the risks associated with voting contrary to what members of the AARP would prefer.

Membership groups are not the only organizations that can rely on votes as a resource. The steel industry is in a unique position to use its electoral resources. The industry is somewhat regional, with many plants located in the Midwest and Middle Atlantic states. It cannot claim the broadly distributed, ubiquitous membership of the

NRA or the AARP. Representatives and senators who are *not* from steel producing states have little incentive to support the struggling steel industry. But big steel has little problem finding champions for their cause among members of Congress representing districts where it is a major presence. Perhaps more importantly, Pennsylvania, with the largest share of the steel industry, is electorally important in presidential politics. Its close partisan division and large number of electoral votes make it an important state for an Electoral College victory. In 2002, the International Trade Commission recommended a 40 percent increase in import tariffs to protect the industry from foreign dumping of steel. As President George Bush considered the recommendation, union members sent the White House over 134,000 handwritten letters.[38] They followed up with a rally outside the White House with a crowd of nearly 30,000 from steel communities.[39] Bush adopted the recommendation despite substantial criticism attributing his decision to electoral considerations.

These several cases illustrate another important aspect of using votes as resources. In some cases, as with the AARP, organizations do not need to mobilize members to ensure that the legislator understands the electoral implications of a decision. The link will be obvious to all concerned. In others, the interest organization must mobilize members to contact legislators to signal both their wide presence in a district and the intensity of their concern. Such **outside lobbying** is sometimes a necessary step in selling a proposal via the inside lobbying of testifying or directly contacting a legislator. Mobilizing members has become common over the last two decades. Sometimes, this grassroots lobbying is really Astroturf—an artificial exercise of forwarding thousands of identical pre-printed letters to legislators. But, over time, legislators have become quite adept at distinguishing real from artificial grassroots lobbying.

How important are constituency considerations in influencing legislators' relationship with lobbyists? A very creative experimental study by Michelle Chin, Jon Bond, and Nehemia Geva compared directly the impacts of constituents and campaign contributions in securing access to members of Congress.[40] They asked actual schedulers for House members to prioritize a set of hypothetical requests for meetings for their representative. Given that there were more requests than times available, the schedulers had to deny access to some of those requesting an appointment. The schedulers showed a strong inclination to give priority to organizations whose members were constituents of the representative. Organizations with a presence in the district got meetings, and organizations that contributed funds to the legislator's campaign were no more likely to secure access than those that did not. But in real life, PAC contributions and constituents are less often pitted against each other than might be expected. Professional lobbyists that represent organized interests sponsoring PACs are much less likely to contribute to and lobby representatives when they do not have geographic ties to the member's district.[41]

Money

Money has been in the background of almost everything discussed to this point. The origins of PACs and the role of campaign contributions in the electoral process were discussed in the previous chapter. There we saw that most interest organizations employ an access strategy — rather than an electoral strategy — in allocating funds to political candidates. In this chapter, we have examined research comparing the relative influence of lobbying contacts and campaign contributions on committee voting. We have also examined research comparing the influence of presence in a district and campaign contributions on gaining access to members of Congress. Such comparisons are not serendipitous. Money has been at the heart of almost all discussions of lobbying for more than a decade. This has also been true for Congress itself, which was immersed in the debate about money and influence through the seven years between introduction of early versions of the Bipartisan Campaign Reform Act (McCain-Feingold) and its final passage in 2002. The debate over whether and how money influences legislative decision making has been equally as intense among those who study campaign finance.

Consistent with the transactions school interpretation of legislatures as markets in which commodities — laws — are bought and sold, some scholars have found strong links between campaign contributions and the floor votes of members of Congress. Dennis Quinn and Robert Shapiro, for example, found that contributions from business PACs are closely associated with votes for lower corporate tax rates.[42] Kenneth Godwin reported evidence that business campaign contributions increased Democratic legislators' support of business and trade interests.[43] The influence of money is not limited to business interests. Allen Wilhite and John Theilmann found that contributions from labor PACs increase the likelihood that legislators will support pro-labor positions.[44] At least some research, then, supports the transactions interpretation.

Many political scientists, however, reject this conclusion. As we have seen, validly determining whether PAC contributions influence votes requires carefully controlling for all of the other influences that determine a legislator's vote, and these many forces can be very difficult to separate. Legislators from districts with a large number of high tech firms will, for example, likely receive campaign contributions from the PACs these firms sponsor. But many of the legislator's constituents may work for the same firms, so, is the legislator representing his or her constituents or responding to a PAC contribution when voting on a bill favorable to the industry? When these and other possible influences were controlled for in statistical studies of the relationship between contributions and votes, many found little evidence of any association.[45] A widely cited study by Janet Grenzke, for example, found that PAC contributions rarely change legislators' votes. Campaign contributions may provide an opportunity for access, a chance for the organization to communicate its views, but Grenzke found that these contributions influenced votes only on minor legislation. On important contested legislation, there was no systematic link between votes and money.[46] Similarly, Lawrence Rothenberg found that PAC contributions from the defense industry had little influence on congressional voting on the MX missile. Rather, district considerations and direct lobbying had a significant influence.[47] These and other studies convinced many political scientists that votes are not bought and sold. At best, PAC contributions may buy access to legislators. But district considerations and direct lobbying matter far more in determining legislators' votes. This conclusion, of course, is consistent with the pluralist's argument that, in the end, constituents' preferences matter the most.

More recently, however, a number of studies have accumulated indicating that, under certain circumstances, money can influence votes. The hallmark of these recent studies is their comparison of the influence of money across multiple votes in Congress, thereby controlling for the context of the vote. These studies suggest that some aspects of context condition whether money can influence legislative voting. PAC contributions are more influential on some issues than others. PACs can matter when the issue is technical in nature or narrow in scope.[48] Also, when the economic benefits of a proposal are narrowly targeted to contributors and costs broadly distributed across the electorate, contributions are more likely to influence votes.[49] And when an issue is non-partisan or non-ideological in nature, PAC contributions can sway votes.[50]

Several studies have found that PAC contributions can influence votes when the visibility of the issue is low[51] or if public opinion is divided.[52] John R. Wright, for example, examined 75 congressional votes on tobacco policy from 1981 to 2000.[53] Tobacco PACs had little impact on the outcome of most votes. This was not surprising, given the public's strong support for regulating smoking, but a portion of the votes involved agricultural issues on which legislators could balance supporting tobacco against defending the popular institution of family farming. On these issues, PAC contributions did influence voting decisions. These findings are consistent with the neopluralist argument that money can influence votes in some situations. The contexts in which money counts should not be overemphasized, however. When the public cares about an issue, money has little direct influence on final votes.

Money may still matter in other ways. Money can be converted into other resources that might influence legislators' votes. Instead of contributing to campaigns, for example, an organization may invest its funds in staff resources or research. Ken Leyden's study of congressional testimony found that organizations' resources are associated with opportunities to testify at **hearings**.[54] As Leyden states, "Groups in the best position to provide the kind of information legislators want to hear are those that can demonstrate they have done considerable research on a topic of interest to legislators, know the political ramifications of different choices, and have the wherewithal to articulately deliver this information in a timely fashion."[55] Wealthy organizations can afford to hire the kinds of contract lobbyists who can make the best use of direct contacts with legislators.[56] So, even if money has a direct impact on voting only under certain circumstances, it may have an important indirect impact by buying other resources.

STRATEGIC CHOICE

Resources — votes, information, and/or money — are important. But access to these resources is not sufficient to influence policy outcomes. Interest organizations must deploy their resources in ways that are telling rather than wasted. Two types of strategic choices are especially important when decisions about deploying resources are made—selecting the right tool to use in the right situation and deciding whether or not to work with other organizations in pursing policy objectives.

Selecting the Right Tool

When asked which resources are useful in gaining access to lawmakers, lobbyists are inclined to cite the resources that their organizations have in greatest abundance. Lobbyists for corporations say that their trustworthiness and reputation for hard work are critical. If all else fails, they might mention money. But corporations must rely on these resources, given their lack of a membership base such as that of the National Rifle Association. Large citizens' groups such as the NRA and the Sierra Club stress strong constituency connections arising from their extensive membership base and their dedication to their particular issues. Lobbyists for professional associations and labor unions also stress the importance of a large membership base. Think tanks emphasize the importance of research and policy expertise. But not all resources are equally useful in all situations. Most importantly, work by two political scientists indicates that the nature of the issue greatly influences whether a particular resource will move legislators.

Mark Smith examined the success of business interests across three different kinds of issues.[57] **Particularistic issues** engage the interests of only one or a few companies or industries. They pursue their own policy goals with little attention on the part of the larger business community or the public. These issues are addressed in a relatively closed process where a limited number of members of Congress, executive officials, and companies cooperate to reach mutually beneficial decisions. Direct contacts based on long-standing relationships and money are more likely to be effective when particularistic issues are at stake, since members of Congress need not be as careful in taking constituent preferences into account.[58]

Conflictual issues, in contrast, involve a real clash of interests. Such conflicts are common within the business community. On some issues, for example, the preferences of trucking interests differ from those of railroad interests. The resolution of conflictual issues involves identifying winners and losers. If one of the competing sets of firms has a strong employment base in a member's district, it will act as a champion by representing constituents' preferences. But for legislators from districts without a strong presence of either side of the dispute, other factors, such as technical policy information, ideological preferences, the position of the party or the president, and even money, may be more important.[59]

Finally, **unifying issues** are those that impact the interests of business as a whole. Unifying issues tend to be partisan, ideological, and highly salient to the public. They often involve major policy changes that bear significantly on a large number of people. Regulations limiting air pollution or improving workplace safety or the relationship between labor unions and management are unifying issues because they have a broad impact on the business community and far-reaching effects. Because these issues affect many members of the business community in a similar way, many types of businesses will share the same position. A unified front might seem to provide the ideal occasion for exercising influence. Paradoxically, however, these are issues on which business interests actually have the least influence. Because they are likely to be salient to a large number of voters, constituency considerations are far more likely to matter to legislators than money or even long-standing personal contacts.[60] For example, almost all businesses opposed at least some elements of the accounting and corporate fraud reforms adopted by Congress in July 2002. Yet, in the face of growing public anxiety about a collapsing stock market, the bill sailed through Congress with hardly a negative word.

Ken Kollman drew similar conclusions from a study of a broader range of interest organizations.[61] As seen in Table 5-2, Kollman distinguishes issues on two dimensions. Issues may be popular or unpopular, and they may or may not be salient to the public. The corporate and accounting reform bill illustrates well how the popularity and salience of an issue constrain the effectiveness of different influence tools.

The top row of the table concerns policies of little salience or where the public is inattentive. With the stock market booming in the late 1990s, the kinds of reforms SEC Chair Arthur Levitt was proposing were hardly on the public's mind, even though the public might have supported many of them. Although potentially popular

TABLE 5-2 Issue Characteristics and Types of Lobbying Strategies

		Popularity of the Issue	
		Low	High
Salience	*Low*	Elitist Strategy	Latent Support Strategy
of the			
Issue	*High*	Classical Group Politics Strategy	Comforting Politics Strategy

Source: Adapted from Ken Kollman, *Outside Lobbying* (Princeton: Princeton University Press, 1998), p. 159.

with the public, Levitt's proposals threatened many corporations and accounting firms benefiting from lax oversight of their operations. An elitist strategy, narrowing the scope of discussion to political elites by mobilizing a handful of key members of Congress to oppose Levitt's proposed reforms, was effective. Direct contacts with key legislators and, perhaps, significant campaign contributions were sufficient to derail the proposals in a low salience environment. Mr. Levitt could only pursue a latent support strategy. He could provide information and expertise to legislators, but he could not rely on support from the larger investing public. As Levitt noted at the time, the investing class "is the most powerful lobbying force in the country and it is the least well organized."[62] As long as they were *both* unorganized and inattentive, the investing public had little sway on legislators.

The effectiveness of different influence resources changes, however, when issues are salient to the public. These strategies are reported on the lower row of Table 5-2. As seen in the lower right of the table, a comforting politics strategy is appropriate when an issue is popular and salient. In such cases, interest organizations actually matter little. After the scandals and sharp declines in stock prices, the public was paying attention, so supporters of the reforms hardly needed to signal the preferences of the public to legislators. Lawmakers knew that the public was furious and looking to them for answers. Public preferences are so influential in such heated situations that there is little that organizations opposed to the issue can do to change the mind of legislators. At best, they can rely on a classic interest group politics strategy of mobilizing information or financial resources to modify the policy at its edges or delay the decision until the public becomes bored or inattentive. In the case of the accounting and corporate fraud bill, such tactics were employed, but were quickly swept aside by the intensity of public opinion.

While organized interests must play the hand dealt them when a vote nears; the popularity and salience of issues are not fixed. In the case of the accounting and corporate fraud bill, external events — the scandals and the stock market — raised the salience of the reform proposals. But as discussed in Chapter 4, much of what interest organizations do entails trying to move issues from one cell in Table 5-2 to another, more favorable configuration. That is, they try to dampen or promote the salience and popularity of issues so that the context in which decisions take place is more favorable, given the kinds of resources they can deploy.

Coalitions

One way to maximize resources of all sorts — money, information, and votes — is by joining a **coalition** of like-minded organizations. Interest organizations often work together. In many cases, the coalitions are very temporary alliances of convenience. The National Rifle Association and the American Civil Liberties Union, for example, both oppose some elements of the Bipartisan Campaign Finance Reform Act of 2002. In such cases, the coalition will be a very loose affair entailing sharing information. In other cases, coalitions represent a stronger form of coordination among long-time allies. A list of the members of one such alliance, the Coalition Against Religious Discrimination, is presented in Table 5-3. Many of the member organizations are stalwart advocates of civil liberties and social policies that often cooperate in challenging or promoting specific proposals. Still other coalitions graduate to become freestanding interest organizations. An example of one such organization, the Financial Services Coordinating Council (FSCC), is discussed in Interest Organization Example 5-2. The FSCC gradually moved from a coalition to become an independent interest organization.

Organizations, at least potentially, gain much by joining a coalition. First, an interest organization shares the cost of lobbying.[63] This is especially important when legislation reaches the floor or if it is considered by a number of different committees. In both cases, many

TABLE 5-3 The Coalition Against Religious Discrimination

THE COALITION

The Coalition Against Religious Discrimination formed in response to the President George W. Bush promotion of faith-based initiatives allowing social service organizations, particularly those that treat alcohol and drug addiction, to include religion as a component of the treatment program. The Coalition Against Religious Discrimination formed to oppose the Bush initiative as a violation of the constitutional provision for the separation of church and state.

ITS MEMBERS

The 51 members of the coalition include many religiously affiliated organizations with long records of opposition to relaxing the wall separating church and state. But the coalition is a veritable who's who of liberal social organizations, including feminist groups, professional social service and education associations, civil liberties groups, and a number of labor unions.

American Academy of Pediatrics, American Association of University Women, American Baptist Churches, USA (ABC), American Civil Liberties Union, American Counseling Association, American Humanist Association, American Federation of State, County and Municipal Employees, American Jewish Committee, American Jewish Congress, Americans for Religious Liberty, Anti-Defamation League, Americans United for Separation of Church and State, Baptist Joint Committee on Public Affairs, Catholics for a Free Choice, Center for Law and Social Policy, Central Conference of American Rabbis, Equal Partners in Faith, Friends Committee on National Legislation, Hadassah, the Women's Zionist Organization of America, Jewish Council for Public Affairs, Jewish Women International, Justice and Witness Ministries, United Church of Christ, Na'Amat USA, National Abortion and Reproductive Rights Action League, National Association For the Advancement of Colored People, National Association of Alcoholism and Drug Abuse Counselors, National Association of School Psychologists, National Association of Social Workers, National Community Action Foundation, National Council of Jewish Women, National Education Association, National Family Planning and Reproductive Health Association, National Gay and Lesbian Taskforce, National Organization for Women, National Partnership for Women and Families, National PTA, National Women's Law Center, NOW Legal Defense and Education Fund, OMB Watch, People for the American Way, Planned Parenthood Federation of America, Rabbinical Assembly, Religious Action Center of Reform Judaism, Religious Coalition for Reproductive Choice, Service Employees International Union, AFL-CIO, Sexuality Information and Education Council of the United States, The Alan Guttmacher Institute, The Interfaith Alliance, Unitarian Universalist Association, Women of Reform Judaism.

Source: http://www.stopreligiousdiscrimination.org, visited July 10, 2002.

legislators must be contacted. Even should such contacts not lead directly to influence, the network is likely to provide a more accurate head count of legislators' votes.[64] A second advantage is that coalitions enhance the opportunities of organized interests to shape legislation. If the coalition's members resolve conflicts among themselves, they can present a unified front to lawmakers. Solving conflicts themselves puts control of the process in their hands rather than allowing legislators to act as arbiters.[65] Third, coalitions lend legitimacy to an organization's goal. If the coalition speaks for — or appears to speak for — a large segment of the population, a large proportion of the interests in an economic sector, or a broad array of interests, the coalition's goal is more likely to be viewed as legitimate and less likely to seem the maneuvering of "special" interests.[66] As James Q. Wilson noted, if a majority of interested parties are behind a policy, then there appears to be one right course of action.[67] This simplifies action for policy makers by creating a public perception of a fair and inclusive decision making process.[68]

Last and most importantly, coalitions are an effective way to increase an organization's clout. One preliminary study has shown that the resources of the coalition as a whole, rather than the resources of the individual members, determine how responsive governmental actors are.[69] This may even be true of very loose alliances in which member organizations may do no more than lend their name to the coalition. But even this small degree of participation benefits both the more active members of the coalition and the organization that participates in name only.[70] The active participants appear to be speaking on behalf of a large group, and those whose participation is peripheral can register their preferences with minimal effort.

There are obvious benefits to participating in a coalition — shared resources, greater influence, a stronger appearance of legitimacy. But there are also reasons why organizations might choose not to participate in a coalition. As discussed in Chapter 2, niche theory suggests that the primary competitors of most organizations are other organizations sharing their goals, sources of finance, and membership base. Interest organizations specialize in policy niches and often avoid competition with similar organizations on closely related issues.[71] Participating in a coalition, then, can weaken niche issue

INTEREST ORGANIZATION EXAMPLE 5-2:

Plays Well with Others!

The Financial Services Coordinating Council (FSCC) is made up of four heavyweight trade associations: the American Insurance Association, the American Council of Life Insurers, American Bankers Association, and Securities Industry Association. During the 1980s, the four principals engaged in a series of ferocious turf battles. Banks began selling insurance, securities companies wanted to merge with banks, and the insurance companies fought to maintain their monopoly on the insurance business. But the Gramm-Leach-Bliley Act of 1999 reshaped the financial sector. Many of the same companies now sell insurance, banking, and securities services. With this overlap, there are now many issues on which the parent associations agree. The partners formalized their loose coalition as the FSCC, representing over 40,000 financial institutions providing services to almost every household in America.

Like many loosely structured coalitions, the FSCC entails coordination of the activities of their parent organizations. In the FSCC's case, four high-powered top lobbyists, representatives from each association, meet twice a month to discuss strategy and decisions (sometimes over cookies, they say). But the FSCC has assumed many of the trappings of an independent interest organization. For example, it maintains it own website. Listed there are 16 FSCC press releases dating from April 2001 to June 2002, including the testimony of FSCC representatives before four congressional hearings. The website also describes and comments on 10 bills FSCC is tracking through Congress. But perhaps the best sign that FSCC has become a freestanding organization is its hiring of two contract lobbyists to represent its interests in Minnesota.[63]

Source: http://www.hillnews.com/052202/influence_industry.aspx, visited July 10, 2002.

specialization. Moreover, while compromising with allies may increase the chances of success, it also means that an organization may have to sacrifice some policy details that are important to it. So, coalitions do not arise automatically.

When do interest organizations choose to form coalitions? Research on the frequency of joining coalitions at both the state[72] and federal levels suggests that several forces are important. First, the level of opposition matters. When there is strong opposition from other organizations or another coalition, organizations are more likely to ally themselves with others to protect and pursue their interests. Second, joining a coalition is more likely when the issue is considered across several legislative committees rather than just one. Alliance history matters, too. When organizations have been allies before, they are more likely to join in coalition when a new issue arises. Fourth, the organization's own needs influence its coalition behavior. When an organization faces severe competition for members and funds from similar organizations, autonomy may be more important than the benefits gained from joining a coalition.[73]

CONCLUSION

The legislative process provides many opportunities for influence on the part of organized interests. Indeed, a legislator's time, energy, and advocacy may matter far more than his or her vote on a final bill. But interest organizations must compete with the influences of party, ideology, constituency, the executive's agenda, and many other factors determining how legislators vote. We have also seen that while money can be a useful resource, information, expertise, votes, and established relationships are extremely important. But no matter how well endowed an organization might be, the context of some issues may severely restrict its influence.

This view of the legislative process is consistent with neither the pluralist nor transaction perspective. Interest organizations have many opportunities for influence beyond simply providing information to better link legislators and their constituents, although this is a key part of their work. Nor can they simply buy policy as transactions scholars suggest. The neopluralist approach provides a much better description of the role of organized interests in the legislative process. It allows for considerable influence on the part of organized interests *under certain circumstances.* But it also suggests that when constituents are mobilized on salient issues, interest organizations have little influence. As a contract lobbyist in Michigan put it, "If the people are united on something, they get it. We have to get out of the way."[74]

KEY TERMS AND CONCEPTS

Champion
Rules Committee
Supply Price of Policy
Policy Information
Political Information
Testimony
Direct Contacts
Contract Lobbying
Credibility

Expertise
District Presence
Outside Lobbying
Hearings
Particularistic Issues
Conflictual Issues
Unifying Issues
Coalition

QUESTIONS ABOUT YOUR INTEREST ORGANIZATION

1. Does your interest organization employ contract lobbying firms in contact with members of Congress or state legislators? Use lobby registration forms to identify the contract firms.
2. Who are the major lobbyists — in-house or contract — representing your interest organization in direct contacts with legislators? Develop a short biography of each.
3. Has your interest organization testified at state or congressional legislative hearings in recent years? Who else testified at the hearings? Was the deck stacked on one side of the issue?
4. Are there any state or federal legislators who work particularly closely with your interest organization? If so, what have they done for it in recent sessions of the legislature?
5. Has your interest organization participated in any coalitions with other interest organizations? If so, what were the issues on which the coalitions lobbied? Were there opposing coalitions?
6. In how many legislative districts does your interest organization have a presence?

7. Does your organization conduct original policy research that it presents to legislators? If so, what are some of its recent policy publications?

NOTES

1. Associated Press, "Congress Passes Corporate Fraud Bill," http://www.msnbc.com/news/785581.asp, visited July 28, 2002.
2. Richard A. Oppel, Jr., and Daniel Altman, "In a Shift, Republicans Pledge to Pass Accounting Bill," *New York Times*, July 18, 2002, p. c1.
3. Richard S. Durham, "The Vindication of Arthur Levitt," http:// www.businessweek.com:/...sh/feb2002/nf20020219_2045.htm? mainwindow, visited July 28, 2002.
4. Gregory Wawro, *Legislative Entrepreneurship in the U.S. House of Representatives* (Ann Arbor, Michigan: University of Michigan Press, 2000).
5. Ken Kollman, "Inviting Friends to Lobby: Interest Groups, Ideological Bias, and Congressional Committees," *American Political Science Review* 41: 519–544 (1997).
6. Richard L. Hall and Frank W. Wayman, "Buying Time: Moneyed Interests and the Mobilization of Bias in Congressional Committees," *American Political Science Review* 84: 797–820 (1990).
7. Mark A. Smith, *American Business and Political Power* (Chicago: University of Chicago Press, 2000), pp. 33–34.
8. Kevin B. Grier and Michael C. Munger, "The Impact of Legislator Attributes on Interest Group Campaign Contributions," *Journal of Labor Research* 7: 349–361 (1986); Jeffrey Berry, *The Interest Group Society* (Boston: Little, Brown, 1984).
9. Beth Leech and Frank R. Baumgartner, "Lobbying Friends and Foes in Washington," In *The Interest Group Connection: Electioneering, Lobbying, and Policymaking in Washington*, Paul S. Herrnson, Ronald G. Shaiko, and Clyde Wilcox, eds. (Chatham, NJ: Chatham House Publishers, 1998).
10. Marie Hojnacki and David C. Kimball, "Organized Interests and the Decision of Whom to Lobby in Congress," *American Political Science Review* 92: 775–790 (1998).
11. Arthur T. Denzau and Michael C. Munger, "Legislators and Interest Groups: How Unorganized Interests Get Represented," *American Political Science Review* 80: 89–106 (1986).

12. Marie Hojnacki, "The Changing Context of Direct Lobbying," paper presented at the Annual Meeting of the Midwest Political Science Association, Chicago, Illinois, April, 2000.

13. Stephen Moore, Sidney M. Wolfe, Deborah Lindes, and Clifford E. Douglas, "Epidemiology of Failed Tobacco Control Legislation," *Journal of the American Medical Association* 272: 1171–1175 (1994).

14. John R. Wright, "Tobacco Industry PACs and the Nation's Health: A Second Opinion." In *The Interest Group Connection: Electioneering, Lobbying, and Policymaking in Washington*, Paul S. Herrnson, Ronald G. Shaiko, and Clyde Wilcox, eds. (Chatham, NJ: Chatham House Publishers, 1998).

15. Virginia Gray and David Lowery, "Where Do Policy Ideas Come From? A Study of Minnesota Legislators and Staffers," *Journal of Public Administration Research and Theory* 10: 573–598 (2000).

16. Christine DeGregorio, "Assets and Access: Linking Lobbyists and Lawmakers in Congress." In *The Interest Group Connection*, Paul S. Herrnson, Ronald G. Shaiko, and Clyde Wilcox, eds. (Chatham, NJ: Chatham House Publishers, 1998).

17. Raymond A. Bauer, Ithiel de Sola Pool, and Lewis Anthony Dexter, *American Business and Public Policy* (New York: Atherton, 1963).

18. Ken Kollman, *Outside Lobbying* (Princeton: Princeton University Press, 1998), p. 35.

19. Kay Lehman Schlozman and John T. Tierney, *Organized Interests and American Democracy* (New York: Harper & Row Publishers, 1986), pp. 150–151.

20. Robert H. Salisbury, "An Exchange Theory of Interest Groups," *Midwest Journal of Political Science* 13: 1–32 (1969).

21. Kevin M. Leyden, "Interest Group Resources and Testimony at Congressional Hearings," *Legislative Studies Quarterly* 20: 431–439 (1995).

22. Jeffrey C. Talbert, Bryan D. Jones, and Frank R. Baumgartner, "Nonlegislative Hearings and Policy Change in Congress," *American Journal of Political Science* 39: 383–405 (1995).

23. Ibid., pp. 383–385.

24. Ibid., p. 388.

25. Jeffrey Berry, *The New Liberalism* (Washington, DC: The Brookings Institution, 1999), p. 20.

26. Kollman, *Outside Lobbying*, p. 35.

27. Sheila Krumholz, "Influence, Inc.: Lobbyists Spending in Washington: Former Members Turned Lobbyists," July 10, 2002 (2002) http://www.opensecrets.org/pubs/lobby00/former.asp. Livingston was also Speaker-designate of the House before he resigned in the wake of the Clinton-Lewinsky scandals due to infidelity in his own marriage.
28. Ibid.
29. Ibid.
30. Interview with Jerry Giovaniello, "The Rainmakers," *TheHill*, March 20, 2002, http://www.hillnews.com/032002/rss_giovaniello. shtm, visited July 10, 2002.
31. John R. Wright, "Contributions, Lobbying, and Committee Voting in the U.S. House of Representatives," *American Political Science Review* 84: 417–438 (1990).
32. Interview with Jerry Giovaniello, "The Rainmakers."
33. Michael Powell, "Call to Arms," *Washington Post* (August 6, 2000), p. W8.
34. "The Gerontocrats," *The Economist* 7914 (335): A32–33 (1995).
35. Steven A. Holmes, "The World According to AARP," *New York Times* (March 21, 2001), p. H1.
36. Thomas J. DiLorenzo, "Who Really Speaks for the Elderly?" *Consumers' Research Magazine*, 15–20 (September 1996)
37. Jeffrey Birnbaum, "Fat & Happy in DC," *Fortune* 11: 94–100 (May 28, 2001).
38. Garry Hubbard and Marco Turbovich, "Thousands from America's Steel Communities Rally at the White House, Imploring the President to Impose 40% Tariffs on Imported Steel," (February 28, 2002), http://www.uswa.org/press/countdownrallyrelease022802. htm, visited June 4, 2002.
39. John Duray, "Countdown to Justice: 19 Days Until President Bush Decides the Fate of the American Steel Industry: Public Support Builds for Strong Tariff Relief to End Unfair Trade in Steel" (February 15, 2002), http://www.uswa.org/press/countdown021502.html, visited June 4, 2002.
40. Michelle L. Chin, John R. Bond, and Nehemia Geva, "A Foot in the Door: An Experimental Study of PAC and Constituency Effects on Access," *Journal of Politics* 62: 534–549 (2000).
41. John R. Wright, "PAC Contributions, Lobbying, and Representation," *Journal of Politics* 51: 713–729 (1989).

42. Dennis P. Quinn and Robert Y. Shapiro, "Business Political Power: The Case of Taxation," *American Political Science Review* 85: 851–874 (1991).

43. Kenneth R. Godwin, *One Billion Dollars of Influence: The Direct Marketing of Politics*, (Chatham: Chatham House, 1988).

44. Allen Wilhite John Theilmann, "Labor PAC Contributions and Labor Legislation: A Simultaneous Logit Approach," *Public Choice* 53: 277–284 (1987).

45. John R. Wright, "PACs, Contributions, and Roll Calls: An Organizational Perspective," *American Political Science Review* 79: 400–414 (1985).

46. Janet M. Grenzke, "PACs and the Congressional Supermarket: The Currency Is Complex," *American Journal of Political Science* 33: 1–24 (1989).

47. Lawrence Rothenberg, *Linking Citizens to Government* (Cambridge: Cambridge University Press, 1992), p. 209.

48. John Frendreis and Richard Waterman, "PAC Contributions and Legislative Behavior: Senate Voting on Trucking Deregulation," *Social Science Quarterly* 66: 401–412 (1985); William P. Welch, "Campaign Contributions and Legislative Voting: Milk Money and Dairy Price Supports," *Western Political Quarterly* 35: 478–495 (1982).

49. Thomas Stratman, "What Do Campaign Contributions Buy? Deciphering the Causal Effects of Money and Votes," *Southern Economic Journal* 57: 606–620 (1991).

50. David B. Magleby and Candice J. Nelson, *The Money Chase* (Washington, DC: Brookings Institution, 1990); Christopher Witko, "Money, Members Goals and Legislative Decision-Making: The Variable Nature of PAC Influence," paper presented at the Annual Meeting of the Midwest Political Association, Chicago, Illinois, April 2002.

51. Margaret M. Conway, "PACs in the Political Process." In *Interest Group Politics*, Allen J. Cigler and Burdett A. Loomis, eds. (Washington, DC: Congressional Quarterly, 1991); Woodrow Jones, Jr., and Robert K. Keiser, K. Robert, "Issue Visibility and the Effects of PAC Money," Social Science Quarterly 68: 170–176 (1987); Alan Neustadtl, "Interest Group PACsmanship: An Analysis of Campaign Contributions, Issue Visibility, and Legislative Impact," *Social Forces* 69: 549–564 (1990).

52. Laura I. Langbein and Mark A. Lotwis, "The Political Efficacy of Lobbying and Money: Gun Control in the U.S. House, 1986," *Legislative Studies Quarterly* 15: 413–440 (1990); Denzau and Munger, "Legislators and Interest Groups: How Unorganized Interests get Represented"; Magleby and Nelson, *The Money Chase: Congressional Campaign Finance Reform.*
53. John R. Wright, "PAC Contributions and Voting on Tobacco Policy in the U.S. Congress, 1981–2000," paper presented at the Annual Meeting of the Midwest Political Science Association, Chicago, Illinois, April 2002.
54. Kevin M. Leyden, "Interest Group Resources and Testimony at Congressional Hearings," *Legislative Studies Quarterly* 20: 431–439 (1995).
55. Ibid., p. 432.
56. Ibid., p. 433.
57. Mark A. Smith, *American Business and Political Power* (Chicago: University of Chicago Press, 2000).
58. Ibid., pp. 13–14.
59. Ibid., pp. 14–15.
60. Ibid., pp. 15, 20–30.
61. Kollman, *Outside Lobbying,* p. 159; Kollman applied the model narrowly to the use of outside lobbying. We are extrapolating from his analysis to the relative influence of all types of resources. He is not responsible for our conclusions.
62. Durham, "The Vindication of Arthur Levitt."
63. Berry, *The Interest Group Society.*
64. Kevin W. Hula, *Lobbying Together,* (Washington, DC: Georgetown University Press, 1999), pp. 34–35.
65. Ibid.
66. Norman J. Ornstein and Shirley Elder, *Interest Groups, Lobbying, and Policymaking* (Washington, DC: Congressional Quarterly Press, 1978); Berry, *The Interest Group Society.*
67. James Q. Wilson, *Political Organizations* (Princeton: Princeton University Press, 1995), p. 317.
68. Hula, *Lobbying Together,* pp. 29–30.
69. Frank R. Baumgartner and Christine Mahoney, "Gaining Government Allies: Groups, Officials and Alliance Behavior," Typescript, Pennsylvania State University (2002).
70. Hula, *Lobbying Together.*

71. William P. Browne, "Organized Interests and Their Issue Niches: A Search for Pluralism in a Policy Domain," *Journal of Politics* 52: 477–509 (1990).

72. Virginia Gray and David Lowery, "To Lobby Alone or in a Flock: Foraging Behavior Among Organized Interests," *American Politics Quarterly* 26: 5–35 (1998).

73. Marie Hojnacki, "Interest Groups' Decisions to Join Alliances or Work Alone," *American Journal of Political Science* 41: 61–87 (1997).

74. Virginia Gray and David Lowery, *The Population Ecology of Interest Representation* (Ann Arbor, Michigan: University of Michigan Press, 1996), p. 25.

CHAPTER 6

Organized Interests and the Executive Branch

On March 27, 2002, President George Bush signed the Bipartisan Campaign Reform Act of 2002, better known as the McCain-Feingold/Shays-Meehan bill. The new law placed strict limits on the soft money political candidates and parties raise from organized interests. It also restricted the use of issue advertisements using candidates' names immediately prior to federal elections. After the torturous seven-year battle leading up to the president's signature, those charging that organized interests were systematically corrupting American politics with cash savored the historic moment. Scott Harshbarger, president of Common Cause, echoed the feeling of many reformers when he claimed that "Americans have won an historic victory to help bring our government back to the people."[1] He should have known better. As Yogi Berra noted, "It ain't over till it's over." And in politics and public policy, it ain't over until the bureaucracy has acted and the courts have ruled.

The Federal Election Commission (FEC) implements federal election laws. Thus, it was up to the FEC to develop the specific rules that candidates, parties, and organized interests must follow to comply with the Bipartisan Campaign Reform Act. In the months following adoption of the act, the FEC developed a draft set of rules. Letters and comments on the proposed rules from interested parties were received and hearings held. And in June 2002, the FEC adopted final rules that govern implementation of the act. Supporters of reform immediately charged that the FEC's rules and guidelines opened numerous loopholes that could allow the flow of soft money to continue. Senators John McCain and Russ Feingold and Congressmen

Christopher Shays and Marty Meehan charged that "the Federal Election Commission has taken upon itself the task of rewriting the newly passed McCain-Feingold/Shays-Meehan bill. This is not a role given to the FEC by Congress or by the Constitution. Congress spent seven years debating complex and difficult policy issues before reaching the judgments contained in the bill. The FEC's job is to implement those judgments, not revisit them — to enforce the law, not undermine it."[2] The sponsors of the legislation announced that they would try to invalidate the FEC's rules by Congressional action. If unsuccessful, they promised to challenge the rules in court.[3]

This story is not unique. The rules that agencies adopt to implement laws can profoundly shape how they ultimately influence behavior. Organized interests, not surprisingly, seek influence with the executive branch. This chapter explores these interactions. We first examine how elected executives interact with organized interests. We then review several different interpretations of the relationship between organized interests and the bureaucracy. Finally, we consider three means organized interests use to influence bureaucratic decisions.

ORGANIZED INTERESTS AND POLITICAL EXECUTIVES

The executive branch is composed of two very different parts. The first includes political executives who provide democratic direction to the executive branch, albeit temporary, given the vagaries of electoral fortunes. Political executives include elected executives and their appointees to departments and agencies. The second component is the permanent bureaucracy.

Political Executives

Who are political executives? While the boundaries between political executives and the permanent bureaucracy can be somewhat fuzzy within any government and can vary greatly across levels of government, the former are best thought of as the elected executive's team. At the federal level, this team has three parts. The White House office, including the offices of legislative affairs, political affairs, chief of staff, intergovernmental affairs, and other offices, serves as the personal staff of the president. The White House office is one part of the second component of the president's team—the **Executive Office of the President** (EOP), which was established in 1939. The EOP includes a number of agencies—the Office of Management and Budget, the National Security Council, the Council of Economic Advisors, and others—employing a mix of political appointees and career officials who assist the president in managing the executive branch. The EOP has nearly 2,000 employees, some seconded from federal departments. The third component of the president's team includes his appointees serving in top leadership positions in departments and agencies. Overall, President Bush had nearly 3,300 appointments to make when inaugurated in 2001.

Governors and mayors, obviously, have far smaller teams through which to manage bureaucratic agencies. This is especially problematic for governors, given the growing policy responsibilities of state governments. For most of our nation's 200-year history, most governors had neither the capacity to propose budgets nor to oversee their execution. Many gubernatorial offices consist of a handful of staff assistants. Nationally, there are over 500 officials elected statewide, including 43 attorneys general, 42 lieutenant governors, 38 state treasurers, and 36 secretaries of state.[4] Independently elected executives can disagree, undermining the unity of the executive branch. When George W. Bush was governor of Texas, for example, he filed suit to stop his attorney general's allocation of funds from a multibillion dollar legal settlement with tobacco companies.[5] Still, many observers conclude that governors are able to combine their relatively limited formal political resources with their considerable advantage in media attention to provide direction to state bureaucracies.

The introduction of this chapter discussed the FEC's implementation of the McCain-Feingold/Shays-Meehan bill. While President Bush had little to do with its long journey through Congress and signed the bill only reluctantly, this is an exception to the usually active role political executives play throughout the legislative process. Presidents and governors do more than sign bills and, through the bureaucracy, implement them. Indeed, among the most powerful expectations we hold about presidents and governors is that they act as agenda setters. Their proposals account for some, but by no means all, of the most important legislation considered by legislatures, especially budget bills. It is not surprising, then, that organized interests seek access to political executives. As illustrated by the National Rifle Association's triumphant claim of direct access to the White House upon the election of George W. Bush, securing the attention of political executives is a major achievement for organized interests.

How common is such access? President Bill Clinton was roundly criticized for allowing more than 360 guests to stay at the White House or the Camp David presidential retreat. The image in some press accounts was one of the executive branch being bought and sold. And some organizations work hard to secure access to presidents, as seen in Interest Organization Example 6-1. In this case, Anheuser-Busch, which contributed to both parties equally prior to the 2000 presidential election, sought the attention of the in-coming president by serving as a major financial supporter of his inaugural festivities. But organized interests rarely have unlimited access to political executives. Unlike legislators, there is only one president or governor of a state at a time. Their offices also have formidable barriers to access, so political executives largely choose to whom they talk. So, while a powerful leverage point, access to executives is rare. Jack Walker's 1985 survey of voluntary associations found that 90.1 percent lobbied the executive branch as a whole.[6] But only 11 percent reported frequent interactions with any part of the EOP, much less securing the ear of the president.[7] And access can be lost if there is a switch in party control. Mark A. Peterson and Jack Walker noted, for example, that "when Ronald Reagan replaced Jimmy Carter in the White House, there was a virtual revolution in the access or denial of access experienced by different segments of the interest community represented in Washington."[8] Thus, betting solely on access to political executives is risky. Formerly advantaged interests may soon be on the outside looking in.

Some view executive secrecy as excessive while others consider it a necessity to ensure that executives have access to unvarnished advice. Secrecy clearly has, however, an unfortunate implication for students of interest representation. That is, we surely know less about interest organizations and political executives than about any other topic considered in this text. Or rather, we know less that is systematic. As we will see, we have any number of stories about specific interactions between presidents and interest organizations. But these cases are probably atypical. Many became stories only when conflicts within and between interest organizations rose to public

INTEREST ORGANIZATION EXAMPLE 6-1:

George, this Bud's for You!

Founded 120 years ago, Anheuser-Busch Companies is the world's largest brewer, operating a dozen breweries in the United States. Its subsidiaries include many theme parks and firms specializing in packaging, glass production, media services, and a railroad. A number of public policies touch on Anheuser-Busch's extended interests, including policies on underage drinking. Not surprisingly, Anheuser-Busch is also among the most politically active businesses in the nation. In 1997, Anheuser-Busch was one of only two organizations registered to lobby in 49 of the 50 states. In addition to its in-house lobbyists, the brewing company spent $1,870,000 employing nine different Washington lobbying firms in 2000. In the 2000 federal election cycle, Anheuser-Busch and its employees contributed the highest total among individual firms in the beer, wine, and liquor industry, distributing $2,124,911, or 16.81 percent of the industry total. Among these funds, $968,281 was contributed as soft money donations.

Anheuser-Busch employees contributed in a bipartisan manner. In the 2000 federal election cycle, 49 percent of the company's contributions went to Democrats, and 51 percent to Republicans. This contribution strategy is low risk in that it makes few enemies. But presidents may be more inclined to grant access to those who bet firmly on their electoral success, so, after elections identify a clear winner, interest organizations will often look for ways to secure enhanced access to new incumbents. Following his 2000 victory, George W. Bush reportedly raised over $40 million in private funds for his inaugural festivities. Anheuser-Busch was among a number of corporations contributing the maximum amount of $100,000.

Sources: Visited June 8, 2002: http://www.anheuser-busch.com; http://www.opensecrets.org

controversies or, as with the Clinton sleepovers, a whiff of scandal surfaced. Lacking access to systematic data on the interactions of political executives and organized interests, we need to be more cautious about generalizing on this topic than on any other.

Types of Interaction with Interests

With limited time and strong gate-keeping capacities, chief executives have considerable discretion in how they interact with organized interests. Indeed, Mark Peterson identified four distinct ways presidents liaison with advocacy organizations.[9] As seen in Table 6-1, two dimensions define these four types. The first concerns the *breadth* of the interaction. A president may adopt an exclusive approach and liaison only with ideologically compatible organizations, or the White House could open itself to organizations of all ideological stripes. The second dimension concerns the *substantive* focus of the contacts. A programmatic focus emphasizes a president's policies, mobilizing support for his program in Congress, or presidents may focus on representational issues, using access to promote their electoral standing.

The first type defined by these two dimensions is **liaison as governing party.** Such contacts are exclusive or limited to organizations supporting a president's program. And its focus is programmatic; organizations are mobilized to support the president's program in Congress. Thus, not all of the interest organizations allied with the president are useful — only those with sufficient clout in the legislature. Mark Peterson found that this was the most typical mode of interaction in the Reagan White House. Organizations with ties to the Republican Party, large staff resources, and an active role in congressional elections were far more likely to have access to the White House. Later we will consider a more recent example of this type of liaising with organized interests: the National Energy Policy Development Group (NEPDG) led by Vice President Dick Cheney. But most presidential scholars believe that this mode of interaction with organized interests is now the model for all administrations.

Peterson labels the second type of interaction between presidents and interests **liaison as consensus building.** This type also focuses on programmatic issues and getting bills through congress,

TABLE 6-1 Typology of White House Liaison with Organized Interests

		Breadth of Interest Organization Interactions	
		Exclusive	Inclusive
Substantive Focus of Interest Organization Interactions	Programmatic	Liaison as Governing Party	Liaison as Consensus Building
	Representational	Liaison as Outreach	Liaison as Legitimization

Source: Mark A. Peterson, "The Presidency and Organized Interests: White House Patterns of Interest Group Liaison," *American Political Science Review* 86: 614 (1992).

but, in this case, access is more inclusive. The object is to avoid or break a logjam in Congress by forging compromises, building coalitions among interests that normally would be in conflict. In its grandest form, this mode of interaction entails the White House hosting summits to forge solutions to national problems. Peterson suggests that President Johnson tried to use White House contacts with interest organizations in this manner before the Vietnam War fatally distracted his administration. And the extraordinarily large number of organized interests included in the more than year-long preparation of President Clinton's 1993 national health care proposal suggests that it might fit this type of liaison strategy. But the grand coalition fractured when Congress considered the proposal. This failure, and the lack of a more recent example, suggest how difficult it is to forge overly broad coalitions among organized interests.

The third and fourth types of interaction focus less on specific policy issues than on group representation for political or electoral purposes. The third type, **liaison as outreach,** is exclusive in that it focuses on narrow "segments of the president's political coalition that otherwise lack close ties to the government establishment, sometimes to the point of bringing somewhat suspect 'fringe' groups into the system."[10] Defining a fringe group, of course, varies. But it is clear that several presidents have appointed special assistants or established White House offices to highlight the importance of specific groups to a president's coalition. President Johnson placed the Office of Economic Opportunity in the EOP to highlight the importance of the disadvantaged to his political agenda. President Jimmy Carter's public liaison assistant, Midge Constanza, was the administration's contact for gay rights organizations. Most recently, Senior Advisor Karl Rove is reputed to be President George W. Bush's special contact for fundamentalist Christian organizations, as is the White House Office of Faith-Based and Community Initiatives established by executive order just days after his inauguration.

The final mode of interaction is **liaison as legitimization.** This type of interaction is neither limited only to those interests supporting a president's program nor focused on building lobbying support for specific legislation. Rather, access is largely apolitical, with the White House open to interests of all kinds. While rare, this was the objective behind President Gerald Ford's establishing the White House Office of Public Liaison in 1974. Ford's situation as a nonelected president following the discredited Nixon administration was unique. Reestablishing the legitimacy of the presidency was of paramount importance. While the Carter administration initially maintained the Ford administration's open access, difficulties with Congress soon led to adoption of the more common liaison as governing strategy.[11]

Peterson's four types describe the variety of ways presidents and organized interests interact. Underlying each is some notion of exchange—presidents provide access in return for some service to the favored interest organization. In the liaison as governing case, which is the most frequent mode of interaction, presidents receive lobbying support in Congress. But, given the black box of secrecy shrouding elected chief executives, we know little about what the president gives to organized interests in return. Perhaps little. The mere election of a president from a party favorable to a given policy may be sufficient for interest organizations representing it to support an administration's legislative agenda, if with a little prodding. In such cases, the president and the interest organization are natural allies, and there is little need for lobbying per se outside of the electoral process. But in other cases, real horse-trading may be required. Even when the president is working with firm allies, the fine details of administration policy may generate controversy. Such real lobbying of the executive is all but invisible.

ORGANIZED INTERESTS AND THE BUREAUCRACY

One of the oldest parables in the study of bureaucracy involves six blind men and an elephant. Each man, touching a different part of the elephant, describes a very different kind of animal. The public agency, as elephant metaphor, highlights the complexity involved in describing the full richness of multiple tasks, external pressures, and internal management issues of a single agency. But even this metaphor does not capture the full range of interactions between organized interests and public bureaucracy. Rather than a single elephant, our blind men are wandering through a zoo with many different kinds of animals. We will first examine the diversity of bureaucracies and then the various interpretations of their interactions with organized interests.

The Diversity of Bureaucracy

Bureaucraies differ in scale, openness to external influences, task complexity, and many other factors that bear on their relationships with interest organizations. Even the 15 federal departments vary greatly in size. The U.S. Department of Veterans Affairs has over 200,000 employees, while the U.S. Department of Education has but 4,900. There are more than a dozen freestanding federal agencies and public corporations, including the Environmental Protection Agency, the Federal Emergency Management Agency, and many other less prominent members of the bureaucracy. The states have their own counterparts to many of these agencies, but also many others, such as public colleges and universities, that have no analogs at the national level. The many agencies of local government, from tax assessors to local school districts, are part of the bureaucracy as well. In short, the bureaucracy is extraordinarily heterogeneous. The U.S. Department of Defense is different from the police department of Auburn, Maine.

Some public organizations are designed to be very open to organized interests, while others are shielded from such influence. The U.S. Department of Veterans Affairs, for example, has close ties to veterans organizations. Its home page prominently lists the websites of dozens of veterans organizations under the heading of "partners."[12]

The National Labor Relations Board (NLRB), established in 1935, represents a quite different form of openness. The NLRB was designed as an arena for organizations representing labor and management to contend over union elections and unfair labor practices.[13] Other agencies are structured to weaken the influence of organized interests, usually by appointing officials in a manner that shields them from influence. Federal Reserve Board members, for example, are appointed for staggered terms overlapping presidential administrations so as to isolate monetary policy from short-term electoral pressures. The shift from elected to appointed local property tax assessors that occurred in most states over the last century was similarly intended to weaken the influence of organized interests on the allocation of tax burdens.[14] In short, contacts between bureaucrats and organized interests appropriate for one kind of agency may be inappropriate for another.

Bureaucracies and organized interests also interact for many different purposes. Our most common image is perhaps that of a traditional economic interest struggling against rules imposed by regulatory agencies. Thus, Ford Motor Company may lobby for revisions of Occupational Health and Safety Administration worker safety rules or Environmental Protection Agency rules on auto pollution. But Ford is a major supplier of goods to public agencies, including the U.S. Department of Defense. Ford relies on the U.S. Department of Commerce to open foreign markets. Ford also works with the public education system in Michigan and other states to ensure access to a trained workforce. And while Ford lobbies against some budget items, it supports others, especially highway spending. Another example of this range of interactions can be seen in Interest Organization Example 6-2. While nurturing a reputation for fighting government growth, the U.S. Chamber of Commerce often lobbies for increased public spending. In short, many organized interests do not have a simple relationship with bureaucracy.

The complexity of these relationships is especially great at the local level. Over the last two decades, many activities formerly provided by public employees have been contracted out to the private sector. By 1990, notes political scientist Robert Stein, "nearly half the service repertoire of municipal governments is planned, financed, produced, or delivered with the active participation of an entity or entities other than municipal government."[15] This transition has

INTEREST ORGANIZATION EXAMPLE 6-2:

Waste Is Someone Else's Spending!

The U.S. Chamber of Commerce was founded in 1912. With over 3 million business members, 3,000 state and local chambers, and 830 business association affiliates, it is the largest business federation in the world. The Chamber is a "peak" association that purports to represent the entire business sector of the economy. But it is the preeminent advocate for small and mid-sized business. Over 96 percent of its members are small businesses with fewer than 100 employees.

The Chamber provides an array of selective benefits for members, including education services and discounts on computers, insurance, and retirement plans. But the Chamber is predominantly an advocacy organization. It lobbies all branches and levels of government using tools ranging from direct lobbying and mobilizing grassroots contacting of legislators and executives, participation in court cases, and commenting on proposed regulations. The Chamber styles itself as an opponent of big government and waste. Its home page states that it "advances your interests through its nationally recognized team of lobbyists and policy experts. Together, they help craft probusiness legislation and block excessive taxes and regulations."

But the Chamber's anti-big-government stance belies its complicated relations with government. From April through June 2002, the Chamber issued 38 press releases on public policy, but a third called for bigger government or more spending. The Chamber applauded establishing the Department of Homeland Security, providing federal terrorism insurance for businesses, opening the Yucca Mountain nuclear waste repository, and expanding the number of agents patrolling the U.S. border. The Chamber opposed cuts in highway spending and supported greater NASA funding for commercial launch vehicles.

Source: Visited June 20, 2002: http://www.uschamber.com.

been especially great in human services. There is often only a single nonprofit firm bidding for these contracts.[16] And these nonprofits often wear another hat as advocates of the interests of those they serve. Thus, a monopoly advocacy organization may contract with government to provide services formerly provided by a monopoly public bureaucracy. Under such conditions, it is difficult to say where public bureaucracy ends and interest organizations begin.

Finally, the political environments in which agencies operate can change over time in ways that advantage some organized interests and disadvantage others. The inauguration of President George W. Bush in 2001 was good news for the Department of Defense, but not so good for the U.S. Environmental Protection Agency. Downsizing the U.S. Justice Department's work on counterterrorism to focus on drug crimes seemed like a good idea to Attorney General John Ashcroft prior to September 11, 2001. But events changed the Justice Department's priorities. The first budget developed by Harvey Pitt, President Bush's chairman of the Securities and Exchange Commission, proposed sharp cuts in the agency's regulatory staff.[17] A year later, after a series of financial scandals, the president proposed increasing the SEC's budget 20 percent. Contrary to their image as stolid and ponderous, bureaucracies change in response to events in ways that embolden some interests, while leaving others with thoughts of what might have been.

While most scholars recognize the incredible diversity of bureaucratic agencies, they disagree sharply about their role in public policy. More than a dozen models or images have been used to describe agencies' power relationships with other political actors.[18] Some of the major models are arrayed across the rows of Table 6-2, grouped according to whether they view the bureaucracy as a weak actor, one of many, or a dominant actor in the policy process. Within each perspective, different models are grouped by our three schools of thought about the influence of organized interests — the pluralist, transactions, and neopluralist interpretations.

Weak Bureaucracy Models

The models in the first row of Table 6-2 view bureaucracies as weak political actors. Agencies do not define their missions, have little control over their budgets, and are highly sensitive to the carrots and sticks wielded by others. This does not mean that all of the weak

TABLE 6-2 Models of Interest Organization Influence with Bureaucracies

		Models of the Influence of Organized Interests			
		Pluralist	Transactions	Neo-pluralist	Other
View of the Power of Bureaucracy as a Political Actor	*Weak Actor*	Neutral Competence with Pure Pluralism	Elitism, Capture, Chicago School	Depends on Structure	Legislative or Executive Dominance
	One of Many Actors	Polyarchy, Representative Bureaucracy	Interest Group Liberalism, Iron Triangle	Advocacy Coalition, Issue Network	
	Strong Actor				Bureaucratic Dominance

Source: authors and adapted from Larry B. Hill, "Who Governs the American Administrative State? A Bureaucratic-Centered Image of Governance," *Journal of Public Administration Research and Theory* 1:216–295 (1991).

actor models agree on the capacity of organized interests to influence policy. In traditional pluralist thinking, policy results from the clash of interests in society where all salient interests are represented in some manner. In this view, policy reflects the balance of power of organized interests.[19] Elected officials, reflecting the balance of interests in society, determine the ends or goals of government. Bureaucrats then merely execute that policy in a politically neutral and technically competent manner. This is a comforting model familiar to us from civics classes. But few scholars now accept its view of the power of either bureaucrats or organized interests.

The upper middle cell of Table 6-2 lists three models that share the pluralist idea that bureaucrats are weak political actors, but adopt the transactions school view of the power of organized interests. In the **elitism** model, best presented in C. Wright Mills' 1956 book, *The Power Elite*, bureaucrats are not weak in the sense of lacking influence, but in terms of lacking a distinctive voice.[20] In Mills' view, upper-level bureaucrats, elected politicians, the leaders of interest organizations are all drawn from the same social class and share the same political views. Whether consciously or unconsciously, they all work toward the same policy goals. While now rarely applied to explain public policy outcomes at the federal level, Mills view provided a popular account of the interactions of urban politicians, interest organizations, and local bureaucrats in the 1950s and 1960s. This perspective survives today in some studies of local economic development suggesting that developers, mayors, and bureaucrats share common perspectives.[21]

The **capture** model highlights the life cycle of agencies.[22] Regulatory agencies are initially established with crusading zeal following a scandal or crisis. But enthusiasm, budgets, and morale can fade as attention shifts to other issues. Further, long-term contacts between regulators and the regulated may render the former overly sympathetic to the interests of the latter. Bureaucrats may find that those they regulate can both make their lives more or less difficult and provide career opportunities outside of the agency. For example, nursing homes can make it more or less difficult for state nursing home inspectors to carry out their charge. The enticements of future employment may generate a revolving door whereby young regulators put in their time and then leave for more lucrative jobs in the regulated industry. In the end, the regulated capture formerly zealous bureaucrats. In the summer of 2002, for example, Senators John McCain and Tom Daschle argued that the Securities and Exchange Commission (SEC) had been captured by the accounting and securities industries it regulates.[23] The SEC staff's low pay, collapsing morale, growing workload, and declining budgets generated high staff turnover, with many leaving for the private sector.[24] Further, President Bush appointed as chairman of the SEC Harvey Pitt, who worked for the SEC early in his career before representing finance and accounting firms as a private lawyer-lobbyist.[25] More telling in light of the capture model, he promised to lead a "kinder, gentler SEC," one far friendlier to the regulated industries.

The **Chicago School** model also emphasizes capture, but it suggests that capture begins on day one in the life cycle of an agency. Growing out of studies of electric utility regulation, economists George Stigler, Robert Barro, and Sam Peltzman argued that it is the regulated who demand regulation.[26] Several goals might explain this counterintuitive outcome. Regulation might smooth out cycles of demand and supply for competitors within a major industry so as to minimize cutthroat competition. Regulation may also raise barriers to entry for new firms, thereby protecting an existing cartel. Both explanations have been used, for example, to explain the adoption of airline regulation. Alternatively, regulations may be used in a predatory manner by major firms. Since the costs of complying with regulations are typically higher for small rather than large firms, they would give large firms a competitive edge.[27] But while the Chicago School model has been employed to explain the role of interest organizations in a few cases, it is not clear that it explains all regulatory events or has much to say about nonregulatory bureaucracies that comprise a much larger proportion of public agencies.

There is no distinct neopluralist weak actor model. Rather, neopluralists argue that all of the prior models might apply in different cases. The key lies in the specific institutional and political configurations governing an agency. As we have seen, some agencies, like the Federal Reserve Board, are highly insulated from political influence. Others, such as the Department of Veterans Affairs, are designed to be exceptionally open to organized interests. Some agencies deal with issues the public cares a great deal about, such as the Social Security Administration. But others toil in narrow technical domains of little concern to most, but of a great importance to a few. The political environment of even these agencies can change markedly, as illustrated by the SEC following the Enron, WorldCom, Merrill Lynch, and Xerox scandals. In a neopluralist world, then, agencies interact with organized interests in a manner running from the extremes of neutral competence to full capture and all of the possibilities in between.

The final set of weak bureaucracy models is listed in an "other category" because they lack an unambiguous assessment of the influence of organized interests over public agencies. Executive and/or legislative dominance models assert that bureaucrats are fully controlled agents of political principals. In this case, however, control results not from a committed neutral competence on the part of bureaucrats, but because principals possess a full array of carrots and sticks to monitor and guide civil servants.[28] The two models, however, identify different principals. **Executive dominance** scholars emphasize the power presidents and governors have in designing agencies and appointing their heads.[29] This view was given a frightening edge in discussions of an evolving imperial presidency following President Richard Nixon's use of the FBI and IRS to quiet opponents.[30] **Legislative dominance** scholars have been more influential within political science over the last decade, although not without vocal critics.[31] To legislative dominance scholars, the budget, mission design, and oversight authority of legislatures are enough to ensure that nothing happens in agencies unless the legislature wills it.

Obviously, both models cannot be right, but in either case the models lack a simple view of the influence of organized interests on bureaucracy. It all depends, of course, on whether organized interests can influence the principal. Pluralists and neopluralists, we have seen, suggest that this influence is limited. But if the transactions school's assertions that organized interests buy and sell legislation in Congress and/or manipulate presidential priorities are correct, then bureaucracies are only one step removed from their influence. Organized interests would play an important role in influencing bureaucracies by warning principals when an application of carrots and sticks is needed. Organized interests would be the crucial fire alarms that tell political principals that it is time to intervene in agency decision making.[32]

Bureaucracies as One of Many Players

Several models view bureaucracy as one of a number of actors that can influence public policy. Among the other actors, of course, are organized interests. As seen in the second row of Table 6-2, two models are consistent with pluralist view of organized interests. **Polyarchy** is a variant of traditional pluralism, viewing public policy as a product of interactions among interests in society where all salient interests are represented. But the polyarchy version of pluralism assumes that government is more than a neutral playing field on which organized interests compete. Government is a player, too. Government agencies have a general interest in resolving conflicts among competing interests.[33] Thus, they may facilitate exchanges among organized interests and work to insure that no one interest captures public policy to the exclusion of others. Agencies also have a specific interest in public policy arising from their technical expertise; thus, agencies may do more than passively wait for political leaders to determine the ends of policy before considering the means to achieve them. They may bring to the debate over ends their own technical skills, albeit in a neutral manner. While constituting something of an idealized image of bureaucracies and organized interests, the public image of at least a few public bureaucracies approaches polyarchy. The U.S. Center for Disease Control, for example, remains open to many interests concerned about public health and is itself an active player in the policy arena based on its acknowledged technical experience. Many state universities also aspire to the polyarchic model. They are both extraordinarily open to a wide range of interest organizations, but also actively lobby state legislatures on their own behalf.

The **representative bureaucracy** model is also consistent with the pluralist view of organized interests. The central idea of this model is that bureaucrats, while unelected, provide a representative function similar to that of legislators and elected executives.[34] The representative bureaucracy model suggests that the more the demographic composition of bureaucracy mirrors society, the more agencies will naturally reflect public preferences. Tests of this hypothesis have found strong evidence, for example, that black and Latino populations are better served by local schools when blacks and Latinos are better represented among school administrators.[35] Still, this form of representative is usually thought of as passive, obviating any need for organized interests to directly represent the preferences of different demographic groups. That is, when the share of minority employees of an agency better matches the community the agency serves, there should be less need for organizations representing the interests of minorities to lobby actively.

A darker image of agency-interest group interaction is provided by the transactions model version of the one player among many view of bureaucracy. Both Theodore Lowi's **interest group liberalism** model and the **iron triangle** model suggest that interest organizations and public agencies compete among and between themselves to shape public policy. But the policy solutions they craft rarely reflect the public interest.[36] These models involve more than simple capture, however. Rather organized interests and bureaucrats also engage in mutually beneficial exchanges. The interest group liberalism model suggests that special interests provide political support for agencies in the legislature. In turn, bureaucrats favor their partner's interests in conducting agency business. A third set of conspirators, legislative committees, are added in iron triangle models.[37] Legislators receive campaign funds from favored organized interests and get to allocate the pork provided by bureaucracies in exchange for larger budgets for agencies to implement policies favored by organized interests. Both models assume that these exchange relationships are exclusive to a narrow set of interests and are long-lasting.

Two models of bureau interactions with organized interests are consistent with a neopluralist interpretation of the latter's influence while viewing agencies as one of many players in the policy process. Like the transactions school models, the **issue network** and **advocacy coalition** models view agencies as active players in the policy process, interacting regularly with organized interests. Again, their relationship is based on an exchange of resources each needs. But issue network and advocacy coalition models add important caveats to the mix. Issue networks consider a wider range of participants, including legislative staffers, journalists, academic researchers, and others interested in a policy issue.[38] Especially important, citizens' groups and other advocacy organizations, not just traditional economic interests, are potential members of a network governing a policy area. In advocacy coalition models, more than one network may co-exist, competing for influence over a policy issue.[39] Control of policy is always subject, therefore, to contestation and may be temporary.

The fluid and variable outcomes of network and advocacy coalition models make them especially suited for neopluralist interpretations of the influence of interest organizations. While neopluralists view the policy process as open over the long term to almost any interest organization willing to devote time and energy to exercising influence, they do not assume that outcomes always or inevitably reflect a compromise among all salient interests. In network and advocacy coalition models, a dominant coalition governing a policy area might be so broad as to resemble polyarchy, or it may be so narrow as to be indistinguishable, except in permanence, from an iron triangle. Indeed, analyses over several decades of the politics of tobacco, pesticide, and nuclear energy policy,[40] which we consider in more depth in Chapter 8, demonstrate that the size and permeability of dominant coalitions ebb and flow over time.

Strong Bureaucracy Models

The last row of Table 6-2 is largely a null set, as indicated by the shaded cells. Simply put, some models of bureaucratic politics view public agencies as so powerful that they totally control executives, legislators, and organized interests. If bureaucracies are so strong, interest organizations can contribute little to the policy process. Given their inattention to organized interests, we need not describe the **bureaucratic dominance** models in detail. In sketch, though, they argue that bureaucrats' technical knowledge,[41] their monopoly over information critical to public policy decisions,[42] and their ability to use bureaucratic routines to narrow policy options,[43] profoundly influence the policy choices of the other actors in the policy process. But strong bureaucracy models have fallen out of favor over recent decades. Scholars now recognize that the motivations of bureaucrats are far more complex than suggested by some of these models.[44] More than technical information determines policy; political information about public preferences matters, too. Most importantly, we now recognize that organized interests represent an alternative source of policy information and expertise. Indeed, elected politicians often use organized interests and public agencies as checks on each other's influence.

MEANS OF INFLUENCING THE BUREAUCRACY

Because of the heterogeneity of bureaucratic interactions with organized interests one can point to examples that are consistent with each of the models just discussed. But it is difficult to say which is typical, given the lack of systematic studies across a representative sample of public agencies. Still, some scholars have examined in a more systematic manner several specific tools organized interests use to influence agency decisions.

Indirectly Influencing Bureaucrats

Organized interests often try to influence bureaucracies indirectly through the efforts of executives and legislators. The tools available to executives and legislators are potentially formidable. State legislatures and Congress have a significant say on the missions and budgets of agencies, and they can hold oversight hearings on agency operations, but scholars disagree about the importance of these tools. Some point out that Congress rarely engages in oversight activities.[45] Except for major scandals, devoting time to oversight serves the interests of members less well than other activities like legislating and providing constituency service. Others argue, however, that oversight activities operate more like fire alarms than police patrols.[46] That is, rather than requiring the constant attention of legislatures like a patrol officer on the beat, oversight needs to occur only when agencies need correction. Organized interests can monitor agencies for legislators, providing them with fire alarm-like signals that action is needed.

Political executives, too, have significant resources that can influence bureaucratic decision making. Presidents, governors, and mayors are also important players in the budget process. Over recent decades, in fact, presidents and governors have increased their control over the executive side of the budget process. Prior to the mid-1960s, for example, agencies had substantial discretion in proposing items for inclusion in the president's budget. Since then, a series of reforms have sharply limited what bureaucrats can propose, replacing a bottom-up process with one emphasizing top-down controls.[47] Presidents also tightened controls over agency actions. When federal agency officials testify before Congress, their testimony must now be cleared by the White House. The Office of Management and Budget, a major agency in the EOP, now routinely reviews proposed agency rules and regulations. But perhaps the most important power political executives have is their ability to appoint the top officials of agencies.

While appointment power is restricted for some governors and mayors when some of their cabinet members are independently elected, it remains a potentially important leverage point for organized interests to indirectly influence agencies. Unfortunately, we have little systematic evidence about the role of organized interests in the appointment process. Most appointments attract remarkably little public attention. Of the many appointments of top agency officials made by President George W. Bush and approved by the Senate, for example, only a few attracted public testimony by even a single interest organization, and almost all of these comments were laudatory. In large part this inattention is strategic. Legislators grant political executives substantial discretion in appointing their management teams. Even if organizations oppose a nominee, their efforts are unlikely to lead to a nominee's rejection. This does not mean, however, that interest organizations are unimportant in the appointment process. A few especially controversial nominees are rejected in most administrations. More importantly, organized interests allied with a political executive play a substantial behind-the-scenes role in vetting nominees.

Controversies occasionally arise that suggest organized interests strongly influence executive appointments. For example, after more than 18 months in office, President George W. Bush had yet to nominate a commissioner of the Food and Drug Administration (FDA). The stalled nomination resulted from a three-sided conflict. The pharmaceutical industry, a strong ally of President Bush, supported only nominees sympathetic to its needs. But Senator Ted Kennedy, chair of the Senate committee that would consider the nomination, was under pressure from consumer organizations opposed to entrusting the FDA to a pharmaceutical industry insider. Compounding the conflict, organizations opposed to abortion, another ally of President Bush, supported only nominees willing the reverse the Clinton administration's FDA decision approving the use of an abortion pill.[48] While perhaps unusual in rising to a very public controversy, this example provides a glimpse of the powerful role interest organizations play in at least some executive appointments and, thereby, agency decisions.

Assuming that organized interests can influence legislative and executive decisions about the bureaucracy, do they really have much impact on agencies? Studies of a number of agencies have produced mixed results. A few studies find that they have little impact.[49] The most systematic set of studies was conducted by B. Dan Wood and Richard W. Waterman. They examined how the outputs of eight federal agencies — the Interstate Commerce Commission, the Equal Employment Opportunity Commission, the Federal Trade Commission, the Nuclear Regulatory Commission, the Food and Drug Administration, the National Highway Traffic Safety Commission, the Office of Surface Mining, and the Environmental Protection Agency — varied with levels of legislative attention and changes in presidential administrations and the appointment of top officials.[50] In the EPA case, for example, Wood and Waterman examined how congressional and presidential actions influenced the number of hazardous waste inspections, litigations, and fines the agency levied from 1981 to 1988.

Overall, Wood and Waterman's analysis drew three major conclusions. First, they found that presidential appointments had the strongest impact on agency behavior. In six of the eight cases, agencies responded to a change in leadership by altering its activities in a manner consistent with the preferences of the appointing president. Second, Congress matters as well. Congressional hearings and budget changes had a marked impact on agency outputs. And third, the impact executives and legislators had on the agencies varied with their structure. Agencies housed in executive departments, like the Office of Surface Mining in the Department of Interior, were more amenable to executive and legislative influence. But the independent regulatory commissions are partially protected from short-term influences; members are appointed with staggered terms overlapping presidential administrations. As a result, they were less responsive to executive and legislative direction. If interest organizations influence legislators or executives, then they can indirectly influence at least some agencies. The influence is limited, however, if the structure of an agency protects it from short-term control by political principals.

Federal Advisory Committees

Organized interests must obviously be concerned about the rules and regulations agencies adopt to implement laws. As with the FEC example introducing this chapter, the regulations that implement a statute can change its intent in significant ways. One way that organized interests participate in the policy process is through membership on advisory committees. At the national level, the Federal Advisory Committee Act of 1972 defines **federal advisory committees** (FACs) quite broadly. They include any committee established by reorganization plans, statutes, the president, or agencies for the purpose of obtaining advice or recommendations except those composed entirely of full-time federal employees. Currently, about a thousand FACs are in operation in the federal government. Given this broad definition and their large number, FACs vary considerably. Some are merely symbolic, while others exercise considerable influence over policy. Some maintain a carefully balanced representation of different interests. Others are clearly stacked to represent one point of view. Two examples illustrate this heterogeneity.

The National Energy Policy Development Group (NEPDG) was established by President George W. Bush shortly after his inauguration in 2001. Chaired by Vice President Dick Cheney, the NEPDG met secretly over a few short months on the new president's comprehensive energy policy. Few environmental and consumer organizations were invited to attend. And they understandably feared that the NEPDG's advice greatly influenced the energy policy proposals the president forwarded to Congress in May of 2001, including a controversial plan to open the Arctic National Wildlife Refuge to oil drilling. In fact, the very large number of organizations rumored to be participating in the NEPDG met for a very short time. This suggests that the advisory committee was more interested in mobilizing organizations to influence Congress — Mark Peterson's liaison as governing party — than about real policy planning.

The secrecy of the deliberations and the controversial proposals in the president's plan led many in Congress and the environmental community to wonder who was on the NEPDG. Vice President Cheney refused to list its members or release the minutes of its meetings, arguing that the president should be unhindered in seeking advice. Congress deferred to the president on the minutes, but maintained its right of access to a list of participants as part of its oversight duties. The General Accounting Office, Congress's audit agency, sued Mr. Cheney to release all documents relevant to the operation, but not the deliberations, of the NEPDG.[51]

While this suit was ongoing, two public interest organizations found an innovative end-run around the vice president's stonewalling. The NEPDG was largely staffed by employees of several federal departments, and their documents related to the meeting were clearly subject to public scrutiny. Thus, the liberal Natural Resources Defense Council sued the Energy Department and the conservative Judicial Watch sued seven different federal agencies for a release of documents related to the meetings of the NEPDG.[52] The documents provided by the Energy Department listed nearly 400 interest organizations participating in NEPDG meetings. The overwhelming majority were energy companies and associations, manufacturing firms, and other business associations. Environmental and consumer organizations were notably absent.

The NEPDG was not, however, typical of federal advisory committees. Most FACs are not established by the president. The greater number established by statute and agencies are appointed in a much more formal manner with explicit criteria for membership. Steven J. Balla and Jack Wright examined one such FAC, the National Drinking

Water Advisory Council (NDWAC) of the Environmental Protection Agency.[53] NDWAC was established by the Safe Drinking Water Act of 1974 to advise and consult with the EPA on issues of water quality and help determine EPA priorities among a variety of potential water-quality initiatives.

The EPA selects the members of NDWAC. But the act sets the membership at 15—five from the general public, five from state and local government agencies concerned with water, and five from private sector organizations with an interest in water quality issues. Each year the EPA solicits nominations for open seats on NDWAC. Of the 110 nominees from 1995 to 1997, 47 percent were nominated or endorsed by interest organizations. And those receiving these endorsements were significantly more likely to win appointments to NDWAC. Further, Balla and Wright found that the endorsing organizations were the same ones who were active in the initial passage of the Safe Drinking Water Act. They concluded that "representation on the advisory committee is broadly representative of interests that were active in the legislative debate over the Safe Water Drinking Act."[54] Thus, the structure and appointment process of FACs like the NDWAC reinforce the balance of forces operating when its authorizing statute was passed, thereby minimizing agency drift from the initial intent of Congress.

Our two examples represent extremes. In one case, the FAC was stacked on one side of a policy issue and operated out of the White House, shrouded by the protections of executive privilege and secrecy. The other FAC was rigorously balanced by statute and operated in the open within a federal agency. Which is more typical of FACs overall? The answer matters because the Federal Advisory Committee Act was passed in 1972 in part to reduce what many perceived as business domination of FACs. Studies in the 1970s and 1980s indicated that business interests were well represented on FACs—more than 20 percent. But consistent with the intent of the act, they did not dominate FAC membership overall. A more recent analysis by Michelle L. Chin and Eric Lindquist of the memberships of 172 health, agriculture, and science FACs in 2000 supports this earlier finding.[55] Two types of FACs they examined—grant review and special policy emphasis panels—were overwhelmingly comprised of academics. The members' affiliations of the remaining panels addressing policy and regulatory issues are reported in Figure 6-1. Academics

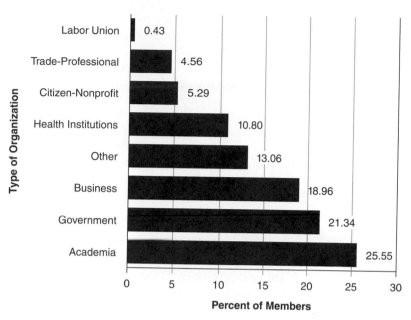

FIGURE 6-1 Affiliation of Members of Federal Health, Agriculture, and Science FACs, 2000

Source: Adapted from Michelle L. Chin and Eric Lindquist, "How Many Fish Swim in a Policy Stream? Federal Advisory Committees and Interest Group Participation in the Policymaking Process," paper presented at the Annual Meeting of the Midwest Political Science Association, Chicago, Illinois, April.

still comprise the largest set of members (25.55 percent), with public agency representatives closely following (21.34 percent). Business, professional, and trade associations together comprise 23.46 percent of members. Representatives of citizens and nonprofit organizations, in contrast, comprise only 5.29 percent. Judging whether a category under- or overrepresents a particular kind of interest is difficult. But it is clear that business interests are both well represented and yet do not fully dominate federal advisory boards.

Participation in Rule Making and Rule Application

Laws governing administrative procedures insure that the public, usually through organized interests, has an opportunity to **comment** on proposed rules and regulations. In some cases, organized interests participate in public **hearings** on applications of regulations to specific cases. We examine both types of influence activities below.

At the federal level, the Administrative Procedures Act requires that agencies publish a notice of intent to adopt or amend a rule in the *Federal Register*, a daily journal publishing federal rules and regulations. The public must then be provided with an opportunity to submit written comments on the proposed rule. The final regulation is published in the *Federal Register* along with an analysis of its statutory and factual basis and purpose. Marissa Golden's study of comments on 11 rule changes adopted by federal agencies in the early 1990s found that commenting on rules was common.[56] Three rules proposed by the Environmental Protection Agency (EPA) concerned acid rain, emission standards, and hazardous waste. The five National Highway and Transportation Safety Administration (NHTSA) rules concerned automobile warning devices, air brakes, child restraints, electric vehicles, and theft prevention. Designs for the elderly and disabled, drug prevention, and income eligibility rules for public housing were addressed by three rules proposed by the Department of Housing and Urban Development (HUD). On average, the proposed rules attracted 43.09 comments. But numbers varied widely. The HUD rule on housing design for the elderly and disabled attracted 268 comments. But its proposed rule on income eligibility for public housing generated only one.

Table 6-3 provides a good example of the participation of organized interests in the rule making process. The Wage and Hour Division of the U.S. Department of Law announced in the March 29, 1996, issue of the *Federal Register* that it proposed to revise the regulations enforcing the Migrant and Seasonal Agricultural Employee Act. Specifically, the department proposed to clarify definitions of "independent contractor" and "joint employment" under the act. The intent of the rule change was to insure that farmworkers employed through a labor subcontractor were still afforded protections provided by the act. In announcing the proposed rule change, the department presented background information on the legislative and judicial rulings associated with the rule change and invited comments from the public.[57]

The public comment period closed on June 12, 1996. In the meantime, 39 comments on the rules were received. Several were one-page statements, including a brief handwritten comment from one of the

TABLE 6-3 Comments on a Proposed Federal Rule Change

THE RULE CHANGE

The Agency: Wage and Hour Division of the Department of Labor

Proposed Rule Change: Amend the regulations of the Migrant and Seasonal Worker Protection Act to include definitions of "independent contractor" and clarify the definition of "joint employment."

Timetable: The proposed rule change was announced on March 29, 1996. The public comment period was closed June 12, 1996. The final rule change was announced on March 12, 1997.

THE COMMENTS

Members of Congress (1): A joint Comment by *Representatives George Miller and Howard Berman* supported of the rule change arguing that it fit the intent of Congress in writing the Migrant and Seasonal Worker Act.

Agricultural Employers and Associations (27): In general, the employers and employers' associations opposed the proposed rule, arguing that it created an overly strict standard that was lacking a sufficient factual basis.

Agricultural Producers, American Farm Bureau Federation, American Forest and Paper Association, American Pulpwood Association, California Grape and Tree Fruit League, Dale Bone Farms, Florida Citrus Mutual, Florida Fruit and Vegetable Association, Hood River Grower Shipper Association, Maine Farm Bureau Association, Marlin Medearis Ranches, Mecca Farms, Michigan Farm Bureau, Midwest Food Producers Association, National Cotton Ginners' Association, National Council of Agricultural Employers, New England Apple Council, Newman Ranch Company, Nisei Farmers League, Pennsylvania Farm Bureau, United State Sugar Association, Ventura County Agricultural Association, Virginia Apples, Virginia Farm Bureau Federation, Washington State Growers Clearing House Association, Washington State Farm Bureau, Zahn Ranch.

Labor Organizations, Farmworker Advocates, Legal Services Organizations and Attorneys (12): In general, the labor and farmworker advocacy organizations supported the rule change and proposed a further tightening of language to avoid ambiguities in its application.

AFL-CIO, California Rural Legal Assistance Foundation, Columbia Legal Services of Washington, Farmworker Justice Fund, Friends of Farmworkers of Pennsylvania, Garry Geffert, Migrant Farmworker Justice Project of Florida, Migrant Legal Action Program, National Council of La Raza, North Carolina Council of Churches, United Farmworkers of America, United Farmers — Texas Division (on behalf of themselves and 14 other organizations).

Source: Compiled by the authors from data provided by Susan Webb Yackee.

co-owners of Zahn Ranch. In contrast, the comment provided by Florida Citrus Mutual was 18 single-spaced pages of legal and economic analysis. One comment was received from two members of Congress stating that the proposed rule was compatible with the intent of Congress when it passed the Migrant and Seasonal Agricultural Employee Act. Another 26 comments were received from agricultural employers and associations. In general, they opposed the rule change, arguing that it was overly strict and lacked a factual justification. Comments were also received from 12 organizations representing labor, farmworkers, and legal advocates. These typically supported the proposed rule change. Thus, critical comments from employers' organizations outnumbered by two-to-one comments provided by those representing the employees who would benefit from the rule change. A review of rule-making across several agencies of the federal government indicates that this pattern is common. Traditional economic organizations are very heavily represented in comments on proposed rules and regulations. Indeed, the agricultural employment case is somewhat atypical in that a relatively large number of comments were submitted by citizens' and labor organizations.

The distribution of comments in the 11 rule proposals studied by Marissa Golden showed a strong presence of business interests.[58] As seen in Figure 6-2, on average, 83.43 percent of the comments on the three EPA rules were received from businesses or utilities. Business presence on the five NHTSA rules was even stronger. On average, 88.34 percent of the comments were submitted by business organizations, but only 17.03 percent of the comments received on the three HUD rule proposals on public housing were from businesses. Citizens's groups played a much smaller role. On average, they submitted only 2.17 percent of the comments on the EPA proposals, 2.22 percent of NHTSA comments, and 7.80 percent of the HUD comments. Other kinds of organizations are notably absent. The 11 rule proposals did not generate a single comment from a labor union. And the HUD rule on housing design for the elderly and disabled was the only one of the 11 rules to generate a comment from a professional association, which is included in the other category. While it is difficult to know how representative these 11 rule proposals are, they suggest that business participation in the rule-making process is substantial.

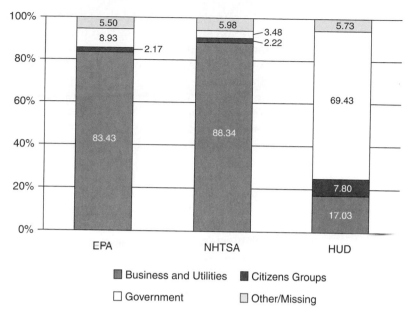

FIGURE 6-2 Comments on 11 Rules in Three Agencies by Type of Organization, 1990s

Source: Adapted from Marissa Martino Golden, "Interest Groups in the Rule-Making Process: Who Participates? Whose Values Get Heard?" *Journal of Public Administration Research and Theory* 8: 245–270 (1998).

Agencies are usually very attentive to comments received on proposed rule changes. When the Wage and Hour Division of the Labor Department published its final rule change in the *Federal Register* on March 12, 1997, a listing of all comments and a summary of the concerns they raised accompanied it. Such extended analysis was no accident. The department had compelling reasons to answer the comments over 11 tightly packed pages of statutory and legal analysis. Rules may be challenged in court if they are unlawful, capricious, or abuse an agency's discretion, so agencies must lay a legal foundation for their rules by addressing the concerns raised in the comment process. More importantly, proposed rules are often modified as a result of comments. In our agricultural employment example, the proposed rule was modified to some extent in response to the concerns of employer groups. This is typical of federal agency responses to the comments they receive on proposed rules. Susan

Webb Yackee's analysis of a sample of proposed rules across several agencies during the 1990s found strong evidence that the number of critical comments is strongly related to the degree of modification occurring in the rule between the time it is proposed and its final announcement.[59] And of the 11 rules examined by Marissa Golden, five had been modified to some degree, while three others were only modestly changed as a result of comments. Only two were not modified at all.[60] While it does not appear that organized interests can forestall the adoption of rules through participating in the comment process, they can modify its final products.

The same pattern of influence is evident in the participation by interest organizations in public hearings on proposed rules and their application. Judy B. Rosener's analysis of over 1,800 applications for building permits heard before three California Coastal Commissions found that their success depended greatly on the level of opposition they encountered.[61] When there was no opposition, 89 percent of the applications were approved. When one or more interest organizations testified against a permit request, the success rate fell to only 66 percent. Indeed, studies of state utility commissions[62] and water quality planning board[63] decisions suggest that environmental organizations are especially successful in using public hearings to influence agency decisions. In short, participation in public hearings can influence bureaucratic decisions, and this influence is not limited to traditional economic interests.

CONCLUSION

Political executives and bureaucrats influence both the laws legislatures adopt *and* how they are implemented. Organized interests cannot, therefore, focus solely on legislatures. But lobbying political executives and bureaucrats can be difficult. Access to political executives is limited for all interest organizations, but especially for those not politically aligned with an administration. And contacts with bureaucracy are usually more formal—through FACs and the rule-making process—than is true for legislators, but interest organizations are heard. Still, we have seen that scholars hold a number of competing views about the policy impacts of these interactions. Bureaucracies have been variously described as reservoirs of neutral competence readily serving political principals, captured by the organized interests they regulate, or dominating both organized interests and political principals.

Still others assume that the relationships among bureaucrats, political principals, and organized interests can vary depending on the political environment at a given time and whether agencies are designed to be open to external influences. This view, of course, is very consistent with the neopluralist interpretation of the politics of interest representation. It suggests that influence is real, but usually limited, modifying policy at the edges. Under some circumstances, however, organized interests can powerfully influence agency decision making, even to the point of being described as capture. But given the findings of studies on executive and legislative control of bureaucracy, it seems that in most circumstances organizations cannot control agencies in order to fully exclude democratic influences. Bureaucracy is rarely so independent that it is immune from either the influence of interest organizations or control by political principals.

KEY TERMS AND CONCEPTS

Executive Office of the President	Polyarchy
Liaison as Governing Party	Representative Bureaucracy
Liaison as Consensus Building	Interest Group Liberalism
Liaison as Outreach	Iron Triangle
Liaison as Legitimization	Issue Network
Elitism	Advocacy Coalition
Capture	Bureaucratic Dominance
Chicago School	Federal Advisory Committees
Executive Dominance	Comments
Legislative Dominance	Hearings

QUESTIONS ABOUT YOUR
INTEREST ORGANIZATION

1. Is your interest organization regulated by any federal or state bureaucracy? Describe the nature of the regulatory activity for up to three agencies.
2. If your organization is regulated by a federal independent regulatory commission, have any of its leaders had a prior career in the industry in which your organization works?

3. Does your interest organization provide goods or services to any federal or state bureaucracy? Describe the nature of the goods or services for up to three agencies.
4. Has your organization provided comments to any rules proposed by federal agencies? If so, describe the most recent proposed rule. What was your organization's position in its comment?
5. Given the interests of your organization, would you describe it as an ally or an enemy to the current White House or is it indifferent? Document your conclusion.

NOTES

1. Common Cause, "Statement by Common Cause President Scott Harshbarger on McCain-Feingold Victory in Senate," http://www.commoncause.org/mccainfeingold/victory/2002.htm, July 3, 2002.
2. Common Cause, "Joint Statement of Congressional Sponsors on the FEC Soft Money Rules," http://www.commoncause.org/publications/june02/062002_2.htm, July 3, 2002.
3. The act, however, may be declared unconstitutional before the rules dispute reaches the courts. After the bill was passed by the Senate, the National Rifle Association and Senator Mitch McConnell filed court challenges charging that it violated First Amendment protection of free speech. Within three months, Senator McConnell's suit was joined by over 60 interest and party organizations (John W. Dean, "Let the Fight Begin: Campaign Finance Reform Goes to Court," wysiwyg://http://writ.corporate.findlaw . . . nter_friendly.pl?page=/dean/200020329.html, July 3, 2002). Ironically, the job of defending the act will fall to Attorney General John Ashcroft and Solicitor General Theodore Olson, long-time opponents of campaign finance reform. The act's sponsors immediately filed court papers to intervene in the case in order to defend the constitutionality of the campaign finance reform law (StraighTalkAmerica, "Members of Congress File Papers to Defend Campaign Finance Reform Law in Court," http://www.StraightTalkAmerica.com/news/NewsPrint.cfm?ID=366&c=6, July 3, 2002).
4. Nelson C. Dometrius, "Governors: Their Heritage and Future." In *American State and Local Politics,* Ronald E. Weber and Paul Brace, eds. (New York: Chatham House Publishers, 1999), p. 64;

for a closer examination of the limits imposed on gubernatorial appointments in one state, see Gary D. Wekkin, "'Hogtied': The Powers of the Arkansas Governor's Office." Paper presented at the Annual Meeting of the Arkansas Political Science Association, Pine Bluff, Arkansas, February 1999.

5. Dometrius, "Governors: Their Heritage and Future," p. 65.
6. Jack L. Walker, Jr., *Mobilizing Interest Groups in America* (Ann Arbor: University of Michigan Press, 1991), p. 109.
7. Mark A. Peterson, "The Presidency and Organized Interest: White House Patterns of Interest Group Liaison," *American Political Science Review* 86: 617 (1992).
8. Mark A. Peterson and Jack L. Walker, Jr., "Interest Groups and the Reagan Presidency." In *Mobilizing Interest Groups in America,* Jack L. Walker, Jr. (Ann Arbor: University of Michigan Press, 1991), p. 150.
9. Peterson, "The Presidency and Organized Interest," pp. 612–625.
10. Ibid., p. 615.
11. Ibid., p. 616.
12. U.S. Department of Veterans Affairs Home Page, http://www.va.gov, July 20, 2002.
13. Terry M. Moe, "Control and Feedback in Economic Regulation: The Case of the NLRB," *American Political Science Review* 79: 1096 (1985).
14. David Lowery, "Public Choice When Services Are Costs: The Divergent Case of Assessment Administration," *American Journal of Political Science* 6: 57–76 (1982).
15. Robert M. Stein, "Arranging City Services," *Journal of Public Administration Research and Theory* 3: 79 (1993).
16. Steven Rathgeb Smith and Judith Smyth, "Contracting for Services in a Decentralized System," *Journal of Public Administration Research and Theory* 6: 277–296 (1996).
17. John W. Schoen, "Is the SEC Up to the Task? Agency Is Underfunded and Outgunned Say Former Staffers," http://www.msnbc.com/779076.asp, July 7, 2002.
18. The following section borrows heavily, if selectively and with modification, from Larry B. Hill: "Who Governs the American Administrative State? A Bureaucratic-Centered Image of Governance," *Journal of Public Administration Research and Theory* 1: 261–294 (1991).
19. David R. Truman, *The Governmental Process* (New York: Alfred A. Knopf, 1951).

20. C. Wright Mills, *The Power Elite* (New York: Oxford University Press, 1956).

21. Floyd Hunter, *Community Power Structure* (Chapel Hill, North Carolina: University of North, Carolina Press, 1953); for a more recent application of the power elite perspective, see G. William Domhoff, *The Power Elite and the State* (Aldine de Gruyter, 1990).

22. Marver H. Bernstein, *Regulating Business By Independent Commissions* (Princeton, N.J.: Princeton University Press, 1955).

23. CNN.com/Inside Politics, "SEC Chairman Says He Won't Step Down," http://www.cnn.com/2002/ALLPOLITICS/07/14/harvey.pitt/index.htlm. July 14, 2002.

24. John W. Schoen, "Is the SEC Up to the Task? Agency Is Underfunded and Outgunned Say Former Staffers," http://www.msnbc.com/779076.asp, July 7, 2002.

25. Prior research has confirmed that former industry insiders who serve on independent regulatory bodies tend to rule in favor of their former employers more often than those coming from other career backgrounds, although the relationship is not a strong one. See William T. Gormley, Jr., "A Test of the Revolving Door Hypothesis at the FCC," *American Journal of Political Science* 23: 665–683 (1979).

26. George Stigler, "The Theory of Economic Regulation," *Bell Journal of Economics and Management* 2: 3–21 (1971); Robert Barro, "The Control of Politicians: An Economic Model," *Public Choice* 14: 19–42 (1973); Sam Peltzman, "Toward a More General Theory of Regulation," *Journal of Law and Economics* 19: 211–240 (1976).

27. Ann Bartel and Lacy Glenn Thomas, "Predation through Legislation: The Wage and Profit Effects of the Occupational Safety and Health Administration," *Journal of Law and Economics* 30: 239–264 (1987).

28. For a general review of the tools used to control bureaucracy, see William T. Gormley, Jr., *Taming the Bureaucracy: Muscles, Prayers, and Other Strategies* (Princeton, NJ: Princeton University Press, 1989); B. Dan Wood, "Principal-Agent Models of Political Control of the Bureaucracy," *American Political Science Review* 83: 970–978 (1989).

29. Jonathan Bendor, Serge Taylor, and Roland Van Gaalen, "Stacking the Deck: Bureaucratic Missions and Policy Design," *American Political Science Review* 81: 873–896 (1987).

30. Arthur A. Schlesinger, *The Imperial Presidency* (Boston: Houghton Mifflin, 1973); Richard P. Nathan, *The Administrative Presidency* (New York: John Wiley and Sons, 1983).

31. Barry R. Weingast, "The Congressional-Bureaucratic System: A Principal-Agent Perspective (with Applications to the SEC)," *Public Choice* 44: 147–191 (1984); Barry R. Weingast and Mark J. Moran," Bureaucratic Discretion or Congressional Control? Regulatory Policymaking by the Federal Trade Commission," *Journal of Political Economy* 91: 765–800 (1983); Terry M. Moe, "An Assessment of the Positive Theory of 'Congressional Dominance,'" *Legislative Studies Quarterly* 12: 475–520 (1987).

32. Matthew McCubbins and Thomas Schwartz, "Congressional Oversight Overlooked: Police Patrols versus Fire Alarms," *American Journal of Political Science* 28: 165–179 (1984).

33. Robert A. Dahl and Charles E. Lindblom, *Politics, Economics, and Welfare* (New York: Harper and Brothers, 1953).

34. Kenneth J. Meier and Lloyd G. Nigro, "Representative Bureaucracy and Policy Preferences," *Public Administration Review* 36: 458–479 (1976); Samuel Krislov and David H. Rosenblom, *Representative Bureaucracy and the American Political System* (New York: Praeger, 1981).

35. Kenneth J. Meier, "Latinos and Representative Bureaucracy: Testing the Thompson and Henderson Hypotheses, *Journal of Public Administration Research and Theory* 3: 393–414 (1993).

36. Theodore J. Lowi, *The End of Liberalism* (New York: W. W. Norton, 1979).

37. Douglas Cater, *Power in Washington* (New York: Random House, 1964).

38. William Gormley, "Regulatory Issue Networks in a Federal System," *Polity* 18: 595–620 (1986).

39. Paul A. Sabatier, "An Advocacy Coalition Framework for Policy Change and the Role of Policy-Oriented Learning Therein," *Policy Sciences* 21: 129–168 (1988).

40. Frank R. Baumgartner and Bryan D. Jones, *Agendas and Instability in American Politics* (Chicago: University of Chicago Press, 1993).

41. Jacques Ellul, *The Technological Society* (New York: Alfred A. Knopf, 1964).

42. William A. Niskanen, *Bureaucracy and Representative Government* (Chicago: Aldine, 1971).

43. Graham T. Allison, *Essence of Decision* (Boston: Little Brown, 1971).
44. John Brehm and Scott Gates, *Working, Shirking, and Sabotage* (Ann Arbor: University of Michigan Press, 1997).
45. Morris S. Ogul, *Congress Oversees the Bureaucracy* (Pittsburgh: University of Pittsburgh Press, 1976); still, others argue that oversight hearings have become more important since Watergate, given the frequency of divided government. From the Iran-Contra in the Reagan Administration to the Whitewater hearings in the Clinton Administration, the party controlling Congress has found opportunities to use hearings to skewer presidents of the other party.
46. McCubbins and Schwartz, "Congressional Oversight Overlooked."
47. Peri Arnold, *Making the Managerial Presidency*, 2nd ed. (Lawrence, Kansas: University of Kansas Press, 1998); Paul C. Light, *The Tides of Reform* (New Haven: Yale University Press, 1997); David Lowery, "The Presidency and the Bureaucracy: A Gentle Plea for Chaos," *Presidential Studies Quarterly* 30: 79–108 (2000).
48. Marc Kaufman, "Top FDA Post Remains Vacant: Politics, Industry Demands Have Delayed Appointment," http://www.msnbc.com/news/780452.asp, July 15, 2002.
49. Daniel P. Carpenter, "Groups, the Media, Agency Waiting Costs, and FDA Drug Approval," *American Journal of Political Science* 46: 490–505 (2002).
50. B. Dan Wood and Richard W. Waterman, *Bureaucratic Dynamics* (Boulder, Colorado: Westview Press, 1994).
51. David M. Walker, "Decision of the Comptroller General Concerning NEPDG Litigation," Washington, DC: General Accounting Office, January 30, 2002.
52. The Center for Responsive Politics, "Energy Task Force Documents," http://opensecrets.org/news/energy_task_force/index.asp, July 4, 2002.
53. Steven J. Balla and John R. Wright, "Interest Groups, Advisory Committees, and Congressional Control of Bureaucracy," *American Journal of Political Science* 45: 799–812 (2001).
54. Ibid., pp. 810–811.
55. Michelle L. Chin and Eric Lindquist, "How Many Fish Swim in a Policy Stream? Federal Advisory Committees and Interest

Group Participation in the Policymaking Process." Paper presented at the Annual Meeting of the Midwest Political Science Association, Chicago, Illinois, April 2002.

56. Marissa Martino Golden, "Interest Groups in the Rule-Making Process: Who Participates? Whose Values Get Heard?" *Journal of Public Administration Research and Theory* 8: 245–270 (1998).

57. We wish to thank Susan Webb Yackee for providing us this example and copies of the comments. The interpretation, however, is our own.

58. Golden, "Interest Groups in the Rule-Making Process," 253–255; The data in Figure 6-1 were recalculated from Golden's data.

59. Susan Webb Yackee, *Interest Group Participation and Bureaucratic Rulemaking*, Dissertation, Department of Political Science, University of North Carolina at Chapel Hill, January 2003.

60. Golden, "Interest Groups in the Rule-Making Process," 260.

61. Judy B. Rosener, "Making Bureaucrats Responsive," *Public Administration Review* 42: 339–345 (1982).

62. William T. Gormley, Jr., "Policy, Politics, and Public Utility Regulation," *American Journal of Politics Science* 27: 99 (1983).

63. David Godschalk and Bruce Stiftel, "Making Waves: Public Participation in State Water Planning," *Journal of Applied Behavioral Science* 17: 597–614 (1981).

CHAPTER 7

Organized Interests and the Judiciary

In the introduction of Chapter 6, we saw how political actors may turn to the courts when they have been disappointed in other arenas. Dissatisfied by the rules the Federal Election Commission (FEC) adopted to implement the Bipartisan Campaign Reform Act, its several congressional sponsors vowed to take the FEC to court if they were unsuccessful in revising the statute's implementing regulations in Congress. Even before the FEC ruled, Senator Mitch McConnell and the National Rifle Association filed separate suits to overturn the act on the grounds that it violated First Amendment protections of free speech. Such legal challenges can have a profound impact on public policy. This potential ensures that organized interests are highly attentive to the actions of the judicial branch as they pursue their policy objectives.

The FEC example, however, does not illustrate the full scope of courts' participation in the policy process nor the many ways that organized interests engage the courts. A much better example is provided by the four-decade-long struggle over smoking, a battle described in detail by Martha Derthick in *Up in Smoke: From Legislation to Litigation in Tobacco Politics*. For four decades, local, state, and national legislatures have passed a number of restrictions on smoking and the advertising of tobacco products. Bureaucracies have been involved, too, from the 1964 U.S. Surgeon General's report identifying the health hazards of smoking to the U.S. Food and Drug Administration's (FDA) attempted regulation of tobacco in 1996. But the battle over tobacco has been fought time and again in the courts. Tobacco companies have defended themselves in numerous individual and class action suits brought by former smokers. While largely successful from the companies' perspective, the costs of this litigation were high. By 1997, the six largest tobacco companies were spending more than $600 million per year in legal fees, and there was no end in sight; more than 300 cases were pending. But suits from smokers and their relatives were only part of the story. Following the 1994 lead of Mississippi Attorney General Mike Moore, most states sued to recover from tobacco companies Medicaid costs attributable to smoking. The attorneys general of 46 states finally settled their case with tobacco manufacturers in 1998, a settlement overseen by the federal courts. Tobacco companies have also skillfully used the courts to block regulation by both national and state governments. The industry successfully fought FDA regulation of tobacco in the federal courts, winning a 5-4 Supreme Court decision in 2000 that the FDA had no jurisdiction over smoking products. And in 2001, the tobacco companies used the federal courts to limit state jurisdiction on the regulation of advertising of tobacco products. Based on this long record of court cases, Martha Derthick concluded that it constituted a national experiment in "regulation by litigation."[1]

The history of tobacco litigation may be an extreme example of the pursuit of public policy in the courts. But like tobacco companies and their opponents, many organized interests are active across the full range of judicial venues provided by American government. On some issues, such as the politics of smoking, organized interests drive public policy issues back and forth from legislatures through administrative agencies to the courts as different venues offer potential advantages in securing their interests. The remainder of this chapter examines how organized interests pursue influence through the judicial branch. We examine first the special nature of the courts as an arena for exercising influence. We then examine both direct and indirect influence strategies organized interests employ, including assessing their effectiveness. Finally, we examine the kinds of organized interests that seek to influence public policy through the judicial branch. In this last topic, we return to our three general interpretations of the politics of interest representations—the pluralist, transactions, and neopluralist schools.

THE SPECIAL NATURE OF COURTS

The judicial branch of government includes a complex array of courts. At the state level, these include both limited jurisdiction trial courts (e.g., small claims courts), general jurisdiction trial courts (e.g., municipal or county courts), and appeals courts. The most recognized state appeals courts are state supreme courts. Most states, however, now employ a system of intermediate appeals courts to reduce the number of cases coming before their supreme courts. Paralleling this structure, federal courts are hierarchically organized from U.S. district and equivalent specialized courts, which hear trials, through U.S. courts of appeal, to the U.S. Supreme Court. Public policy claims may be pursued through all of these venues.

Lobbying the courts, however, is not like lobbying a legislature or the public. More than any other arena of lobbying, courts are highly *formalized, stylized,* and *specialized.* These traits limit the methods that organized interests can employ to directly influence the decisions of juries and judges. Judicial decision making is *formalized* in the sense that it centers not on public policy issues and their merits per se, but on the individual cases that come before them and the specific legal issues these cases raise. This simple fact has important implications for pursuing a policy agenda through the courts. Most importantly, it means that not just anyone concerned about an issue can approach the courts. No matter how concerned environmentalists are about the global warming or how opposed right-to-life advocates might be to abortion, such concern alone does not merit access to the courts. This is quite different from interactions with other institutions of government. No matter what stake they have in the outcome of a policy controversy, citizens can always take their concerns to legislators or executives. By contrast, those who want to use the courts must be specifically and directly involved in a concrete legal dispute with another party. To put it technically, they must have **standing.** Courts must often decide whether would-be litigants have standing, and their increasingly strict standards can make it difficult for organizations to pursue policies through the judicial branch.[2] Still, organized interests often show that they have a stake in the policy issues *raised by a case* and that the case poses a genuine legal dispute, not merely an abstract question of public policy.

Even granted standing, interest organizations find that influencing courts entails a highly *stylized* form of lobbying. Indeed, it is not lobbying in anything like the conventional sense in which we often employ the term—sitting down with a judge and talking through a broad range of policy and political concerns as a lobbyist might do with a legislator. Simply put, courts are expected to consider a narrower range of issues than those addressed in other political venues. Policy disputes in the electoral, legislative, and executive arenas might address public opinion, the technical merits of a policy, and/or its impact on electoral coalitions. But only legal and factual issues matter in courts, at least directly. Thus, the moral issues motivating opposition to abortion by right-to-life advocates or the financial burdens of regulatory policies that lead corporations to seek relief from courts can be obscured in court proceedings. These concerns, are, of course, still there, but they are often hidden behind legal issues concerning constitutional rights or the regulatory procedures agencies use. Naturally, courts, especially appellate courts, are often concerned about the policy ramifications of their decisions. Nevertheless, they must be linked to the issues of law raised by the cases that come before them.

Influence with the courts is also highly *specialized.* Mobilizing constituents and contacting legislators, we have seen, constitute the heart of legislative lobbying. Doing these tasks well often requires deep substantive information about public policy and knowledge about politics. But perhaps with the exception of elected judges, an issue we consider later, courts are rarely concerned about public opinion. And contacting a judge to discuss a case or its political implications is inappropriate. He or she would have to withdraw from considering the case.[3] Rather, direct contacts between judges and interest organizations are limited to briefs filed with a court on the legal issues before it and arguments about them within court. So, while lawyers are well represented among the ranks of lobbyists working at all stages of the policy process, they necessarily dominate efforts to directly influence courts. Both through their training and the tasks they perform, lawyers are among the most specialized professionals in the lobbying community,[4] and not just any lawyer will do. Research by Kevin McGuire on U.S. Supreme Court cases indicates that experience matters a great deal.[5] Cases are far more likely to be decided in favor of a lawyer's client if the lawyer has prior experience before the Court, especially if a lawyer had served as a clerk of the Court earlier in his or her career.

INFLUENCING THE COURTS

Organized interests try to influence judicial decision making in three ways. Paralleling the distinction between indirect and direct lobbying of legislators examined in earlier chapters, influence with the courts is sought both before judges are seated and while they decide cases.

Influencing Judicial Appointments

The first method is indirect. We have seen that legislative scholars distinguish between electoral and access strategies. Electoral strategies try to influence who votes in legislatures by supporting candidates for office who are friendly to an organized interest and opposing those less likely to favor its policy goals. Access strategies, in contrast, try to influence the behaviors of sitting legislators. While sometimes engaging in both types of strategies, organized interests tend to emphasize access strategies when it comes to legislators. But relying on an access strategy may be less useful with courts. That is, the highly stylized, formalized, and specialized nature of the courts limits access to judges and the kinds of direct influence organized interests can employ. Therefore, it makes sense for organized interests to try to influence who the judges are in the first place. If the "right" judges end up serving on a court, an organization may not need to employ more direct modes of influence. And when access is needed, it may be obtained more easily.

Influencing judicial appointments, rather than trying to directly influence judicial decisions, has a further advantage in that appointments take place in arenas in which organized interests are very active. The president, with the consent of the Senate, appoints all federal judges. State judges secure their appointments in a variety of ways. In 10 states, they run for office in partisan elections. Judges are elected in nonpartisan elections in 12 states. Sixteen states employ the Missouri Plan, whereby governors first appoint judges recommended by a committee. The judges then stand in retention elections after serving on a court. And judges in the remaining 12 states arrive on the bench by some combination of gubernatorial appointment and legislative election. While methods of appointment vary, they all occur within legislative, executive, or electoral arenas in which organized interests are regular players. And the means they employ to influence judicial appointments are not limited to the legal tools used in courts. Rather, they include the full set of influence tactics routinely used while lobbying legislatures or shaping elections. In short, influencing who makes decisions, rather than directly influencing the decisions per se, may be especially attractive when it comes to influencing courts.

Gregory Caldiera, Marie Hojnacki, and John Wright conducted the most comprehensive study of lobbying activity on federal judicial appointments.[6] They examined lobbying activities on 15 appointments by 170 of the 299 interest organizations that had taken a position on at least one judicial nomination from 1984 through 1991. They found that lobbying activity varied considerably across the 15 appointments. This finding is important because two controversial Supreme Court nominations — the failed nomination of Robert Bork by President Reagan in 1987 and the successful nomination of Clarence Thomas by the first President Bush in 1990 — were marked by intense conflict among organized interests. Many critics decried what they viewed as an intense politicization of judicial appointments. Many interest organizations lobbied actively on the Bork (145 interest organizations) and Thomas (81) nominations. But these were atypical. Only eight organizations lobbied over one lower federal court nomination. And even the 1987 nomination of Anthony Kennedy to the U.S. Supreme Court, coming between the highly charged Bork and Thomas nominations, generated lobbying activity by only 39 interest organizations. Thus, while organized interests can play an active role in federal judicial nominations, they do not always to do so. And, in general, lobbying over appointments decreases as we move from Supreme Court nominations down to district courts in the federal hierarchy.

Caldiera, Hojnacki, and Wright also found, however, that once organizations decide to become active, they tend to employ the full array of influence tools available to them. They organize letter writing and phone call campaigns, dispense leaflets, inform the media about research on the nominees, testify, lobby legislators, and work in coalition with like-minded organizations. Thus, the influence activities used by organized interests on federal judicial nominations are similar to those used to influence the passage of legislation. An example of a more recent effort by one organization, the National Organization for Women, to influence the Senate's confirmation of a federal judge is discussed in Interest Organization Example 7-1. Consistent with the findings of Caldiera and his colleagues, NOW employed everything in its arsenal to stop the appointment of D. Brooks Smith to the Third Circuit Court of Appeals, including research of his prior decisions, email and phone calls to senators, and a public protest.

Electoral tactics are not available as a way to exercise influence with the federal judiciary, but state courts provide us a valuable opportunity to look at the impact of elections on judicial decision making. Do organized interests engage actively in judicial elections in states that select judges in this manner? The anecdotal evidence suggests that they do not always take advantage of this opportunity to influence judicial selection; most judicial elections are fairly quiet affairs in which incumbents are routinely reelected. But some judicial elections attract considerable attention on the part of organized interests.[7] In a few notable cases state judges have been denied reelection over controversial decisions they have made, elections in which interest organizations played a prominent role. In one such case, outrage by women's organizations led to the recall and defeat in a subsequent special election of Wisconsin judge Archie Simonson in 1977 after he justified reduction of a convicted rapist's sentence because the female victim's manner of dress "invited" the assault.[8] As with appointments to the federal bench, organized interests can become heavily involved in state and local judicial elections, but they do not always or routinely do so.

Still, even the potential of contested elections may influence judicial decisions. If judges think that their decisions may have electoral consequences, they may be more inclined to vote on cases in a manner more consistent with the electorate's preferences. This will advantage organized interests whose goals coincide with public opinion, while disadvantaging others less in tune with the electorate. Research indicates that public opinion does influence judicial decisions in states that elect judges. An examination of state supreme court actions from 1974 to 1973 found that elected courts are more likely to review conservative abortion decisions of lower

INTEREST ORGANIZATION EXAMPLE 7-1

Here Comes the Judge — Not!

Founded in 1966, the National Organization for Women (NOW) has half a million members, making it the largest feminist organization in the United States. Organized in 550 chapters, NOW charges dues of $15 to $35. NOW chapters sponsor a number of activities for members. NOW holds an annual national conference, and members receive a copy of *National NOW Times* five times a year. While active on a range of issues, NOW is especially active on issues concerning economic equality for women and abortion and reproductive rights. NOW lobbies state and national legislators directly as well as by mobilizing member letter, phone, and email campaigns. NOW also sponsors PACs to support friendly candidates for both national (NOW/PAC) and state and local (NOW Equality PAC) office. Judicial appointments are a special focus for NOW.

In the summer of 2002, NOW campaigned against President George Bush's nomination of D. Brooks Smith to the Third Circuit Court of Appeals. NOW argued that Smith had reneged on a 1988 promise when appointed as a federal district judge to resign from an all male social club. NOW also claimed that Judge Smith's decisions were insensitive to claims of employment discrimination and violence against women. To defeat Smith's nomination, NOW conducted and publicized in-depth reports on his prior decisions as a federal judge, organized a phone/e-mail campaign to urge Senators to vote no, and publicly protested his nomination outside of the federal court building in Philadelphia. NOW was especially critical of a handful of Democratic senators who voted for Smith on the Judiciary Committee. A press release, for example, pointed out that Senator John Edwards "hid out in his office across the hall from the hearing, and didn't even have the courage to cast his 'yes' vote in public."

Source: http://www.now.org, visited June 20, 2002

courts if their state electorates are more liberal.[9] Elected supreme court judges are also less likely to vote to overturn death penalty convictions and less likely to invalidate state laws restricting abortion rights than are appointed judges.[10] Fear of electoral retribution, it seems, provides at least a potential influence lever for some organized interests. But it is a lever only available to interest organizations with public opinion on their side.

Engaging in Litigation

Except for state judges who must stand for reelection, the highly formalized, stylized, and specialized nature of the courts provides only a limited number of ways for organized interests to directly influence court decisions. Two are especially important. First, interest organizations engage directly in litigation. While most cases in trial courts do not involve organized interests, they are not strangers to trial courts. Indeed, one study of civil suits filed with the Minnesota federal district court, for example, found that organized interests were involved in fully 18.52 percent of the cases.[11]

Organized interests may become involved in litigation in several ways. First, trade and professional associations and some membership groups, such as labor unions, often defend members in court on issues that are important to all of their members. New York City's 29,000-member Patrolmen's Benevolent Association, for example, maintains a legal defense fund to support its members when they are challenged in court for actions the union construes as part of their official duties. Such defensive efforts sometimes can be quite proactive. For example, New York City's Captains Benevolent Association, the police captains' union, sued to dissolve the Mollen Commission as it prepared to examine charges of police corruption.[12] Similarly, institutions such as corporations and local governments often appear in court to defend their interests. Like the tobacco companies discussed earlier, the Microsoft Corporation spent considerable time and money in the courts during 2000 and 2001 fending off U.S. Justice Department charges that it engaged in monopolistic practices undermining the computer software market. Public institutions also defend their interests in court. During its 2001 term, for example, the U.S. Supreme Court considered the case of *Clark County School District* v. *Shirley A. Breeden,* in which the Nevada school system defended itself against complaints that it had retaliated against an employee who had earlier charged the district with sexual harassment.

Direct litigation is usually limited to defending the institution or a member of a voluntary organization. In some cases, however, the interests of a broader set of plaintiffs than just the members of an organization may be defended in **class action suits.** Class action suits represent the interests of similarly situated individuals whether or not they are active participants in the case. Any member of the class can petition the court to be head plaintiff in the case. When the rules governing standing in class action suits were relaxed somewhat in the 1960s, class action suits became a popular tool of citizens' groups working on environmental and consumer issues. But these rules have tightened considerably in recent years. Members of the class must be notified of the pending case, and plaintiffs must show that members of a class have a direct and important stake in a case's outcome. As a result, the number of class action suits has declined from over 3,000 per year in the mid-1970s to well under a thousand in recent years. Whether litigation is on behalf of an individual, an institution, or a class of citizens, public policies can change in marked ways as a result of a court decision. For most cases, however, it should always be remembered that these larger public policy consequences are more inadvertent than intended. To reemphasize this critically important point, the goal of most litigation has less to do with public policy per se than redress of a specific grievance.

Less frequently, however, organized interests litigate by sponsoring **test cases** with the explicit purpose of shaping broader public policy. In such cases, the interest organization is not defending its own interests or those of a member per se. Rather, they provide a legal team to prepare and argue a case on an issue important to the organization. For example, civil liberties organizations, like the American Civil Liberties Union, often support criminal defendants. This is not because they sanction crime. Rather, criminal cases provide a good context in which to litigate many questions regarding the meaning of important provisions of the Constitution's Bill of Rights. The interest organizations sponsoring test cases are often ideologically oriented issue advocacy groups with strong views about public policy. Whether working on their own or as a subsidiary of a larger interest organization, many of these organizations have been labeled **public interest law firms.** They often develop and test novel legal arguments that might advance an interest. In this sense, public interest law firms share some characteristics with think tanks, as discussed in Chapter 4. Both seek to develop new ideas that might frame a public policy issue in a new light. In the case of law firms, these new ideas are presented in court.

In the hands of a public interest law firm, the right case can act as a powerful lever to move public policy closer to its preferred position. The NAACP's Legal Defense Fund victory in *Brown v. Board of Education of Topeka, Kansas* is surely the most famous example of a test case. Following the NAACP's lead, liberal organizations were for many years especially active in promoting test cases. More recently, however, conservative interest organizations have also followed the lead of the NAACP. For example, The American Center for Law and Justice (ACLJ), a public interest law firm founded in 1990 by the Reverend Pat Robertson's Christian Coalition, sponsored *Campbell v. St. Tammany Parish School Board*. The ACLJ argued that the Louisiana school district's facilities should be open for use by the Louisiana State Christian Coalition for discussion of issues from a Christian point of view, given that they were made available to other groups in the community.[13] Although it is a highly specialized form of advocacy, sponsoring test cases is now common among organizations on both sides of the ideological spectrum.

How successful are interest organizations in court? Based in part on the NAACP's record, organized interests were often reputed to be highly successful litigants. Lee Epstein and C. K. Rowland examined this question more systematically by examining decisions on the merits of cases in U.S. district courts from 1968 to 1980.[14] They matched a series of cases that were similar in all respects — topic, legal issue, year, and judge — except for the litigant. In one set of cases, the litigant was an interest organization. Private counsels filed the other set of cases. Contrary to the strong reputation of organized interests, the cases filed by interest organizations were no more successful than those brought by private litigants. So, while litigation can be an important policy lever for organized interests, it is not a certain one.

Filing Amicus Curiae Briefs

While sponsoring test cases can powerfully affect public policy, they are also very expensive. A legal team must be supported over what may be years of effort. For example, it took the NAACP's Legal

Defense Fund 15 years and an estimated $500,000 to secure its 1954 victory in *Brown* v. *Board of Education* after first committing itself to challenge the "separate but equal" doctrine.[15] Obviously, sponsoring a test case today can be far more expensive, so a second means organized interests employ to directly influence judicial decisions is filing of **amicus curiae** or "friend of the court" briefs. Amicus curiae filings are briefs submitted by interested parties other than those directly participating in a case. At one time, amicus briefs were viewed, in the words of one student of the U.S. Supreme Court, as "sources of dispassionate advice, a way to help guarantee that the members of the court would make fully informed decisions."[16] Now, however, they are used by organized interests to highlight their concerns about a case. In effect, friend of the court briefs allow organized interests to chime in on any case they believe may bear on their concerns.

Courts will not accept friend of the court briefs from just anyone. An organization must have the permission of the parties to the case or, lacking permission of the parties, they can petition the court for permission to submit a brief. But courts rarely refuse permission, given a reasonable argument that an organization has something at stake in the decision or special expertise bearing on its merits. Filing amicus briefs is expensive. One estimate from the late 1980s suggested that preparing a friend of the court brief costs from $15,000 to $20,000.[17] But given that this is still much less expensive than sponsoring a test case, it is not surprising that use of amicus briefs has increased markedly over recent decades. Amicus briefs were filed in only 20 percent of the cases decided by the U.S. Supreme Court in the 1950s. In the last decade, however, the rate of amicus filings rose to over 90 percent.[18] While only a handful of amicus briefs are filed on most cases, others attract the attention of many organized interests. *Webster* v. *Reproductive Health Services,* for example, a key abortion rights case in 1980, generated 78 amicus briefs signed by more than 400 interest organizations.[19]

A more recent example of a politically charged case is *Zelman* v. *Simmons-Harris,* decided by the U.S. Supreme Court in 2002. The Court upheld on a 5-4 vote the constitutionality of Cleveland, Ohio's publicly funded school voucher program. As seen in Table 7-1, this case generated 13 friend of the court briefs at the **merits stage** of the case when the decision is made. Ten briefs, submitted by 43 interest organizations, supported the use of school vouchers. The remaining

TABLE 7-1 *Amici Curiae* in *Zelman* v. *Simmons-Harris*

AMICI IN SUPPORT OF CLEVELAND SCHOOL VOUCHER PROGRAM

American Center for Law and Justice

American Education Reform Council

Becket Fund for Religious Liberty

Black Alliance for Educational Options

Center for Education Reform, American Legislative Exchange Council, Arizona
School Choice Trust, California Parents for Education Choice, Coalition for Parental
Choice in Education, Education Excellence Coalition, Floridians for School Choice,
Illinois Coalition for Parental Choice, Maine School Choice Coalition, United New
Yorkers for Choice in Education, Center for Equal Opportunity, Center for Public
Justice, Children First: CEO Kansas, Citizens for Education Freedom, Educational
Freedom Foundation, Commonwealth Foundation of Pennsylvania, Excellent
Education for Everyone, "I Have a Dream" Foundation, Hispanic Council for
Reform and Educational Options, Minnesota Business Partnership, Nevada
Manufacture's Association, Pennsylvania Manufacturers Association, Associated
Industries of Vermont, Texas Justice Foundation, Toussaint Institute, Urban League
of Miami, Beatrice D. Flower of the Brevard County School Board, Kyle Persinger of
the Marion School Board

Center for Individual Freedom, Cato Institute, Milton and Rose D. Friedman
Foundation, Goldwater Institute

Claremont Institute Center for Constitutional Jurisprudence

Pacific Legal Foundation, Independent Voices for Better Education, Teachers for
Better Education, Ira J. Paul, Robert N. Wright

United States Government

Vermonters for Better Education

AMICI IN OPPOSITION TO THE CLEVELAND SCHOOL VOUCHER PROGRAM

Anti-Defamation League

Ohio School Boards Association, Ohio Association of School Business Officers,
Buckeye Association of School Administrators, Ohio Coalition for Equity and
Adequacy of School Funding, Coalition of Rural and Appalachian Schools, Ohio
Association of Secondary School Administrators

American Jewish Committee, Baptist Joint Committee on Public Affairs, Hadassah,
Jewish Council for Public Affairs, National Council of Churches of Christ, National
Council of Jewish Women, Union of American Hebrew Congregations, United
Church of Christ's Justice and Witness Ministries

Source: http://www.findlaw.com

three briefs, signed by 15 organizations, urged the Court to find Ohio's program to be unconstitutional. It is not surprising that many of the organizations on both sides are citizens' groups concerned about education or church-state relations. But think tanks (such as the Cato Institute) and public interest law firms (such as the Pacific Legal Foundation) filed briefs as well, as did several business associations with less obvious interests in school vouchers. Such conservative organizations are strong supporters of vouchers. This case also illustrates how court cases and the policy issues they raise can sometimes make for strange bedfellows. Three fundamentalist Christian organizations sided with a number of usually liberal Jewish organizations in opposing voucher programs. Both sets of groups were fearful of government intrusions into the religious sphere of life. And several typically liberal black and Hispanic organizations, faced with decaying urban schools, joined forces with many libertarian groups in supporting the Cleveland voucher initiative.

Amicus curiae briefs provide the court with additional arguments that may not be provided in the briefs of the parties to a case. First, they provide courts with information about the importance of a case by identifying how a decision will impact segments of society. Conflicting amici, especially, tell judges that there is a real controversy and that it matters to somebody. Such signals are vitally important for those appellate courts, like the U.S. Supreme Court, that are not required to hear all of the cases submitted for their consideration. Indeed, the great demand for review of cases by the Supreme Court, coupled by its broad discretion over its docket, means that it considers only a fraction of the cases submitted to it. In the 2000 term, for example, 7,852 cases were filed with the U.S. Supreme Court. During the same term, the Supreme Court heard oral arguments on only 86 cases. Thus, appellate courts with discretionary dockets must first sort through cases to identify those that most merit their attention. This is the **certiorari stage** or cert stage of the judicial decision process in which courts decide what to decide. That is, before a case can be heard, plaintiffs must file a petition for a writ of certiorari, asking the appellate court to review the decision of a lower court. Most petitions, we have seen, are denied. Courts employ a variety of criteria to decide which cases are important, including conflicts among lower court decisions, who the parties in the case are, and the preferences of the judges.[20] But the impact of a decision on society also matters, and amicus curiae briefs provide direct evidence for justices that interests in society care about the outcome of a case.

Do amicus curiae briefs influence case selection by courts with discretionary dockets? We have seen in earlier chapters that it is very difficult to demonstrate that the lobbying behavior of organized interests has a substantial impact on the behavior of public officials. But research on the judicial agenda setting power of interest organizations indicates that amicus briefs matter a great deal, at least insofar as getting a hearing is concerned. Having one or more amicus briefs filed with petitions for review of a case by the U.S. Supreme Court greatly increases its likelihood of being reviewed.[21] Moreover, the positive impact of an amicus brief on the chances of a case being considered by the U.S. Supreme Court is especially great if the brief is submitted by parties acknowledged to be experts on the issue under review.[22]

A second type of information provided by amicus briefs concerns the merits of cases. At the merit stage, amicus briefs provide justices access to expertise on the substantive and legal issues raised by a case. This is illustrated by the AIPLA as discussed in Interest Organization Example 7-2. As the bar association representing lawyers specializing on patent, trademark, and copyright law, the AIPLA obviously has special expertise that judges may attend to in deciding cases involving intellectual property. Submitting amicus briefs at the merits stage also allows interest organizations to introduce novel arguments not found in the briefs provided by its direct participants. This is important because amici allow interest organizations to step outside the formalized bounds of a case to raise a broader range of policy concerns. As James Spriggs and Paul Wahlbeck have noted, "Since litigants are more likely to be narrowly focused on the case outcome, the broader policy ramifications may not be discussed in their briefs."[23] Indeed, Spriggs and Wahlbeck found that 64 percent of petitioner amici and 70.3 percent of respondent amici filed with the U.S. Supreme Court in the 1992 term provided information not found in the briefs of the parties. But do judges cite these novel arguments? The answer seems to be no. Spriggs and Wahlbeck found that opinions written by the justices were somewhat less likely to cite amicus briefs that cited arguments not raised in the briefs of the parties to the case.[24] This does not mean, however, that the briefs of the organized interests are unimportant. Again, reiteration of arguments across many briefs is likely to signal judges that an issue is important.

INTEREST ORGANIZATION EXAMPLE 7-2

Nyuk, Nyuk, Nyuk!

The American Intellectual Property Law Association (AIPLA) is a bar association for lawyers working in the field of patents, trademark, copyright, and unfair competition law. Founded in 1897, the AIPLA has 13,000 members who pay dues ranging from $40 per year for students to $225 for lawyers in the private sector. Headquartered in Arlington, Virginia, the AIPLA hosts three conferences per year, conducts professional training seminars, and publishes a quarterly journal.

The AIPLA engages in a wide range of advocacy activities. In 2001 and the first half of 2002, the AIPLA lobbied on 46 bills before the U.S. Congress, ranging from the Genomic Research and Diagnostic Accessibility Act of 2002 to the Music Online Competition Act of 2001. During the same time period, the AIPLA testified before Congressional committees on eight occasions. From 1995 to 2001, the AIPLA filed 24 amicus briefs before state and federal courts. These included cases contesting the assignment of patents for sexually reproducing plants and the copywriting of menu commands in computer software programs.

In 1999, the AIPLA filed an amicus brief in the case of *Comedy III Production, Inc.* v. *Gary Saderup, Inc.* before California's supreme court. Mr. Saderup had reproduced the image of the Three Stooges on posters and T-shirts for commercial benefit. Mr. Saderup claimed a First Amendment right of free speech in defending his use of images of the Three Stooges. The AIPLA argued that the First Amendment provided him no protection because there was no speech associated with the images. The AIPLA also argued that should a First Amendment defense be accepted by the court, it must be balanced against a celebrity's right of publicity to his or her name, image, and other identifying attributes.

Source: http://www.aipla.org, visited June 20, 2002

Whether cited or not, do amicus curiae briefs actually influence court decisions on the merits? The answer is far from clear. Two studies on obscenity and gender discrimination cases decided by the U.S. Supreme Court found that having more amicus curiae briefs filed for a given side of a case improves its chances of winning.[25] And a study of Georgia, North Carolina, and South Carolina Supreme Court decisions found that the number of amicus curiae for and against a given side significantly influenced judicial decisions.[26] But studies considering a wider range of cases before the U.S. Supreme Court have found that the number of amicus curiae briefs for or against a given side in a case made no difference in its probability winning.[27] While amicus briefs appear to influence case selection at the cert stage of the judicial process, evidence that they influence judicial outcomes is limited, at least at the federal level.

THE USE OF JUDICIAL LOBBYING

Given the formalized, stylized, and specialized nature of courts, it should not be surprising that relatively few interest organizations seek influence through the judiciary in comparison to other venues. In Jack Walker's 1980 survey of associations and membership organizations operating in Washington, only 31.6 percent of the respondents indicated that litigation was an important part of their influence strategy.[28] This percentage was far lower than that reported for either legislative (78 percent) or administrative (80.1 percent) lobbying. Ken Kollman's survey of a somewhat broader range of Washington interest organizations during the early 1990s found that only 22 percent of respondents indicated that their organizations regularly participated in some form of litigation over public policy issues.[29] In contrast, 96 percent reported regularly contacting members of Congress, and 68 percent indicated that they regularly contacted officials in federal agencies. Relying on a judicial strategy is relatively uncommon among organized interests, but even these relatively low percentages indicate that many organized interests seek to influence public policy through the courts. And as seen in our earlier discussion of amicus filings, participation rates are increasing.

Why do some organized interests pursue a judicial strategy while others do not? For many years, students of the politics of organized interests posited a **have nots hypothesis** in explaining use of judicial lobbying. Based on a number of notable and widely recounted successes by a handful of liberal organizations, the judicial strategy was thought to be especially attractive for organizations that are disadvantaged in other arenas. The courts are more insulated from public opinion and electoral pressures. Unpopular interests or those with limited electoral clout, it was argued, would find better odds by working through the courts. Further, courts are especially attuned to protecting statutory and constitutional rights, issues that often form the core of claims by society's disadvantaged. And last, while pursuing a legal case through the courts can be very expensive, a single positive decision can have significant effects on public policy. For a variety of reasons, then, the courts seemed to many an especially favorable venue for organized interests representing the interests of the "have nots" of society.[30]

All of these factors played a part in the NAACP's success in the landmark 1954 *Brown* v. *Board of Education* decision of the U.S. Supreme Court.[31] Having limited success in promoting civil rights in the executive and legislative branches of the national government and no success whatsoever in southern states, the NAACP turned its attention to the federal courts. The NAACP's rights-focused legal strategy became a model for other organizations representing liberal social interests. Several successes in the courts during the 1970s by environmental, social welfare, and women's organizations seemed to validate the wisdom of following the NAACP's lead. It is not surprising, then, that a 1980 survey of the lobbying activities of Washington organizations found that those concerned about human services were more likely to engage in a number of litigation strategies than were those with other substantive interests.[32]

While few reject the have nots hypothesis in its entirety, students of judicial lobbying have recently modified it in important ways.[33] First, many of early studies of the have nots hypothesis focused on liberal organizations pursuing controversial claims of constitutional rights. But many more organizations, such as labor unions, trade associations, and business firms, have for years pursued narrower interests in the courts not based on claims about constitutional rights. As Jack Walker and Kim Scheppele have observed, "The rights claiming groups do act in the ways that the case studies reveal, but rights claims are not the largest part of the picture of interest group litigation."[34] The simple number of court cases in which labor unions and trade associations defend their members and business firms pursue narrower goals overwhelm the number of cases based on rights claims, no matter how significant they might be.[35]

Second, the 1990s saw a sharp upsurge in litigation by conservative interest organizations using the kinds of rights claims used by liberal interests. The Christian Coalition's American Center for Law and Justice was discussed earlier. Similarly, the Pacific Legal Foundation was founded in 1973 to oppose liberal environmental organizations using many of their own tactics.[36] Even traditional business interests have begun to employ rights claims in courts similar to those used by organizations representing society's have nots.[37] These developments do not indicate that the core idea of the have nots hypothesis is wrong. Many liberal social organizations have found the courts to be useful venues for pursuing their interests. Rather, they may be victims of their own success in that many conservative organizations, having belatedly discovered the utility of rights claims, are now imitating the NAACP's judicial strategy.

A third and more serious threat to the have nots hypothesis lies in recognizing that reliance on a judicial strategy is costly in time and money. It can take years for a major case to proceed through the courts, and many more years may be needed to defend a successful court decision in follow-on suits. Indeed, a single test case rarely constitutes the final word on a legal issue. The legal battles over the implications of the 1973 *Roe* v. Wade decision striking down state prohibitions on abortion have hardly abated over the last quarter century. And the costly time of lawyer-lobbyists, especially those with the most experience in particular courts, cannot be readily replaced by even the most enthusiastic of grassroots amateurs. Given the costs of using a judicial strategy, we might expect that wealthier, long-lasting interest organizations would be more likely to employ it than fledgling groups.

The have nots hypothesis is broadly consistent with the pluralist interpretation of the politics of interest representation. That is, the pluralists maintained that almost all organizations have access to some governmental arena in which to defend their interests. Even if they might have limited political and economic resources in other arenas, those who feel disadvantaged, whether racial minorities facing southern sheriffs or fundamentalist Christians threatened by the dominant secular culture of the United States, have access to the courts. In contrast, the "haves" hypothesis fits well with the transactions approach's assessment of the power of traditional economic interests. Organizations defending traditional economic interests are more likely to be larger, older, and better financed. Given the cost of using judicial strategies, they may have greater than average access to the judiciary.

There are only a handful of systematic studies of the relative access of different kinds of interest organizations to the courts. Those focusing on organizations' resources have very mixed findings. Consistent with the haves hypothesis, Kim Scheppele and Jack Walker's study of interest organizations' ratings of the importance of different lobbying techniques found that large, wealthy, and long-lived organizations are more likely to use the courts to promote their interests.[38] There is little doubt that organization resources and experience matter in trial courts and at the appellate level in courts that do not control their own docket.[39] The ability to hire better lawyers and search longer and harder for evidence and legal precedent surely matter once in court. Still, more comprehensive surveys of the frequency of resort to the courts by organized interests have failed to find that organizational resources matter.[40]

Studies of interest organization influence through the courts, moreover, generally fail to find evidence that traditional economic interests are dominant. First, consider lobbying on judicial nominations. Caldiera, Hojnacki, and Wright found that institutions, trade and professional associations, and unions comprised on average only 37.9 percent of the organizations lobbying on the 15 judicial nominations they examined. In contrast, 45 percent of active organizations were citizens' groups and public interest law firms.[41] A second mode of lobbying is participating in litigation. Susan Olson's analysis of the participation of interest organizations in private civil cases heard in Minnesota federal district court found that citizens' organizations participated in many more cases than did businesses and trade and professional associations.[42] A third mode of judicial lobbying is through filing amicus briefs. As seen in Figure 7-1, the largest single type of organization filing amicus curiae briefs at both the cert and merits stage of U.S. Supreme Court decisions is state and local governments.[43] This is not surprising in that many are commenting on public policy issues of concern to them or offering

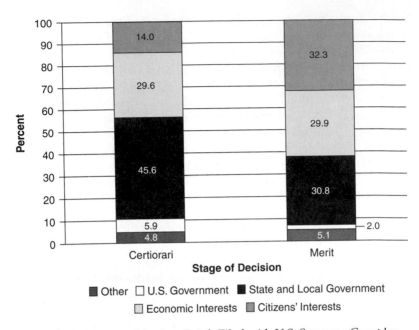

FIGURE 7-1 Percent of Amicus Briefs Filed with U.S. Supreme Court by
Type of Filer, 1982
Source: Adapted from Gregory Caldiera and John R. Wright, "Amicus Curiae before the Supreme
Court: Who Participates, When, and How Much?" *Journal of Politics* 52: 782–806 (1990).

comments on legal cases similar to those being processed in their
own courts. But the haves represented by traditional economic interests—corporations, unions, and professional and trade associations—file just under a third of all friend of the court briefs at both
the cert (29.6 percent) and merit (29.9 percent) stages of cases. Citizens' interest organizations—individuals, charitable and community groups, public interest advocacy organizations, and public
interest law firms—have a smaller presence (14 percent) at the cert
stage in which the Court selects the cases it will rule on. But they
filed more friend of court briefs (32.3 percent) at the merits stage
than traditional economic interests. Fourth and most importantly,
organizational resources do not seem to influence actual U.S.
Supreme Court decisions. A study of litigation success in 36 years'
worth of U.S. Supreme Court decisions (the court controls its own
docket and can thereby avoid frivolous suits) found that the relative
resources of the parties mattered little in terms of final decisions.[44]

Thus, citizens, represented by agencies of the public sector and public interest organizations, are quite active in the courts across a broad range of actual lobbying behaviors.

The traditional have nots hypothesis almost certainly overemphasized the special advantage that organizations representing the disadvantaged have in the courts. Many organized interests, including those representing traditional economic interests, attempt to influence public policy through the courts, and many are successful. But if organizations representing the interests of the disadvantaged of society are not uniquely advantaged in the courts, it seems to provide them an especially level playing field.

CONCLUSION

Organized interests do not stop promoting their interests at the courthouse steps. While fewer organized interests lobby the judicial branch than the executive and legislative branches, lobbying the courts is common and growing. However, the special nature of the courts certainly influences how they must lobby judges. Still, through participating in appointments and elections to the bench, filing and defending against suits, and submitting friend of the court briefs, organized interests have found a number of ways to express their policy preferences.

In the end, though, we must be concerned about how these expressions of policy preferences shape public policy. The pluralist approach argues that organizations only provide information to decision makers. This information may change how an official sees a particular case, but the organization cannot change the core values an official applies in making a decision. While neopluralists allow that organized interests can influence some decisions, they see such influence as limited and highly contingent. In contrast, the transactions approach assumes that efforts to apply influence all too frequently work.

While research on judicial decision making does not provide a single answer to the issue of influence, on this most critical issue it seems that the pluralists and neopluralists have it more nearly right, at least in terms of amicus briefs and decisions on the merits of cases. Yes, the information organized interests provide to judges through their briefs seems to influence their selection of cases, but the systematic studies of amicus participation on U.S. Supreme Court cases indicates that this influence has little impact on the decisions judges make about their merits. In addition, studies of cases decided on the merits indicate that interest organizations are no more successful in court than are private litigants. Rather, consistent with pluralists and neopluralists, the preferences of the judges seem to matter most when making decisions on the merits. This attitudinal model of judicial decision making is now the prevailing interpretation of most judicial scholars, even if students of the courts do not universally accept it. While presenting it in detail is beyond the scope of this book, a large body of research has found that the attitudes of the judges predict very well how they vote on legal cases.[45] Pluralists and neopluralists, therefore, would not be surprised that the balance of amici has little impact on judicial decisions on the merits. And they would not be surprised that organized interests are no more successful in court than are private litigants.

KEY TERMS AND CONCEPTS

Standing

Class Action Suits

Test Cases

Public Interest Law Firms

Amicus Curiae

Merits Stage

Certiorari Stage

Have Nots Hypothesis

QUESTIONS ABOUT YOUR
INTEREST ORGANIZATION

1. Has your interest organization sued or been sued on a significant issue of public policy? Use legal websites to identify cases.
2. If your interest organization was sued or has been sued on an issue of public policy, what arguments were raised in the briefs of the parties? How were the cases settled?
3. Has your interest organization filed amicus curiae briefs in state or federal court? Use your organization's website and legal websites to identify cases raised in the amicus briefs.
4. If your organization has filed amicus briefs, on what grounds did it claim a stake in cases?
5. If your organization has filed amicus briefs, did any of its briefs raise policy or legal issues not raised by the parties to a case?

NOTES

1. Martha A. Derthick, *Up In Smoke* (Washington, DC: CQ Press, 2002).

2. As discussed below, however, these requirements are not especially rigorous for amicus briefs. See Gregory Caldiera and John R. Wright, "Amici Curiae before the Supreme Court: Who Participates, When, and How Much?" *Journal of Politics* 52: 782–806 (1990).

3. For a particularly telling example of this sort involving lobbyist Thomas G. Corcoran and two U.S. Supreme Court justices, see Karen O'Connor, "Lobbying the Justices or Lobbying for Justice?" In *The Interest Group Connection*, Paul S. Herrnson, Ronald G. Shako, and Clyde Wilcox, eds. (Chatham, New Jersey: Chatham House, 1998), pp. 267–268.

4. John P. Heinz, Edward O. Laumann, Robert L. Nelson, and Robert H. Salisbury, *The Hollow Core* (Cambridge: Harvard University Press, 1993), pp. 87–155.

5. Kevin T. McGuire, "Lobbyists, Revolving Doors, and the U.S. Supreme Court," *The Journal of Law and Politics* 16: 113–137 (2000); Kevin T. McGuire, *The Supreme Court Bar* (Charlottesville, Virginia: University Press of Virginia, 1993).

6. Gregory A. Caldiera, Marie Hojnacki, and John R. Wright, "The Lobbying Activities of Organized Interests in Federal Judicial Nominations," *Journal of Politics* 62: 51–69 (2000).

7. Marie Hojnacki and Lawrence Baum, "'New Style' Judicial Campaigns and the Voters: Economic Issues and Union Members in Ohio," *Western Political Quarterly* 45: 921–948 (1992).

8. http://www.wort-fm.org/kiosk/sept/htm, visited November 29, 2002.

9. Paul Brace, Melinda Gann Hall, and Laura Langer, "Placing State Supreme Courts in State Politics," *State Politics and Policy Quarterly* 1: 81–108 (2001).

10. Brace, Hall, and Langer, "Placing State Supreme Courts in State Politics;" Melinda Gann Hall, ""Electoral Politics and Strategic Voting in State Supreme Courts," *Journal of Politics* 54: 427–446 (1992); Melinda Gann Hall, "State Judicial Politics: Rules, Structures, and the Political Game." In *American State and Local Politics*, Ronald E. Weber and Paul Brace, eds. (New York: Chatham House Press, 1999), pp. 114–138; Melinda Gann Hall, "Constituent

Influence in State Supreme Courts: Conceptual Notes and a Case Study," *Journal of Politics* 49: 1117–1124.

11. Susan M. Olson, "Interest-Group Litigation in Federal District Court: Beyond the Political Disadvantage Theory," *Journal of Politics* 52: 854–882 (1990).

12. Human Rights Watch, *Shielded from Justice: Police Brutality and Accountability in the United States—New York*, http://www.hrw.org/reports98/police/usps106.htm, June 15, 2002.

13. The American Center for Law and Justice, "ACLJ to Ask U.S. Supreme Court to Consider Equal Access for Christian Coalition in Louisiana," http://aclj.org/news/nr_001031.asp, October 31, 2000.

14. Lee Epstein and C. K. Rowland, "Debunking the Myth of Interest Group Invincibility in the Courts," *American Political Science Review* 58: 206–217 (1991).

15. Karen O'Connor and Bryant Scott McFall, "Conservative Interest Group Litigation in the Reagan Era and Beyond." In *The Politics of Interests*, Mark P. Petracca, ed. (Boulder, Colorado: Westview Press, 1992), pp. 266.

16. Kevin T. McGuire, *Understanding the U.S. Supreme Court* (Boston: McGraw-Hill, 2001), p. 149.

17. Gregory Caldiera and John R. Wright, "Organized Interests and Agenda Setting in the U.S. Supreme Court," *American Political Science Review* 82: 1109–1107 (1988).

18. McGuire, *Understanding the U.S. Supreme Court*, p. 151.

19. O'Connor, "Lobbying the Justices or Lobbying for Justice?" pp. 280–281.

20. McGuire, *Understanding the U.S. Supreme Court*, pp. 55–90.

21. Caldiera and Wright, "Organized Interests and Agenda Setting in the U.S. Supreme Court."

22. Kevin T. McGuire and Gregory A. Caldiera, "Lawyers, Organized Interests, and the Law of Obscenity: Agenda Setting in the Supreme Court," *American Political Science Review* 87: 717–726 (1993).

23. James F. Spriggs II and Paul J. Wahlbeck, "Amicus Curiae and the Role of Information at the Supreme Court," *Political Research Quarterly* 50: 365–386 (1997).

24. Spriggs and Wahlbeck, "Amicus Curiae and the Role of Information at the Supreme Court."

25. Robin Wolpert, "Explaining and Predicting Supreme Court Decision-Making: The Gender Discrimination Cases." Paper presented at the Annual Meeting of the Midwest Political Science Association, Chicago, April 1991; Kevin T. McGuire, "Obscenity, Libertarian Values and Decision Making in the Supreme Court," *American Politics Quarterly* 18: 47–67 (1991).
26. Donald R. Songer and Ashlyn Kuersten, "The Success of Amici in State Supreme Courts," *Political Research Quarterly* 48: 31–42 (1995).
27. Donald R. Songer and Reginald S. Sheehan, "Interest Group Success in the Courts: Amicus Participation in the Supreme Court," 46: 339–354 (1993).
28. Jack L. Walker, Jr., *Mobilizing Interest Groups in America* (Ann Arbor: University of Michigan Press, 1991), p. 109.
29. Ken Kollman, *Outside Lobbying* (Princeton: Princeton University Press, 1998), p. 35.
30. Richard C. Cortner, "Strategies and Tactics of Litigants in Constitutional Cases," *Journal of Public Law* 17: 287–307.
31. Clement E. Vose, *Caucasians Only* (Berkeley: University of California Press, 1959); Stephen L. Wasby, *Race Relations in an Age of Complexity* (Charlotte: University of Virginia Press, 1995).
32. Kim Lane Scheppele and Jack L. Walker, Jr., "The Litigation Strategies of Interest Groups." In Jack L. Walker, Jr., *Mobilizing Interest Groups in America* (Ann Arbor: University of Michigan Press, 1991), pp. 157–184.
33. For a discussion of the many ways in which the hypothesis has been modified, see Olson, "Interest-Group Litigation in Federal District Court: Beyond the Political Disadvantage Theory."
34. Scheppele and Walker, "The Litigation Strategies of Interest Groups," p. 182. However, others have found that cases concerning redistributive policy actually constitute a higher proportion of cases heard at least by federal district court than cases involving regulatory policy. See Olson, "Interest-Group Litigation in Federal District Court."
35. Lee Epstein, "Courts and Interest Groups." In *The American Courts*, John B. Gates and Charles A. Johnson, eds. (Washington, DC: CQ Press, 1991), pp. 335–371.
36. O'Connor and McFall, "Conservative Interest Group Litigation in the Reagan Era and Beyond," pp. 236–284; Karen O'Connor

and Lee Epstein, "The Rise of Conservative Interest Groups," *Journal of Politics* 45: 479–489 (1983); Gregg Ivers, "Please God, Save This Honorable Court: The Emergence of the Conservative Religious Bar." In *The Interest Group Connection*, Paul S. Herrnson, Ronald G. Shako, and Clyde Wilcox, eds. (Chatham, New Jersey: Chatham House, 1998), pp. 289–301.

37. Wayne V. McIntosh and Cynthia L. Cates, "Interest Groups and the Courts: Free Speech for Corporations." In *The Interest Group Connection*, Paul S. Herrnson, Ronald G. Shako, and Clyde Wilcox, eds. (Chatham, New Jersey: Chatham House, 1998), pp. 302–317.

38. Scheppele and Walker, "The Litigation Strategies of Interest Groups."

39. Donald R. Songer and Reginald S. Sheehan, "Who Wins on Appeal? Upperdogs and Underdogs in the United States Courts of Appeals," *American Journal of Political Science* 36: 235–258 (1992).

40. Patrick J. Bruer, "Washington Organizations and Public Policy Litigation: Explaining Reliance on Litigations as a Strategy of Influence." Paper presented at the Annual Meeting of meeting of the Midwest Political Science Association, Chicago, April 1987.

41. Caldiera, Hojnacki, and Wright, "The Lobbying Activities of Organized Interests in Federal Judicial Nominations," p. 58.

42. Olson, "Interest-Group Litigation in Federal District Court."

43. Caldiera and Wright, "Amicia Curiae before the Supreme Court."

44. Reginald S. Sheehan, William Mishler, and Donald R. Songer, "Ideology, Status, and the Differential Success of Direct Parties before the Supreme Court," *American Political Science Review* 86: 464–471 (1992).

45. Indeed, the prevailing attitudinal model of judicial decision making emphasizes the role of judges' preferences in explaining their votes. See Jeffrey A. Segal and Harold J. Spaeth, *The Supreme Court and the Attitudinal Model* (New York: Cambridge University Press, 1993).

CHAPTER 8

Consequences and Reforms

*I*n two days of hearings in December, 2002 supporters and opponents of the **Bipartisan Campaign Finance Reform Act** (BCFRA, or the McCain-Feingold/Shays-Meehan Act) argued its merits and, more to the point, its legality before the U.S. District Court in the District of Columbia. The act, passed by Congress earlier in the year and signed into law by President George Bush on March 27, is the latest confrontation between those who view organized interests as inimical to democratic politics and others who view their activities as its essence. The district court will make a decision on the Bipartisan Campaign Finance Reform Act, which surely will be reviewed by the U.S. Supreme Court, but the larger issue is unlikely to disappear whatever the courts decide. Organized interests are hardly likely to vanish from politics, and so efforts to regulate their behavior will continue. Are more regulations needed? Will they work? Are they wise? We try to answer these questions in this concluding chapter.

These questions are, however, difficult to answer for two reasons. First, they raise almost all of the issues we have already considered in previous chapters. Our views of regulation, for example, are surely influenced by our understanding of how well interest communities mirror interests in society and whether the behaviors of the public and political elites can be readily manipulated. Second, the regulation of organized interests does not align neatly along the usual liberal-conservative split in American politics. The *New York Times,* for example, claimed that "McCain-Feingold is an effort to address deep and growing problems in the political system. Our democratic ideals about 'one person one vote' are fast being buried under a mountain of special-interest money."[1] Yet former Wyoming senator Alan K. Simpson, a conservative Republican, asked the three judge panel, "Who, after all, can seriously contend that a $100,000 donation does not alter the way one thinks about—and quite possibly votes on—an issue?"[2] In contrast, the conservative Heritage Foundation argued that greater regulation would constitute an unconstitutional abridgment of free speech rights,[3] a position shared by the American Civil Liberties Union and the AFL-CIO.[4] In short, the issues surrounding the regulation of organized interests are not aligned in such a simple, familiar manner that we need not think deeply about them. To sort through these complexities, we examine two topics. First, we assess the overall impact of organized interests on American politics and public policy. Second, we examine a menu of reforms and consider how each relates to the alleged sins of organized interests.

POLITICAL AND POLICY CONSEQUENCES

The preceding four chapters reviewed the many means organized interests employ to influence the public, legislatures, the executive branch, and the courts. We have seen that organized interests are not always, or perhaps even routinely, successful in shaping their decisions. What cumulative impact, then, do they have on politics and public policy? This is a critical question, given that reform proposals generally are not aimed at isolated examples of improper behavior by organized interests. They are designed instead to tackle a broad class of behaviors that are seen as a threat to democratic politics or sound public policy. This means that to assess the appropriateness of reform proposals, we must first consider how organized interests collectively influence politics and policy. This, of course, is the final stage of the influence production process outlined in Table 1-2 of Chapter 1: the political and policy outcome stage.

Summary judgments about the cumulative impact of organized interests on politics and public policy are, unfortunately, often based on very weak foundations. Some journalists, for example, broadly indict organized interests based on collections of horror stories generated from nonrepresentative samples of organized interests and policies.[5] Some social science indictments of the dominance of organized interests leap too readily from noting the dominance of business interests in lobbying communities to claims that public policy invariably serves elite interests.[6] Instead, we need to examine systematic studies testing specific hypotheses about the cumulative impacts of organized interests on politics and public policy. Research of this type has been conducted on four specific indictments of organized interests.

Political Participation

Americans are increasingly cynical about government and are participating in elections in ever diminished numbers. The facts underlying this assertion are often repeated. While 70 percent or more of survey respondents said that they trusted government most of the time in the 1960s, only 30 percent did so in the 1990s.[7] As seen in Figure 1-2, more citizens now say that government is run by a few big interests rather than for the benefit of all. Over the same period, voting turnout in U.S. presidential elections has declined from 70 percent to the point that only half of the voting age population bothers to show up at the polls. From the mid-1970s to the mid-1990s, the percentage of citizens indicating that they have participated in many standard forms of civic engagement—attending a public meeting, writing to legislators or to a newspaper, signing a petition, and so on—declined, in some cases by more than a third.[8]

Scholars have spent a considerable amount of time over the last decade debating the reality of this **crisis in civic engagement**,[9] its implications for democratic politics,[10] and its causes.[11] Many of the purported causes go far beyond our concern about organized interests. Still, organized interests are often pointed to as a major culprit. The indictment of organized interests rests on three observations. First, critics note the tremendous growth in populations of organized interests operating both in state capitols and Washington. We documented this population explosion in Chapter 3. But growth in the number of organized interests engaged in politics is not in and of itself a problem. Rather, the problem arises from how these organized interests now participate in politics. Thus, the second part of the case against organized interests emphasizes the growing intensity of policy conflicts arising from more and more interest organizations engaging in politics. As competition increases, it is claimed, the volume and shrillness of the claims made by organized interests turn off citizens' interest in politics. To citizens, suggests Morris Fiorina, "the result is unnecessary conflict and animosity, delay and gridlock, and a public life that seems dominated by 'quarrelsome blowhards.'"[12] The third element of the indictment concerns money. Organized interests introduce large amounts of money into politics through contributions to political campaigns. Whether or not the transactions school's assertion that campaign contributions influence policy outcomes is true, the ever larger sums of money that organized interests bring to politics certainly create at least the appearance of corruption. Journalists and organizations supporting campaign finance reform have not been shy in trying to convince Americans that cynicism and mistrust are entirely appropriate responses to a political system awash in interest organization money.

The last argument about perceptions of corruption associated with the free flow of money is perhaps the most telling. We saw in Chapter 5 that there are good reasons to think that the transactions school overemphasizes the role of money in securing either access or desired policy outcomes. Yet against the avalanche of voices decrying the corrupting power of money in politics, very few are willing to assert publicly that campaign contributions by organized interests have any legitimate role to play in the democratic process.[13] One of the few exceptions is the Cato Institute. As seen in Interest Organization Example 8-1, the Cato Institute's amicus brief in the challenge to the Bipartisan Campaign Finance Reform Act heard by the U.S. District Court in December 2002 fully acknowledges that money is one among several influences on legislators' votes. While not countenancing direct bribes, Cato claimed that, when laundered through free speech by supporting favored candidates, money is as legitimate an influence as election endorsements. Such direct arguments about money are rare. It is not surprising, then, that the public widely views interest organization money as inevitably corrupting.

When we go beyond perceptions of corruption, however, claims that organized interests are responsible for declining civic participation rest on very shallow foundations. There is, for example, no relationship between the number of organized interests active in states and voting turnout and other forms of individual political

INTEREST ORGANIZATION EXAMPLE 8-1

Opposing Reform

Edward H. Crane founded the Cato Institute in 1977. Along with the Heritage Foundation, it is the embodiment of the modern conservative advocacy tank. Cato's take on conservatism emphasizes its libertarian or market-liberal strains, rather than social conservatism. The institute brings to ongoing policy debates "the traditional American principles of limited government, individual liberty, free markets and peace." Cato publishes numerous books and monographs and sponsors conferences on a wide range of policy issues. The Cato Institute does not accept government funding, relying instead on contributions from corporations, individuals, and foundations. Members can join for as little as $50, for which they receive selected policy studies, the Cato Policy Report, and Ed Crane's bimonthly report on the work of the Institute.

An opponent of campaign finance reform, the Cato Institute cosigned (with the Institute for Justice, a libertarian public interest law firm) an amicus curiae brief filed with the U.S. District Court challenge to the Bipartisan Campaign Finance Act by Senator Mitch McConnell (R-Kentucky). The institute's brief emphasized the threat posed to free speech by the act, but it made three additional arguments that are less commonly heard. First, the brief argued that reporting requirements associated with the act violate the anonymity and privacy inherent in the right to freely association with others. Second, the brief argued that all politics are based on a quid pro quo relationship between constituents and elected officials; money mediated through speech is no different than other kinds of influences. And third, the Cato lawyers asserted that the government had no compelling interest in reducing the mere appearance of corruption.

Source: http://www.cato.org, visited December 19, 2002.

engagement.[14] We further saw in Chapter 2 that group membership promotes individual political participation. Membership teaches us how to become involved in politics, enhances individual feelings of efficacy, and informs us about our stakes in the policy process.[15] While the money-fueled shrillness of political campaigns surely leads to more negative views of politics, hot campaigns and the media attention they attract also increase citizens' attention to politics.[16] Thus, if there is a crisis in civic engagement in American politics, it is not at all clear that the smoking gun belongs to organized interests.

Political Gridlock

Critics of organized interests assert that they are responsible for political **gridlock** — the failure of governmental institutions to address important policy problems in a timely manner. Political analyst Kevin Phillips, for example, claimed that the growing policy gridlock observed in Washington during the 1990s was due to "the enormous buildup and entrenchment of the largest interest group concentration the world has ever seen."[17] Intense competition among these many interest organizations makes it difficult, critics argue, for legislators to accomplish anything. A Michigan lobbyist observed that "almost every group has something to say on every issue. The legislature has little wiggle room. Some group squeals about everything they do."[18] Securing majority support for any position may be difficult in these circumstances.

Gridlock is a uniquely neopluralist complaint. Transactions scholars assert that organized interests can all too readily translate their preferences into policy. Pluralists assume that public officials are able to sort through the cacophony of voices of even crowded interest communities to discover the public's will. Indeed, conflict among organized interests may be an essential signal to public officials that policies and the venues in which they are considered must change. Conflict among organized interests may be necessary to break policy logjams.[19] Neopluralists generally agree with pluralists that organized interests contribute to democratic government by better linking citizens' preferences to the decisions of elected officials. But some neopluralists also note that the policy process can suffer from too much of a good thing. When so many organized interests seek influence, discovering the public's will may take so much time that it is difficult for government to respond to even severe policy problems in a timely manner.

Tests of the gridlock hypothesis have produced very mixed results. Virginia Gray and David Lowery examined the relationship between the density of state interest communities and the numbers of bills introduced and passed by state legislatures in 1990 and 1991.[20] Controlling for a number of other factors, such as when government control is divided between the two major political parties, they found strong evidence of gridlock. Legislatures in states with dense interest communities considered and passed far fewer bills into law than those in states with less crowded interest systems. But research on Congress has not supported the gridlock hypothesis. Jeffrey Berry's analysis of several sessions of Congress found that bill passage rates did not vary with the number of organizations engaged in lobbying.[21] Within each year, moreover, bills on which many organizations lobbied were no more likely to fail than those on which few were active. Why has Congress avoided interest-induced gridlock? First, lobbying congestion is almost surely overstated. While some bills attract the attention of many organized interests, most attract very little.[22] Second, as the Washington interest community has grown, Congress has increasingly relied on omnibus legislation—combining provisions that might once have been addressed in single bills into larger packages addressing many issues—to weaken the influence of interest organizations opposed to specific policy changes.[23] In sum, while there is some evidence of gridlock arising from interest community density at the state-level, Congress has so far been able to avoid this consequence of the politics of interest representation.

Economic Sclerosis

Transactions scholars are not concerned about gridlock. They assert instead that organized interests are all too successful in shepherding their proposals through legislatures and the bureaucracy. Transactions scholars do not, however, envision this success as evidence of a pluralist heaven. Rather, they see a pluralist hell based on three insights discussed earlier. First, as seen in Chapter 2, Mancur Olson argued that large economic interests, facing less severe collective action problems, are mobilized more easily than other interests.[24] The latter will, therefore, be better represented within interest communities. Second, as discussed in Chapter 6, George Stigler, Sam Peltzman, and Robert Barro have argued that most organized interests pursue changes in public policies that insulate them from competition through special tax breaks, spending subsidies, and regulations that make it more difficult for new competitors to enter the market.[25] Third, as noted in Chapter 5, transactions scholars assume that money, a resource that traditional economic interests have ready access to, is invariably successful in securing their preferences.[26] Mancur Olson combined these insights in *The Rise and Decline of Nations* in the institutional sclerosis hypothesis.[27] As interest communities grow ever larger, more and more restrictions on market competition will be adopted. Over time, these erode economic efficiency so that ever more dense interest communities generate ever slower rates of economic growth.

Despite the fanfare that the institutional sclerosis hypothesis attracted initially, very little evidence supports it. For example, there is little relationship between the density of state interest communities and either economic growth or the number of regulations in states.[28] This failure is almost certainly due to problems with the hypothesis's premises. We saw in Chapter 2 that the mobilization advantages of traditional economic interests are not as great as often suspected. Further, the size of interest communities is self-limiting, with growth slowing as interest systems become large. The proportion of traditional economic organizations in state interest systems has been stable for more than two decades.[29] While special protections from competition may make it difficult for rivals to enter the market, it does not stop them from entering the political fray and trying to eliminate these barriers to entry.[30] Perhaps most importantly of all, we have seen in the last four chapters that money does not inevitably advantage traditional economic interests.

Political Power

Perhaps the most important indictment of organized interests is that they are far too powerful in American politics. The presence of ever more organized interests in the political process and the continuing dominance of traditional economic interests constitute prima facia evidence that big interest organizations now exercise too large a role in American politics. This indictment reflects, of course, the transactions school view of organized interests. We have examined in considerable detail the many premises and hypotheses underlying the transactions school perspective, and many have been found wanting. Recent research indicates that problems of collective action do not inevitably undermine the mobilization efforts of citizens' organizations. The balance of citizens' organizations and traditional economic interests has remained constant over recent decades. The campaign contributions of PACs to legislative candidates generally follow an access rather than an electoral strategy. Even so, money does not always win access; district presence matters far more. The amicus briefs filed by organized interests do influence the cases that appellate courts review, but not their outcomes. Most importantly, when the public cares about an issue, organized interests find it very difficult to reshape policy outcomes.

These results would not surprise traditional pluralists. To pluralists, the presence of organized interests in politics reflects less their power than their uncertainties about real issues they care about. The preferences of voters are sharpened by the efforts of organized interests to frame issues and the policy proposals developed by think tanks. The communication of these preferences to public officials is a key means, along with voting, through which they assess the popularity and salience of policy issues. Indeed, the linkage of interest organizations, voting, and political parties via campaign activities is, from a pluralist perspective, essential to effective democratic control of government by citizens. As Todd Graziano of the Heritage Foundation expressed it, "The only effective way for most citizens to be heard during an election campaign is to band together in interest groups like unions, fraternal organizations, and community groups."[31] In short, organized interests are a necessary part of democracy.

Still, research findings do not always support pluralists' optimistic assessments. Most of the interest organizations petitioning government are not, as suggested by Graziano, bands of citizens. They are institutions — businesses, schools, churches, and other organizations without members. Not all organizations have equal access to all government institutions, especially the executive branch. When presidents employ a "liaison as governing party" strategy, organizations opposing his legislative agenda will have little opportunity to be heard in the White House. While citizens' organizations are well represented in some stages of the policy process, such as in testimony in legislative hearings, they are often underrepresented relative to business interests in bureaucratic settings where the regulations implementing laws are developed. Perhaps most importantly, when the public does not care about issues, organized interests have significant opportunities to promote their own, more specialized causes. This neopluralist view rejects both the extreme pessimism of the transactions school and the overly optimistic vision of traditional pluralism. The neopluralist school suggests that while organized interests are an essential part of democratic politics, their activities must be closely monitored. At times, specific reforms may well be needed to correct specific abuses of power by organized interests.

        While these earlier findings tell us much about the power of organized interests, none of them really addresses their full cumulative impact on public policy. Two studies on state organized interests are instructive because they assess their overall power across multiple political systems. Thomas Hrebenar and Clive Thomas have for almost two decades surveyed political scientists across the country about the relative power of each of their state's organized interests. Respondents were asked to rank on a five-point scale running from dominant to subordinate the "extent to which interest groups as a whole influence public policy compared to other components of the political system, such as political parties, the legislature, [and] the governor."[32] Their 1998 survey found that organized interests were dominant in five states, a decline from nine states in their initial survey 15 years previously. Still, organized interests were important in many states and in none were they completely subordinate to other political actors. Importantly, the power of organized interests seems unrelated to either the size of a state's interest community or to its diversity.[33] While individual interest organizations are surely important powers in some states, simply having many organized interests registered to lobby does not make them collectively powerful in state politics.

        The second study built on earlier work by Erikson Wight and McIver that found that the liberalness of public opinion in a state strongly influences how liberal its policies are.[34] Virginia Gray and colleagues examined whether the density and diversity of state interest communities weakened this democratic link between public opinion and public policy.[35] The density of state interest systems had no influence on the translation of public opinion into public policy. But interest system diversity did have a small impact. States with larger proportions of lobby registrations by business interests tend to have slightly less liberal public policies than would be expected. Together these studies suggest that organized interests do not fully dominate state politics relative to other political actors, as suggested by transaction scholars. But unlike pluralist interpretations, organized interests do more than passively convey information.

PROPOSED REFORMS

Reforms to check what some perceive as the excessive power of organized interests have been with us for a century. Alan Rosenthal identified the political logic of reform when he noted that "legislatures pass **ethics laws** usually because they have to—they're under pressure from a scandal, or the press is beating on them, or there are reformers within who see it as a good issue to use politically."[36] This was certainly true of the granddaddy of reforms, the Tillman Act of 1907. Industrialist Mark Hanna contributed $100,000—worth more than a million dollars today—to President William McKinley's 1896 presidential campaign. But Hanna's contribution paled compared to banker J. P. Morgan and Standard Oil's contributions of $250,000.[37] To restrict such business power, the Tillman Act prohibited banks and corporations (and, after 1943, labor unions) from giving funds directly to political candidates. The next significant federal reform effort, the amending of the Federal Election Campaign Act in 1974, followed on the heels of the Watergate scandal.[38] The Watergate scandal also initiated the first major wave of lobby regulation by states in the 1970s. New scandals in Arizona, California, Kentucky, and a handful of other states during the 1990s—with legislators sometimes caught on tape accepting bribes or extorting funds from organized interests—initiated a second round of reforms.[39]

While both politicians and most organized interests are typically brought into the reform tent with all of the enthusiasm of a wine connoisseur attending a temperance meeting, laws governing lobbying and campaign activity can have significant effects on their behavior. How, then, should we assess reform efforts? Several questions seem pertinent. First, what was the specific problem a given reform effort was designed to address? Second, was the reform effort effective in addressing this problem? Third, what unintended consequences did the reform generate? And last, what are the costs of reform? We apply these questions to four classes of reforms.

Restructuring Interest Communities

There have been occasional efforts to influence the density or diversity of lobbying communities. Reforms targeted at density try to minimize the number of organized interests influencing public policy. The most draconian was Georgia's law in the early 20th century that declared lobbying a crime! Not surprisingly, few organizations admitted that they lobbied in Georgia.[40] Of course, such simple prohibitions do not work. As we will see in the next set of reforms, the federal government and all states now register organizations engaged in lobbying. Some scholars believe that these requirements act as "barriers to entry" into lobbying communities. That is, even the small costs of registering, and the potential public scrutiny registration might bring, may discourage attempts to influence public policy.[41] Research on variations in state registration requirements indicates, however, that they have little impact on numbers of lobby registrations.[42] Tax laws are also thought by some to influence the size of interest communities. Federal tax law grants significant advantages to 501(c)(3) nonprofit organizations. There is a tradeoff, however. While they may disseminate information, they cannot in a strict sense lobby. A few nonprofits have lost their tax-exempt status for violating this rule. While this might be expected to make them reluctant to lobby, nonprofit organizations routinely register. Quite simply, they are unlikely to be challenged as long as their lobbying efforts are restricted to talking about the merits of an issue and they do not engage in electioneering.[43] Overall, then, efforts to restrict the size of lobbying communities have been ineffective.

Fewer — but far more controversial — efforts have tried to alter the diversity of interest communities. We saw in Chapter 2 that government has often provided the initial impetus in the mobilization of many membership organizations, including the National Rifle Association and the National Organization for Women. However, efforts to promote greater participation on the part of underrepresented interests have waxed and waned with changes in the partisan and ideological composition of government. Lyndon Johnson's Great Society legislation of the 1960s required "maximum feasible partici- pation" by the recipients of public services in their planning and provision, which in turn stimulated the mobilization and political engagement of many organizations representing the interests of the poor and racial minorities. Such efforts were an anathema to the Rea- gan administration, which tried to "defund the left" in the 1980s by "killing the grant programs that supported these groups."[44] How- ever, conservatives are not opposed to all such assistance. In 2001 President George Bush promoted conservative Christian organiza- tions by establishing by executive order the White House Office of Faith-Based and Community Initiatives. Overall, however, efforts to reshape the diversity of interest systems are not likely to have much success. While they may provide a short-term stimulus for the mobilization of some kinds of organized interests, it is doubtful that they have any lasting impact on the mix of organizations registered to lobby given the high birth and death rates typical of lobbying communities.

Registration and Reporting Requirements

By far the most successful reforms adopted to alter the way orga- nized interests conduct their business are registration and reporting requirements. These directly restrict neither the number of interest organizations that lobby nor how they lobby. Rather, these reforms bring their efforts into the open for all to see. The most important re- quirement is simply the duty to register to lobby. While a few states required organized interests to register to lobby as early as 1890, the Watergate scandal initiated a wave of new laws so that by 1988 Arkansas became the last state to require registration.[45] State **regis- tration laws** vary considerably. They do not define lobbying in a common manner, they have different thresholds of activity trigger- ing registration requirements, and enforcement provisions and penalties vary markedly.[46] The federal government, in contrast, was quite tardy in adopting a strong registration law. The Foreign Agents Registration Act of 1938 and the Legislative Reorganization Act of 1946 were limited in scope and weakly enforced. Only with the Lobby Disclosure Act of 1995 did the federal government have a meaningful registration requirement.[47] The act requires registration of all organizations directly contacting members of Congress and spending at least $20,500 over a six-month period. Similarly, the Federal Election Campaign Act of 1971 both defined political action committees (PACs) and later required that they register with the newly created Federal Election Commission (FEC). Not all states allow PACs to contribute to state and local campaigns, but those that do vary in terms of limits on the kinds of organizations that can sponsor PACs.[48]

Reporting requirements add content to registration laws by compelling organized interests to list who is lobbying on their behalf, whom they lobby, and how much they spend in trying to influence the course of public policy. **Reporting laws** vary considerably across the states. For example, only 39 states require that lobbyists report the specific legislative or administrative action they seek to influence.[49] In contrast, the federal reporting requirements of the 1995 Lobby Disclosure Act are quite extensive. For example, the Sierra Club's nine page 2000 report, like those of all registrants, is available online at the FEC's website. It indicates that the membership group supported 19 bills, opposed 22 others, and supported or opposed portions of five more legislative proposals. In addition to lobbying the Congress and three units in the Executive Office of the President, the Sierra Club reported lobbying nine different federal agencies or departments. The report also listed the names and positions of 20 Sierra Club lobbyists. Finally, the report indicates that the Sierra Club spent $105,000 in lobbying.

The quality of registration and reporting requirements vary, and they surely do not capture all lobbying. Still, they have taken a large step toward opening the lobbying process to public scrutiny. While not restricting any lobbying practices per se, the media, political challengers, and other organized interests have obvious incentives to publicize the information provided by lobbying reports. This was no more evident than in the financial and accounting scandals of 2002, when press reports routinely reported the lobbying activities of Enron and other corporations accused of questionable business practices. Even before these scandals, one evaluation of registration and reporting reforms concluded that they led to greater restraint on the part of organized interests in dealing with public officials, an enhanced concern on the part of organized interests for their public image, and a growing professionalization of the lobbying industry.[50]

Registration and reporting requirements also had one unintended impact. The availability of valid registration rolls allowed social scientists for the first time to study in a systematic way the population dynamics of lobbying communities at the federal level, as seen in Chapter 3.

Conflict of Interest Laws

Since New York first acted in 1954, all states and the federal government have adopted some form of ethics legislation going beyond simply prohibiting bribery. Ethics laws do not bear directly on organized interests, but on the public officials they lobby. That is, they try to restrain the influence of lobbyists indirectly by restricting their targets' susceptibility to lobbying practices raising potential **conflicts of interest**.[50] First, 20 states and the U.S. Congress prohibit legislators from receiving *honoraria* from organized interests for speeches or related activities on their behalf. Second, many conflict of interest laws restrict public officials from receiving gifts from lobbyists. Some limit gifts to a maximum dollar value. Other states have adopted Wisconsin's "no cup of coffee" rule, which prohibits legislators from receiving anything of value from lobbyists, including the aforesaid cup of coffee. Third, public officials in many governments are now subject to *revolving-door* restrictions that prohibit them from lobbying old colleagues for some time period after leaving elected or appointed positions. Fourth, many state governments now prohibit or at least limit legislators who are *lawyers* from conducting legal business with state agencies. Finally, 40 states and the federal government now require legislators to provide *personal financial disclosure statements*.[51] In many states, these requirements extend further to candidates for legislative office, judges, and/or agency officials.

Conflict of interest laws vary widely in terms of the behaviors that are prohibited and their application to legislators, executives, and judges. In large part, this variation arises from different states' experiences with scandal. As with registration and reporting rules, recurring scandals seem to drive adoption of ever stricter conflict of interest rules.[52] Their effectiveness varies too on the specific goals ascribed to them. At the broadest level, ethics legislation is designed to minimize perceptions of corruption arising from the influence activities of organized interests. While hard to measure, it does not seem that ethics rules have diminished sometimes extraordinarily cynical views of public officials, as reported in Figure 1-2. In this regard, then, ethics laws must be counted a failure. On the other hand, they have greatly changed the way lobbying is conducted. Clive Thomas and Ronald Hrebenar credit ethics legislation, along with disclosure and reporting requirements, with "the apparent disappearance of the old wheeler-dealer lobbyist from the states and to some extent the federal political scene, and the increased professionalism of lobbyists in general."[53] In short, while ethics laws have changed lobby practices, they have not yet altered the public perceptions that were their main focus.

Another type of conflict of interest law deserves special attention. Since 1992, 21 states have adopted **term limits** restricting the number of years legislators may serve.[54] The term limits movement claimed that reelection incentives insure that legislators will depend too heavily on the organized interests providing them critical campaign resources. Viewing registration and reporting requirements and ethics laws as piecemeal approaches, term limits strike at the core of politicians' reelection incentive. Eliminate this incentive, it is argued, and lawmakers will reflect the people's will rather than special interests' desires. Pluralists and neopluralists respond to this quintessential transactions school reform in three ways. First, they reject the notion that organized interests inevitably misrepresent the public's preferences. As we have seen, pluralists view the preferences of organized interests as reflections of public preferences, albeit weighted for the salience of given issues. Opponents of term limits also suggest that politicians' desires to secure reelection constitute an essential check on their drifting too far from their constituents' interests. Finally, critics claim that the expertise legislators develop from long terms of service is an important check on organized interests. Having seen many proposals over the course of long careers, experienced legislators are far less likely than neophytes to be misled by special interest claims. Unfortunately, since the earliest states adopting term limits are only now experiencing their full effects, we cannot yet evaluate these competing hypotheses.

Campaign Finance Reforms

Over the last decade, campaign finance reform has been at the center of efforts to restrict the power of organized interests.[55] We have seen, however, that not all interest organizations are opposed to such reforms as the Bipartisan Campaign Finance Reform Act. In fact, several public interest organizations and think tanks are major supporters of the act. As seen in Interest Organization Example 8-2, Common Cause has been at the forefront of efforts to pass the McCain-Feingold/ Shays-Meehan bill and continues both to monitor its implementation by the FEC and to defend its provisions in court. Common Cause and other proponents of campaign finance reform anchor their support on a transactions school interpretation of the role of money in politics. Campaign money affords large and wealthy interest organizations undue access and influence that distort the democratic translation of constituents' preferences into public policy. Others reject this view but still favor reform because the presence of large sums of money in politics creates at least the impression of corruption and, thereby, undermines the legitimacy of government. In either view, campaign contributions from organized interests, unregulated by the ethics laws discussed earlier, constitute a fundamental conflict of interest for elected officials.

We described the history and structure of campaign finance laws in Chapter 4. Federal regulation of campaign finance has evolved in significant ways since the adoption of the Federal Election Campaign Act of 1971 and the 1974 amendments. These numerous abridgments have set the context of the ongoing debate over campaign finance reform in general and the Bipartisan Campaign Finance Reform Act in particular. Critics lodge three indictments of the campaign finance system, charges addressed by the 2002 act.[56] First, they argue that the original purpose of soft money — strengthening political parties — has become a mask for unlimited contributions to what are really campaign efforts. The BCFRA bans soft money contributions. Second, critics argue that many issue ads run by organized interests are, while not explicitly endorsing or opposing a candidate, thinly veiled campaign ads. The BCFRA bans issues ads referring to a candidate or candidates 30 days before primaries and 60 days before general elections. Third, to critics, independent expenditures by organized interests in support or opposition to candidates are a loophole used to avoid FECA limits on direct contributions to campaigns. The BCFRA more strictly specifies when such contributions must be considered "coordinated" with campaign expenditures and requires their more timely disclosure. To partially compensate for

INTEREST ORGANIZATION EXAMPLE 8-2

Supporting Reform

John Gardner founded Common Cause in 1970. Mr. Gardner had previously served as Secretary of the Department of Health, Education, and Welfare in the Johnson Administration. Common Cause now has over 200,000 members. Financed by dues and individual contributions, the bipartisan organization does not accept government grants or support from foundations, labor unions, or corporations. Nearly 100 volunteers assist the 50 person staff in Common Cause's Washington headquarters. Common Cause also employs 60 staff members working on state and local government reforms. While Common Cause has worked on a variety of issues, its central focus has always been on government openness and accountability. Common Cause frequently testifies before Congress, conducts and publishes research, and joins legal cases bearing on these issues. In 2000, 11 Common Cause staff members were registered as lobbyists with Congress, and the organization reported $1,420,000 in lobbying expenses.

Given its goals, it is not surprising that Common Cause has been a major supporter of lobbying reform in general and the Bipartisan Campaign Finance Reform Act in particular. Common Cause testified in support of the proposed legislation. With Democracy21, the Center for Responsive Politics, and the Campaign and Media Legal Center, Common Cause filed a complaint with the Federal Election Commission asserting that the major political parties began undermining its implementation just months after the act was signed into law. Common Cause also worked with the Congressional sponsors of the Bipartisan Campaign Finance Reform Act to defend the legislation against legal tests of its constitutionality.

Source: http://commoncause.org, http://www.opensecrets.org, visited December 19, 2002.

these losses of campaign funds, the BCFRA also doubles the amount of "hard" money that individuals can give to candidates and allows those amounts to be indexed for inflation.

Supporters and opponents of the BCFRA agree on little, as seen in Table 8-1. The items in the table are abstracted from two commentaries on the act with strikingly similar titles: "Top Ten Myths about Campaign Finance Reform," by Todd Gaziano of the Heritage Foundation,[57] and "Myths and Realities about the Bipartisan Campaign Reform Act of 2002," by Thomas Mann of the Brookings Institution.[58] Todd Gaziano suggests that attempts to limit interest organization money will inevitably fail, are unconstitutional abridgments of the right of free speech, will further entrench incumbents in office, and will diminish the voices of lower- and middle-class citizens in politics. Thomas Mann rejects all four arguments. These are not the only sources of disagreement. Opponents of the BCFRA also claim that the ban on soft money will seriously weaken party building and get-out-the-vote efforts. Supporters, in turn, argue that parties will compensate for the loss of soft money by raising, under the new, higher limits, larger amounts of regulated "hard" contributions. Only one of these and many other disputes will be settled anytime soon. Courts will decide whether the act or portions of it are consistent with First Amendment protections of free speech. Should all or portions of the act survive ongoing legal challenges, however, social scientists eventually—by following the money—will be able to determine which of Mr. Mann or Mr. Gaziano's interpretations is more nearly correct.

Finally, one proposal not currently on the political agenda would fully solve the real or imagined threats posed by the money that organized interests bring to politics: full public financing of political campaigns. As noted earlier, presidential campaigns are now partially supported by the federal treasury, and 22 states have some sort of public funding of campaigns. While few can be characterized as full public funding, initial research on the state programs provides only mixed assessments of their effectiveness.[59] Public financing seems to reduce the number of uncontested legislative elections and narrows the spending gap between incumbents and challengers. But these outcomes tap only a few of the goals of public funding. We do not know, for example, if public funding reduces the influence of organized interests on public policy or whether citizens

TABLE 8-1 Competing Arguments about the Bipartisan Campaign Finance Reform Act

Opposing: Todd F. Gaziano, The Heritage Foundation	Supporting: Thomas E. Mann, The Brookings Institution
THE EFFECTIVENESS OF THE ACT	
Enacting convoluted campaign regulations, constitutional or not, is like trying to dam a stream with a pile of sticks. Campaign spending eventually will flow through the dam, over the dam, or find another path. But because such indirect spending is often less effective, the amount of money chasing the same end will increase.	Yes, it is difficult to formulate policies regulating money and politics that are workable and sustainable. But that doesn't mean that all efforts to regulate reforms are counterproductive. Some well-conceived reforms have achieved their stated objectives for a period of time, but they need ongoing maintenance and repair.
THE CONSTITUTIONALITY OF THE ACT	
If the First Amendment means anything, it means that Congress shall not try to limit the amount of campaign speech or spending. The Supreme Court has made clear that this is a prohibited purpose. . . . It is a fundamental tenet of the First Amendment that government has no business trying to limit the amount or type of political discourse.	Nothing could be further from the truth. No speech is banned by the new law — not a single ad nor any word or combination of words would be muzzled. Individuals and groups retain their full First Amendment rights. The only new requirements relate to the disclosure and sources of funding for television and radio ads close to an election.

(continued)

TABLE 8-1 continued

Impacts on the Power of Incumbency

No bill would pass if it hurt incumbents, and [the act] substantially helps incumbents. The Canadian experience with reforms similar to those proposed by Shays-Meehan confirms this: Incumbents lost even fewer elections and, because of new spending caps, campaign ads became almost totally negative.

For challengers, getting over the threshold of recognition that all incumbents have is crucial, and higher television costs . . . make that threshold painfully higher. Reducing ad demand by parties and groups will help challengers by lowering costs and freeing up . . . time . . . for candidate ads.

Who Will Be Harmed

[The Act] would restrict the rights of poor and middle-class citizens to engage in campaign activity through [membership] groups, but it leaves wealthy individuals and huge media corporations alone. Plutocrats and powerful media corporations should be free to speak, but it is wrong to increase their power artificially at the expense of less affluent citizens.

Many [of the organized interests] that contribute soft money to parties do so only reluctantly, as "access insurance"—out of fear that if they don't, their more obliging competitors will get privileged access—or to avoid retribution by officeholders. Take away the soft money and much spending on politics from corporate treasuries will end.

Source: http://heritage.org/Research/LegalIssues/, visited April 11, 2003.

Source: http://www.brook.edu/views/articles/mann/20020507.htm, visited April 11, 2003.

in states with publicly funded election campaigns are less likely to assume that politicians always and with certainty dance to the tune of organized interests.

CONCLUSION

Social science, in fact, can help answer many questions about the politics of interest representation. We have organized the many candidate answers to several of these queries into three perspectives: the pluralist, transactions, and neopluralist schools. On balance, the best evidence to date seems to provide stronger support for the neopluralist perspective than for the relatively more extreme pluralist and transactions perspectives. But the social science debate over organized interests is far from over. We have seen that evidence remains ambiguous on many specific hypotheses about the behavior of organized interests. Even if the neopluralist school seems to provide a better account of the world of organized interests, neopluralism is a label covering a significant range of intellectual territory. Some neopluralists lean toward the benign assessment of traditional pluralists, while others credit important elements of transactions scholars' more cynical evaluation. We have not been shy in pointing out important gaps in our knowledge about several important issues. On these, social science research, at least so far, offers little guidance. Still, we hope that our survey provides students with a useful map of current knowledge and some hints about the direction of future research.

In the end, however, social science can never answer *all* of our questions about the politics of interest representation. Some of these questions are quite broad. How, for example, should our political institutions weigh the various and sometimes competing expressions of public preferences received from the three major instruments of democratic participation—voting, political parties, and organized interests? Which provides the most legitimate expression of the public's will? Other questions are narrower in focus, but no less important. Perhaps most importantly, does money—when used to fund issue ads, lobbyists, and campaign contributions—constitute constitutionally protected free speech, or is it more rightly viewed as an instrument of nondemocratic influence? Whether the focus is narrow or broad, these are normative questions that we must answer on our own. Indeed, we have a responsibility as citizens to answer these questions. Virtually all of us already participate or soon will participate in the politics of organized interests. For many of us, this participation will take a very active form as members or leaders of membership groups or as appointed or elected public officials. Some students will even pursue, whether by intention or by accident, careers as lobbyists. For others, participation will be more passive, through the churches we worship in, the schools we attend, the clubs we join, and the places we work. In either case, a robust view of democratic citizenship requires that each of us take at least some measure of responsibility for the behavior of these—*our*—interest organizations throughout the influence production process.

KEY TERMS AND CONCEPTS

Bipartisan Campaign Finance Reform Act   Registration Laws
Crisis in Civic Engagement   Reporting Laws
Gridlock   Conflicts of Interest
Ethics Laws   Term Limits

QUESTIONS ABOUT YOUR INTEREST ORGANIZATION

1. Has your interest organization expressed support or opposition to the Bipartisan Campaign Finance Reform Act or other reform proposals? If so, how?
2. Will the Bipartisan Campaign Finance Reform Act alter how your organization seeks to influence politics and the policy process. If so, how?
3. In the end, does your interest organization contribute to democratic politics in a positive, supportive manner, or does it thwart or distort democratic government?

NOTES

1. *New York Times*, "Campaign Finance Reform on Trial," December 4, 2002, http://www.democracy21.org, visited December 20, 2002.

2. http://www.democracy21.org, visited December 20, 2002.
3. Todd F. Gaziano, "Top Ten Myths About Campaign Finance Reform," February 12, 2001, http://www.heritage.org/Research/LegalIssues/LM5.cfm, visited December 10, 2002.
4. Gaziano, "Top Ten Myths About Campaign Finance Reform."
5. Elizabeth Drew, *The Corruption of American Politics* (Woodstock, New York: Overlook Press, 1999).
6. G. William Domhoff, *The Power Elite and the State* (Aldine de Gruyter, 1990).
7. Morris P. Fiorina, "Extreme Voices: A Dark Side of Civic Engagement." In *Civic Engagement and American Democracy*, Theda Skocpol and Morris P. Fiorina, eds. (Washington, DC: Brooking Institution Press, 1999), p. 404.
8. Robert D. Putnam, *Bowling Alone* (New York: Simon and Schuster), pp. 31–47.
9. Michale P. McDonald and Samuel L. Popkin, "The Myth of the Vanishing Voter," *American Political Science Review* 95: 963–974 (2001).
10. Fiorina, "Extreme Voices."
11. Theda Skocpol and Morris P. Fiorina, *Civic Engagement and American Democracy* (Washington, DC: Brookings Institution Press, 1999).
12. Fiorina, "Extreme Voices," p. 412.
13. Instead, opposition is usually based on free-speech concerns and their doubtful effectiveness.
14. David Lowery and Virginia Gray, "Reinforcing or Compensatory Biases? Interest Representation and Democratic Participation in the American States," Comparative State Politics 19: 1–18 (1998).
15. Sidney Verba, Kay Lehman Schlozman, and Henry E. Brady, *Voice and Equality* (Cambridge: Harvard University Press, 1995); Steven J. Rosenstone and John Mark Hansen, *Mobilization, Participation, and Democracy in America* (New York: MacMillan Publishing Company, 1993); Jan Leighley, "Group Membership and the Mobilization of Political Participation," *Journal of Politics* 50: 447–463 (1996).
16. Melissa Ring, "Americans' Attention to Campaign Rises, As Does Their Perception That the Campaign Has Turned Negative," The Joan Shorenstein Center on the Press, Politics, and Public Policy,

http://www.vanishingvoter.org/releases/02-25-00.shtml; Eric
Anderson, "News Coverage Propels Election Interest," The Joan
Shorenstein Center on the Press, Politics, and Public Policy,
http://www.vanishingvoter.org/releases/09-20-00.shtml.

17. Cited in Jeffrey M. Berry, "Interest Groups and Gridlock." In *Interest Group Politics*, 6th ed., Allan J. Cigler and Burdett A.
Loomis, eds. (Washington: CQ Press, 2002), p. 335.

18. Cited in Virginia Gray and David Lowery, *The Population Ecology
of Interest Representation* (Ann Arbor: University of Michigan
Press, 1986), p. 200.

19. Frank R. Baumgartner and Bryan D. Jones, *Agendas and Instability in American Politics* (Chicago: University of Chicago Press,
1993).

20. David Lowery and Virginia Gray, "Interest Representation and
Democratic Gridlock," *Legislative Studies Quarterly* 20: 531–552
(1995).

21. Berry, "Interest Groups and Gridlock."

22. Frank R. Baumgartner and Beth L. Leech, "Interest Niches and
Policy Bandwagons: Patterns of Interest Group Involvement in
National Politics," *Journal of Politics* 63: 1191–1213 (2001).

23. Glen S. Krutz, "Omnibus Legislation: An Institutional Reaction
to the Rise of New Issues." In *Policy Dynamics*, Frank R. Baumgartner and Bryan D. Jones, eds. (Chicago: University of Chicago Press, 2002): 205–229.

24. Mancur Olson, *The Logic of Collective Action* (Cambridge: Harvard University Press, 1965).

25. George Stigler, "The Theory of Economic Regulation," *Bell Journal of Economics and Management* 2: 3–21 (1971); Robert Barro,
"The Control of Politicians: An Economic Model," *Public Choice*
14: 19–42 (1973); Sam Peltzman, "Toward a More General Theory of Regulation," *Journal of Law and Economics* 19: 211–240
(1976).

26. Fred S. McChesney, *Money for Nothing* (Cambridge: Harvard
University Press, 1997).

27. Mancur Olson, Jr., *The Rise and Decline of Nations* (New Haven:
Yale University, 1982).

28. Gray and Lowery, *The Population Ecology of Interest Representation*, pp. 219–236. But for a partially contrasting view, see Paul
Teske, "Testing Interest Group and Institutional Theories of State

Regulation." Paper presented at the Annual Meeting of the State Politics and Policy Conference, College Station, Texas, March 2001.

29. Virginia Gray and David Lowery, "The Institutionalization of State Communities of Organized Interests," *Political Research Quarterly* 54: 265–284 (2001); David Lowery and Virginia Gray, "The Expression of Density Dependence in State Communities of Organized Interests," *American Politics Research:* 374–391 (2001).

30. Gary S. Becker, "Public Policies, Pressure Groups, and Dead Weight Costs," *Journal of Public Economics* 28: 329–347 (1985).

31. Gaziano, "Top Ten Myths About Campaign Finance Reform."

32. Clive S. Thomas and Ronald J. Hrebenar, "A Reappraisal of Interest Group Power in the American States." Paper presented at the Annual Meeting of the American Political Science Association, Atlanta, Georgia, September 1999.

33. Gray and Lowery, *The Population Ecology of Interest Representation,* pp. 236–242.

34. Robert S. Erikson, Gerald C. Wright, and John P. McIver, *Statehouse Democracy* (New York: Cambridge University Press, 1993).

35. Virginia Gray, David Lowery, Matthew Fellowes, and Andrea McAtee, "The Opinion-Policy Linkage in the American States: The Effect of Legislative Professionalism and Organized Interests on Policy Responsiveness." Paper presented at the Annual Meeting of the State Politics and Policy Conference, Milwaukee, Wisconsin, May 2002.

36. Rob Gurwitt, "Reform in the Unlikeliest Places," *Governance,* January 1994, p. 37.

37. Mark J. Wilcox and Clyde Wilcox, *Interest Groups in American Politics* (Washington, DC: CQ Press, 1999), p. 4.

38. Frank J. Sorauf, *Inside Campaign Finance* (New Haven: Yale University Press, 1992), pp. 7–28.

39. Virginia Gray, "The Origin and Impact of Lobbying Laws in the United States." Paper presented at the Annual Meeting of the Law and Society Association, Glasgow, Scotland, July 1996.

40. Belle Zeller, *American State Legislatures* (New York: Thomas Y. Crowell, 1954), p. 233.

41. Margaret F. Brinig, Randall G. Holcombe, and Linda Schwartzstein, "The Regulation of Lobbyists," *Public Choice* 77: 377–384 (1993).

42. David Lowery and Virginia Gray, "How Some Rules Just Don't Matter: The Regulation of Lobbyists," *Public Choice* 91: 139–147 (1997).

43. Nonprofits are sometimes surprised to receive surveys based on lobby rolls, saying, "We don't lobby; we just talk to legislators." Nonprofits now routinely lobby with little fear. See Marca Avner, *The Lobbying and Advocacy Handbook for Nonprofit Organizations* (St. Paul, MN: Minnesota Council on Nonprofits/ Amherst H. Wilder Foundation, 2002).

44. Jeffrey M. Berry, *The New Liberalism* (Washington, DC: The Brookings Institution, 1999), p. 29.

45. Clive S. Thomas and Ronald J. Hrebenar, "Regulating Interest Groups in the United States: National, State, and Local Experiences." Paper presented at the Annual Meeting of the American Political Science Association, San Francisco, California, August 1996, p. 10; for those who appreciate irony, the Council of Government Ethics Laws (COGEL), an association of state ethics agencies, traces its founding to a 1974 meeting held in the Watergate Hotel.

46. Cynthia Opheim, "Explaining the Differences in State Lobbying Regulation," *Western Political Quarterly* 44: 405–421 (1991); for a current listing of definitions and prohibited activities, see The Council of State Governments, *Book of the States: 2002* (Lexington, Kentucky: Council of State Governments, 2002), pp. 413–414.

47. Thomas and Hrebenar, "Regulating Interest Groups in the United States: National, State, and Local Experiences," p. 9.

48. Clive S. Thomas and Ronald J. Hrebenar, "Political Action Committees in the State: Some Preliminary Findings." Paper presented at the Annual Meeting of the American Political Science Association, Washington, DC, August, 1991.

49. The Council of State Governments, *Book of the States: 2002,* pp. 415–416.

50. Beth A. Rosenson, "Conflict of Interest Laws in the American States: Explaining Variation in Ethics Restrictions for State Legislators." Paper presented at the Annual Meeting of the American Political Science Association, Boston, September 1998.

51. The Council of State Governments, *Book of the States: 2002,* pp. 421–422.

52. Rosenson, "Conflict of Interest Laws in the American States."

53. Thomas and Hrebenar, "Regulating Interest Groups in the United States: National, State, and Local Experiences," pp. 30–31; also see Alan J. Rosenthal, *The Third House* (Washington, DC: CQ Press, 2001), pp. 99–107; Adam J. Newmark, "Personal Relationships and the Importance of Information in State Lobbying." Paper presented at the Annual Meeting of the Southern Political Science Association, Savannah, Georgia, November 2002.

54. The Council of State Governments, *Book of the States: 2002*, p. 66.

55. It should not be surprising that campaign finance reform has attracted significant scholarly attention. A sample of recent works on both sides of the issue not otherwise cited include Diana Dwyre and Victoria A. Farrar-Myers, *Legislative Labyrith* (Washington, DC: CQ Press, 2001); Anthony Corrado, *Campaign Finance Reform* (New York: The Century Foundation Press, 2000); Annelise Anderson, *Political Money* (Stanford, California: Hoover Institute Press, 2000); Bradley A. Smith, *Unfree Speech* (Princeton, New Jersey: Princeton University Press, 2001).

56. The Center for Responsive Politics' FEC Watch provides a fuller discussion of each of these three issues at: http://www.fecwatch.org/loopholes.

57. http://heritage.org/Research/LegalIssues/, visited April 11, 2003.

58. http://www.brook.edu/views/articles/mann/20020507.htm, visited April 11, 2003.

59. For a review of the limited literature on the impact of public funding of political campaigns and related issues in the states, see Graham P. Ramsden, "State Legislative Campaign Finance Research: A Review Essay," *State Politics and Policy Quarterly* 2: 176–198 (2002).

Suggested Web Sources on Interest Organizations

Students wishing to pursue answers to the questions about specific interest organizations at the end of the chapters will find the following web sources useful. Not listed is perhaps the most important source—each organization's own website. Further, the sites listed below are not the only websites that might be of use; more come on-line everyday. And last, ready access to the web does not mean that a walk to the library and exploring its old-fashioned paper holdings is likely to be fruitless or uninteresting.

1. *The Center for Responsive Politics.* CRP provides the most extensive information on-line about lobbying and campaign expenditures from interest organizations, individuals, and PACs. For example, this site contains information on PAC's campaign contributions each election cycle, total PAC contributions to members of Congress, a list of individual contributors to the PAC, the amount of an individual's contribution to the PAC, the state of residence and profession of each individual contributor to the PAC, the date of individual contributions to the PAC, the industry and sector affiliations with each PAC, and a link to the FEC website which has all of the PAC campaign contribution filings made to the FEC. (*URL*—http://www.crp.org)

2. *Lexis-Nexis.* If you are on campus with a Lexis-Nexis link, this URL will link you to the L-N Congressional testimony page listing texts of interest organizations' testimony before Congressional Committees. (*URL*—http://web.lexis-nexis.com/congcomp/)

3. *The Federal Election Commission.* This URL provides a list of federally registered PACs with their sponsoring, connected, or affiliated organization (if not readily identifiable from the full committee name). (*URL*—http://www.fec.gov/pages/pacronym.htm)

4. The Internet Public Library's Associations on the Net. This is a collection of links to over 2000 Internet sites providing information about

professional and trade associations, cultural and arts organizations, political parties and advocacy groups, labor unions, academic societies, and research institutions. (*URL* — http://www.ipl.org/ref/AON/)

5. *Find Law.* This is an on-line supermarket of legal information. You can, for example, find information about law offices, legal professionals, court cases, federal and state courts, legal organizations, among many other items. (*URL* — http://www.findlaw.com/)

6. *The Urban Institute's National Center for Charitable Statistics.* The NCSS is the national repository of nonprofit sector submissions to the Internal Revenue Service (IRS). These data enable researchers to conduct in-depth analyses of specific nonprofit groups and to examine general nonprofit sector trends. (*URL* — http://ncss.urban.org)

7. *Guidestar's National Database of Nonprofit Organizations.* This site provides a searchable database of more than 700,000 U.S. nonprofit organizations. The data is collected from the IRS Business Master File (BMF), IRS Forms 990 and 990-EZ, and the nonprofits themselves. Guide Star provides, in some but not all cases, information about nonprofit missions, programs, services, and goals. (*URL* — http://www.guidestar.org/index.jsp)

8. *The Independent Sector.* IS is a coalition of corporations, foundations, and voluntary organizations. The IS site includes links to academic centers, research associations, institutes, foundations, Internet-based resources, nonprofits, and think tanks. (*URL* — http://www.independentsector.org/pathfinder/resources/index.html)

9. *The National Council of Nonprofit Associations.* This organization is comprised of a network of 38 state and regional associations of nonprofits representing more than 17,000 nonprofits throughout the country. The URL provides a link to the association chapter in each state, which (in most cases) has the names and web page links to all of the state members. (*URL* — http://www.ncna.org/states.htm)

10. *The Political Index.* The Political Index has a very extensive list of organizations sorted by policy areas, and, in most cases, direct links to organizations. There is also a staggering amount of information and links relevant to all things political on their homepage. (*URL* — http://www.politicalindex.com)

11. *The Voter Information Service.* This site provides a large, searchable database on their homepage containing information about 45 major interest groups' position on Congressional legislation, among other data. Users have to be somewhat proficient in Microsoft Access to get around this site. (*URL* — http://www.vis.org/visweb/html/visdb.htm)

12. *Indiana's Lobby Registration Commission.* Indiana's Lobby Registration Commission has posted on this page links to the homepages of the Lobby Registration Commission in every state. It also provides links to

specific information about lobbying in Indiana. (*URL* — http://www. in.gov/ilrc/links/otherLinks.html)

13. *The National Conference of State Legislatures.* This site can search through more then 500,000 documents from the states that includes information on legislative policy reports, current and past legislation, state statutes, and answers from a select group of surveys. (*URL* — http://www. ncsl.org)

14. *The Council on Governmental Ethics Laws.* This site includes information on governmental ethics, elections, campaign finance, and lobby laws in all fifty states. (*URL* — http://www.cogel.org/)

15. *The Center for Public Integrity.* CPI is a Washington-based institution that operates on a broad agenda devoted to investigative journalism on federal and state government affairs. This site posts the products of that work, which includes many publications of interest to scholars of interest organizations, including reports on state lobbying expenditures and interactions between legislatures, lobbyists, and constituents, among hundreds of other reports. (*URL* — http://www.publicintegrity.org/ dtaweb/home.asp)

16. *The Aspen Institute's NonProfit Sector Research Fund.* The Aspen Institute's Nonprofit Sector Research Fund contains valuable research and reports important sector trends, which are nicely indexed (with links). This is a great site to provide context for a case study. (*URL* — http:// www.nonprofitresearch.org/newsletter1531/newsletter.htm)

17. *Faculty Homepages.* Many of the academic scholars studying the politics of organized interests now provide the data they have collected on their homepages. Professors Frank Baumgartner of Pennsylvania State University and David Lowery of the University of North Carolina at Chapel Hill provide two such sites. Dr. Baumgartner's site includes data on interest organizations active at the federal level, including: 1.) datasets on Congressional hearings, statutes, the federal budget, and selected stories from the *Congressional Quarterly Almanac* and *The New York Times* on interest organizations, 2.) information on lobbying and government advocacy efforts by interest groups and others involved in a sample of governmental decisions in 1999–2000, and 3.) financial information from lobbyists, among many other data. Dr. Lowery's site includes data on state interest organizations including: 1.) totals of state lobby registrations by organizations in 1980, 1990, 1997, 1998, and 1999, and 2.) lists of the individual interest organizations lobbying the states in 1997. (*URL* — http://polisci.la.psu.edu/faculty/ Baumgartner/welcome.htm#research) (*URL* — http://www.unc.edu/ depts/polisci/Lowery/index.html)

Index